MEMORIES

OF MASS

REPRESSION

NARRATING LIFE STORIES IN THE
AFTERMATH OF ATROCITY

MEMORIES
OF MASS
REPRESSION

NANCI ADLER
SELMA LEYDESDORFF
MARY CHAMBERLAIN
LEYLA NEYZI

EDITORS

TRANSACTION PUBLISHERS
NEW BRUNSWICK (U.S.A.) AND LONDON (U.K.)

Library of Congress Catalog Number: 2008035350
ISBN: 978-1-4128-0853-8
Printed in the United States of America

Library of Congress Cataloging-in-Publication

Memories of mass repression : narrating life stories in the aftermath of atrocity / Nanci Adler ... [et al.], editors.
    p. cm.
Includes bibliographical references and index.
ISBN 978-1-4128-0853-8
    1. Historiography—Social aspects. 2. Historiography—Political aspects. 3. Collective memory—Political aspects. 4. Memory—Social aspects—History—20th century. 5. Memory—Political aspects. 6. Social history—20th century. I. Adler, Nanci.

D13.M437 2008
907.2—dc22

2008035350

Contents

Acknowledgments   vii

Introduction   ix
Nanci Adler, Selma Leydesdorff, Mary Chamberlain,
and Leyla Neyzi

Part I: Truth-Seeking and Memory Failure in Stories
of Chaos and Misery

Srebrenica in the History of Genocide: A Prologue   3
Norman M. Naimark

1. When Communities Fell Apart and Neighbors   21
   Became Enemies: Stories of Bewilderment in Srebrenica
   Selma Leydesdorff

2. Localizing the Rwandan Genocide: The Story of Runda   41
   Jacob R. Boersema

3. Memories and Silences: On the Narrative of an   61
   Ingrian Gulag Survivor
   Ulla-Maija Peltonen

Part II: Aftermath: Trauma and Emotions

4. "My Entire Life I Have Shivered": Homecoming   83
   and New Persecution of Former Slave and Forced
   Laborers of Nazi Germany
   Christoph Thonfeld

5. Resisting Oppression: Stories of the 1980s' Mass   99
   Insurrection by Political Activists in the Eastern
   Cape Province, South Africa
   Jan K. Coetzee and Geoffrey T. Wood

6. Struggling with a Horrendous Past: Rwandans   119
   Talk about the Aftermath of the Genocide
   Hessel Nieuwelink

7. Leaving Silence Behind? Algerians and the   137
   Memories of Repression by French Security Forces
   in Paris in 1961
   Jim House

Part III: The Transmission and Distortion of Memory

8. "Privatized Memory?" The Story of Erecting the   157
   First Holocaust Memorial in Budapest
   Andrea Pető

9. Recalling the Appalling: Mass Violence in Eastern   175
   Turkey in the Twentieth Century
   Uğur Ümit Üngör

10. Multiple Framings: Survivor and Non-Survivor   199
    Interviewers in Holocaust Video Testimony
    Michele Langfield and Pam Maclean

List of Contributors   219

Index   223

Acknowledgments

This volume is comprised of a number of outstanding contributions that emerged from various professional gatherings. We are grateful to the authors for the high quality of their work, and for their forbearance during a rather long editorial process. We would like also like to take this opportunity to express our gratitude to four institutions for organizing the forums that inspired this collection. In November of 2005, Sabancı University in Istanbul organized a workshop on "Memory, Narrative and Human Rights" that generated discussion on fundamental issues related to remembering mass repression. The idea of a collective volume on this theme came about during this time. The subject was further explored in March of 2006 when the Center for Holocaust and Genocide Studies (Royal Netherlands Academy of Arts and Sciences and the University of Amsterdam) hosted a symposium entitled "Memory and Narrating Mass Violence." There, a number of young scholars shared the results of their field work, and many cross-cultural similarities were observed. We also reflected on the critical differences in the way in which mass violence is remembered and related, and this discussion is set forth in the present volume. Also in March of 2006, the Oral History and Life Stories Network of the European Social Science History Conference organized two panels in Amsterdam on "repressed memories and memories of repression." A number of the panelists addressed increasingly topical issues relating to memory and recalling mass repression. We were eager to become acquainted with their work, and to be able to include it in this volume. Lastly, in November of 2007 the University of Salzburg provided a forum, "The Meaning of Narrative," which gave the opportunity to reflect upon the volume's conclusions. Finally, and in fact in the first place, we are deeply grateful to the subjects for their willingness to be interviewed. In the pages that follow, readers will better understand the extent of their feat, not only in their experience of repression itself, but in the very act of talking about it.

Introduction

Nanci Adler, Selma Leydesdorff, Mary Chamberlain,
and Leyla Neyzi

After years of extensive academic debate, there is consensus among most researchers that the accounts of survivors form an important basis for the study of genocide and mass violence. For a long time, some historians had argued that not only what former victims said, but also what they remembered was biased, and thus belonged to the realm of emotions.[1] Memories were only accepted for purposes other than the writing of history, because testimony so many years after the event was not considered a viable, reliable source. The history writing on mass atrocities also avoided so-called subjective information. In later years, when historians accepted new sources they restricted themselves to the traditional grid of subjectivity such as letters, memoirs, and autobiography. Oral testimonies were relegated to other venues that dealt with the past like the courts, movies, or televised documentaries. It was in these forums that it became apparent how volatile and changing memories could be. Especially in the courts, where the criminal character of the perpetrators of mass violence was already judged at an early stage on the basis of testimonies, psychologists and other specialists on memory were increasingly called upon to argue that little credibility should be given to that which was remembered. Even so, memories were still needed to reconstruct what had happened, but the chronicling of those memories followed different rules than would historians basing themselves on written sources.[2]

In the last decade, the landscape has changed and massive efforts have been undertaken to integrate memories of mass violence into the writing of its history,[3] not just out of respect for the survivors (as its detractors argue), but because any history writing that would exclude the voices of those who suffered would be incomplete.[4] This is not limited to the use of oral sources.[5] There are also events for which oral testimonies and written personal memories are our only source for investigation.[6] The Armenian genocide and more recent genocides such as that which took place in Rwanda are clear instances in which written records (if they even exist) are not sufficient for reconstructing what happened. It follows that in the writing of the history of genocide, "emotional" memory and "objective" historical research are interwoven and inseparable. It is as much the historian's task to decipher witness accounts, including their inherent charged emotional language, as it is to interpret whatever "traditional" written sources may be available.[7] These sometimes antagonistic narratives of memory, fashioned and mobilized within public and private arenas, together with the ensuing conflicts, paradoxes, and contradictions that they unleash, are all part and parcel of efforts to "come to terms" with what happened. Mining memory is the only way in which we can hope to arrive at a truer, and less biased, historical account of certain events. Undoubtedly, the rise of interdisciplinary research on memory has had its own influence on the ways historians now view remembered data.[8]

Memories of Mass Repression: Narrating Life Stories in the Aftermath of Atrocity presents some of the results of researchers working with the voices of witnesses. We do not view either the volatility of the voices nor the subjective experiences as negative attributes, but rather consider the vast field of subjectivity problematized in this research to be open to exploration.[9] The chapters presented here not only include the voices of the witnesses, victims and survivors; they also reflect the subjective experience of the study of such narratives. In that sense, the series *Memory and Narrative* follows—and contributes to—the development of the field of oral history, where the creation of the narrative is considered an act of interaction between the text of the narrator and the listener, whereby the text of the narrator itself constitutes only part of what is studied. We are particularly interested in the ways in which memory is created, and sometimes molded, and in the interaction with different—and even conflicting—memories of other individuals and society as a whole. On each side of the victim/ perpetrator divide, we often find a different recollection of the same event. A relevant question is: How is the experience articulated, and how do its complexities shape the many meanings of the narratives told to the historian in communicative tropes that try to convince the audience?

It is also here that we place the volume within the field, which is as broad as anthropology, journalism, genocide studies, and other disciplines that pursue the study of mass repression.[10] The present collection, and hopefully future investigations with similar methodology, claims a niche in the historiographical writing where the interaction between the narrator of history and the listener to histories is central. This type of writing is widely interdisciplinary, as illustrated by the variety of geographic and academic backgrounds of our authors. *Memories of Mass Repression* can also be placed within the field of micro history, somewhere between anthropology and history—traditions that enable us to place seemingly unimportant or unrelated incidents within a wider context. These accounts include daily life, and the ordinary and seemingly insignificant. This approach enables us to better grasp the meaning subjects impart to what happened, and the ways people survive.

The taking of oral testimony and the giving of oral history are emotional experiences, whereby the historian listens, processes the information, and transmits it to an imagined audience/reader. There are also other forces at work between the told story and the recorded history. Oral historian Alessandro Portelli has addressed this issue as follows: "The historian must work on both the factual and the narrative planes, the referent and the signifier, the past and the present, and, most of all, on the space between all of them."[11] In order to do so, the historian needs to make use of what we know about memory, about listening to trauma, and compassion, but most of all, the historian has to find ways to work with the kind of data that usually do not figure in historical discourse. Such an approach renders less and less important the fact that these voices narrating a past that has not been mastered are not neutral. That does not make them less true, they simply belong to another truth.

Such narratives sometimes leave the historian empty-handed, since we are still in the process of exploring how to deal with the complex layers and shifts in emotion. Academic descriptions fall short because they do not seem to be able to sufficiently convey the magnitude of the horror; they lack forms, models, and even words. This situation, and our need to transmit our empathy, forces us to look for new styles of communicating what we hear.

We still do not know exactly where the contours of traumatized memory lie. In the field of oral history and life stories we search for them, and once found, often deal with them within the framework of the varied findings of psychotherapy.[12] Those who listen to these stories are fully exposed to the victims' pain, chaos, grief, and mourning.[13] But it is not only the listener that is confronted with facts and realities that challenge their emotional capacity to cope. Remembering and recounting also forces the survivors to once again confront the cruelty, humiliation, pain, and death that they had previously encountered. When victims tell their story to a receptive audience, whether that is a therapist or an oral historian, the experience becomes co-processed, which sometimes results in the narrator feeling a little better, and the listener feeling a little worse.[14] We know that certain events seldom become integrated into the life story, even though they play a formative role in that story. In most cases, the victims prefer to forget these memories, or to compartmentalize them into memories that stay unchanged and depersonalized.[15] Some survivors have adapted to speaking about what happened to them without even touching these emotions, they have found—created—genres in which to talk. This sometimes even goes so far that witnesses tell a story about their own suffering without the feeling that they actually took part in it, as if it were someone else they were talking about. Alternatively, sometimes they tell their own story as others have described them, merging their individual memories with the collective conception of how events ensued. Many such cases could be observed in the flood of memoirs and memories of Stalinism that was unleashed during Gorbachev's campaign of glasnost.[16]

Narrator and listener can be trapped together in an interaction of emotions. The historian/listener is confronted with stories so disturbing that they are sometimes unbearable even to listen to. Listening to trauma, after all, had hitherto belonged to the realm and task of psychotherapists. Historians are still learning how to deal with these types of painful, sometimes fragmented stories which constitute a very particular, and unique historical source. We argue and illustrate in this volume how even seemingly incoherent stories and memories can facilitate a reconstruction of historical events in which human suffering also has a place.

Dominique LaCapra has argued that being able to relate a past through the critical reflection of memory is fundamental to maintaining the values of a democratic culture. This requires incorporating memories that are not pleasant, are not ours, and do not belong to the image a nation or individual would perhaps like to maintain. When political systems or individuals cannot allow for this because they lack either a sufficient degree of democracy, or have something to hide, the result is official censure or self-censure. All memory is at some level selective, even that which we try to accurately recount. It follows that memory is also about forgetting. Looking back, we can become ambivalent or ashamed about who we were and what we did, or what we believed in. Most believers in political movements that turned out to be the opposite of what they promised confront such emotions. When given a proper forum, stories that are in opposition to dominant memories, or in conflict with our own memories, can effectively battle collective forgetting, and the way in which we think about and commemorate events.

The problem of individual memory versus collective memory is acute in the case of mass atrocity. The histories we present in this volume are based on narrated experiences, which happened a relatively short time ago. Most of the stories had not been previously accessed, since so little time had elapsed between what happened and the interviews. They are narratives of people who are more or less able to tell their stories, albeit in emotional and broken language. This group has found ways to talk about what happened amongst themselves, and to others. For some, the telling itself has kept them sane or has connected them to someone in the world again.[17] As noted above, telling a story, and finding someone to bear witness, can also help survivors to connect again to the world. It can ensure a place for them in history, too. When stories are not—or no longer—possible, they can be replaced by sites of memory, which bring the past into the public realm.[18] Such sites can provide a way of compartmentalizing memory so that it is not as confrontational.

The question arises as to whether one can ever forget atrocities, or forgive abusers. Religious discourse, and truth commissions as well, suggest that there will be a final reconciliation for the wronged and the wrongdoers alike. But postponing accountability to the afterlife is insufficient for many victims. At minimum, they want recognition, an accurate and public record of what happened, and they want to be remembered. Today, we live in an age in which it is generally accepted that past wrongs—genocide, terrorist attacks, political mass violence, and brazen personal injustices—should be constantly remembered. The question remains open as to whether letting go of such memories—after a certain point, and under certain conditions—may actually be more appropriate.

Oral historians struggle more with what is *not* said than with what is said. The stories contain ruptures that can sometimes be explained by a trauma, but it is a particular challenge to discern the interaction between memory and forgetting, and to understand what determines the selection process. The discussion on the similarity between remembering and forgetting, introduced in several of the *Memory and Narrative* volumes throughout the years, thus continues.[19]

Part I, Truth-Seeking and Memory Failure in Stories of Chaos and Misery, begins with a contribution by Norman Naimark (author of *Fires of Hatred,* a comparative study of ethnic cleansing[20]) entitled "Srebrenica in the History of Genocide." It opens with a harrowing account of the killings in Srebrenica, the largest mass killing in Europe since the Second World War. But the meaning of Srebrenica was more than this: it revealed the easy elision between ethnic cleansing and genocide, and the failure of the international community's duty to protect. As a result, new norms for international intervention in the interests of protection are emerging which could over-ride the sovereignty of a nation state—an argument used in Iraq, but not, for instance, applied in Darfur. Naimark makes a powerful argument for the need to remember in order for the past to be explored to pave the way for long-term accommodation. The problem, however, is that there is a real risk that the genocide at Srebrenica will become the defining *motif* of Bosnian identity. If so, Naimark argues, "then it is hard to imagine a multi-national state can succeed in the future."

In the next chapter, Selma Leydesdorff argues on the basis of interviews with survivors that while the events in Srebrenica are officially memorialized, scant attention is given to the stories of the women who survived the massacre. She maintains that their traumatized memories are silenced not only by the forces of politics and the outside world, but also by the silence within the survivors themselves. Looking at the events on the level of micro-history, she shows how memory for the women she interviewed has become impossible, because they were betrayed by those whom they trusted and befriended most; their neighbors and classmates had become hunters and perpetrators.

In "Localizing the Rwandan Genocide: The Story of Runda," Jacob Boersema explores the ways in which massive mobilization for killing in Rwanda was organized locally, and he places these events in the larger context of the violence. Using a small community as a starting point, the author tries to understand the widespread adherence to the call for violence by looking at the micro level. According to Boersema, what happened locally was closely tied to what happened on a national scale, so exploring local experience may facilitate a better understanding of the Rwandan genocide. Central is the community and the way in which the narrators relate not only the events, but also the way in which local life was organized, and how social relations were part of how the genocide was enacted.

Ulla-Maija Peltonen[21] also takes up the relationship between the micro-story and the macro story in her essay on the Ingrian man Tauno (born in 1922), who lived on the Finnish-Russian border. This is a little known story of people living on a piece of land who had to shift nationality as result of a decision made by those who were controlling history. Peltonen has focused her research on the offense, shock, fear, and terrorization that had previously only received wide attention through the writings of ex-prisoners like Shalamov and Solzhenitsyn.[22] The man Peltonen interviewed lived on the fine line between life and death, which may have been his incentive to reflect on memory, and to revisit memories and argue against them. As she writes: "Tauno was silent for almost forty years, until he decided to tell his story, to bear witness to what had happened." The narrator has become the one who bears witness, as is the case with the women of Srebrenica. Sometimes such narratives can develop a testimonial quality that hinders the free speech so common and so necessary to the field of oral history and storytelling.

Part II, Aftermath: Trauma and Emotions, commences with a chapter by Christoph Thonfeld on how the return home was often the beginning of a new trauma. Forced laborers who returned home at the end of the Second World War were often not welcome. The interviews incorporated into this piece are part of the International Forced Labourers Documentation Project that collected stories from former slave laborers in over twenty countries. Thonfeld focuses on those forced laborers that were considered second-class victims after they came back to Slovenia and former Yugoslavia. The arbitrariness of the violence was not accepted, and it became hard to make new social connections in a world that had a hierarchy of suffering. The essay shows a history that is partly known as collective memory, but it is also a silenced memory. It shows how the narrators, despite the absence of recordable speech, nevertheless told their story. But they did so in very particular ways, such as by pretending to stick to the "facts and by talking in a way that demonstrated lack of emotional involvement."

Jan K. Coetzee[23] and Geoffrey T. Wood describe the mass movement against apartheid in the 1980s in Grahamstown in their chapter, "Resisting Oppression: Stories of the 1980s' Mass Insurrection by Political Activists in the Eastern Cape Province, South Africa." The focus once again is on the relationship between changes on a micro scale and what was happening in the larger world. The regime was in its waning years, but people did not know that at the time. While much has been written on the macro level, these authors look at what happened in the lives of the grassroots activists. By shedding light on the individual lives of twelve activists they aim to get a better understanding of this violent and severely repressed movement. There had been "reforms" and varied reactions to them, which created huge division within the community. Repression, however, was sometimes so severe that those divisions disappeared. This essay shows how individuals living under the worst conditions became involved. Some reacted with fear to the extreme violence, others used their time in jail as a moment for learning. They had initially organized themselves spontaneously, sometimes individually. Later, they started to understand more about what was happening. Though these activists paid an enormous psychological price, they ended the period as different people.

Hessel Nieuwelink also based his chapter, "Struggling with a Horrendous Past: Rwandans Talk about the Aftermath of the Genocide," on a small sample of interviews. He talked with survivors or surviving family members of the Rwandan genocide, and visited the traditional "gacaca" lawn court sessions. His subjects were generally ready to speak about the various waves of violence they had survived. The focus here is not so much on what has happened, as is the case in other life stories in this volume, but that those responsible admit their crimes. Some victims consider a verdict and sentence, whether it be monetary, or in kind, to be some form of compensation for the pain they have suffered. In that sense these local courts help to piece together fragments of lives and function at the same time as truth commissions. While Jean Hatzfeld has profoundly documented why killers became perpetrators, and how they talked about it afterward, in his impressive book on the tales of survivors and perpetrators,[24] this essay by Nieuwelink moves one step beyond the narrative of the atrocities by looking at the way people tried to adapt in the post-genocide period, and what the process of transitional justice meant for them personally. He also touches on the way in which the gacaca sessions facilitate in the creation of a shared collective memory.

Collective forgetting is the theme of Jim House's chapter, "Leaving Silence Behind: Algerians and the Memories of Repression by French Security Forces in Paris in 1961." This essay examines the French inability to deal with its colonial past. In riots in 1961 in the streets of Paris, dozens of protesting Algerians were clubbed to death. The French government wanted the events to be forgotten as much as did the Provisional Government of the Algerian Republic. There was no place for the transmission of the memories, which created what House terms a strategic silence. This history is now emerging, as the time seems ripe for more revelations on France's violent past in the wars of independence, where more and more groups from all non-French sides speak up.[25] Silence had been a way to move on with life, but that silence was accompanied by shame and fear. There is shame over the fact that people were forced into nudity, and about the sexual abuse they went through. There is also a fear about what happens when the survivors speak out. They initially assume that no one will listen to them. House listens to the personal motivations for people to have been silent for decades, and he describes the multi-vocal counter narrative that has emerged now that they are speaking out. The possibility to speak about proscribed subjects is still hindered by the post-colonial condition of the Algerian migration to France. Since Algerians, even as French citizens, are still treated as outsiders, there is as yet little room for a full history that would integrate the formerly colonized.

In Part III, The Transmission and Distortion of Memory, we start with a piece from Hungary, where after World War II reconciliation failed and distortions in memory were institutionalized in silence and forgetting. In "'Privatized Memory'? The Story of Erecting the First Holocaust Memorial in Budapest," Andrea Pető describes the killing of Jews at a place that unconsciously became a site of mourning in Budapest. The scene was an apartment building that was looted in 1944; its tenants were massacred. The legal procedures in the post-war period were heavily influenced by the Communist Party's struggle for power. Consequently, a very particular memory was constructed around the female war criminal Piroska Dely who made the victims into heroic anti-fascist resisters. The case became so convoluted that the contradictions in the story diminished the memory of the victims, which was even further aggravated by the silence of the survivors. Only in private memories was it recalled that Jews were actually the victims of this massacre. In the post-Communist period memory became the center of a heated debate about how the Holocaust should be remembered. Pető argues that it is time to create "sites of remembering," so that the Hungarian holocaust can be given its appropriate place.

In his essay on the Xerzan region in eastern Turkey largely populated by Kurds, "Recalling the Appalling: Mass Violence in Eastern Turkey in the Twentieth Century," Uğur Üngör shows how silence, like memory, is transmitted over generations. The violence there is closely linked to the building of the Turkish nation-state, which brought about several waves of violence against religious and cultural minorities. In Xerzan this involved the assimilation of several tribes and their leadership. But more importantly, Xerzan became one of the theaters of the Armenian genocide. The mass killing of the Armenian middle class brought social rupture, and in that region Kurdish families proceeded to occupy the houses of murdered Armenians. However, since Kurdish nationalism—which originated in the very same Turkish state formation where other languages were forbidden and assimilation was obligatory—was considered a threat, the state reinforced its military presence. The clashes that ensued from 1926 live on in Kurdish oral culture. After 1932 the tribes were "subdued" in an atrocious way. The region became a forbidden zone and the former inhabitants could no longer live there. It spurred local identification with the tribe, and accompanying defiance of the Turkish state. It gave rise to new violence continuing a history of war and a chain of interwoven memories of violence.

Our last contribution, "Multiple Framings: Survivor and Non-Survivor Interviewers in Holocaust Video Testimony," addresses the heritage of the Holocaust as reflected in the form of the tremendous archive of audio and video material, and the literature surrounding it. The desire to interview survivors about the Holocaust has coincided with the great availability of new technologies. The best-known collections are the Fortunoff Video Archive[26] and the Survivors of the Shoah Visual Foundation. Here we present an essay by Michele Langfield and Pam Maclean that centers on the far less known archive of the Jewish Holocaust Museum and Research Center in Melbourne. Assuming that testimony is always mediated by the culture and society in which the interviewers and interviewees live, the authors investigate the role of the interviewer, and show how much insider-outsider positions influence the interview. They argue that it is urgent to establish the basis of the narrative's authority, and they show how the interviewer is in control of the testimony that is created. Since video testimonies and the scholarly articles analyzing them understandably focus on the narrator[27] as the natural center of every story, we thought it fitting to revisit the old adage that oral testimonies are made by two parties. Focusing on both parties and their interactions with one another offers researchers opportunities to explore the co-creation of the narrative.

To what extent video testimonies may replace one of the original tasks of the writing of oral history remains an open question. Telling, illustrating, and publishing about atrocities were among the original goals of oral historians. It is clear that stories can be better transmitted when we look at them, or when we listen to them, than when we read them. We hear hesitation and sadness; we see tears. Listening and looking were the first step. But secondary, comparative analysis, and analysis of the silences have always been crucial. Those are the tasks of scholars, and our work confronts us again and again with new questions and new areas of focus.

Already early on, oral historians tried to go one step beyond just listening, to searching for new ways to present findings.[28] We are aware that the historical consciousness of crimes committed during mass repression is a construction that is remade over time.[29] Consequently, the stories presented here as representations of events that make us emotional will change over time. Until now, the model for these representations and perceptions has been the oral history of the Holocaust.[30] But it is apparent that the oral histories of other genocides and mass atrocities have to eventually look beyond known models in order to examine the uniqueness of the cultural setting of their genocide. We might find out that the whole valorization of silence as a symptom of trauma is not suited for societies where people talk. We might recognize displays of trauma that are unexpected, represented by artifacts that we struggle to understand, and we might find different ways of expressing the story in songs and prayers,[31] in movement such as dance or physical rituals, or the ripping of clothes, the weaving of tapestry, or the writing of poems. Depending on the culture, all of these mediums represent what has happened as much as telling a story does. It is crucial that we not only expand the boundaries of our knowledge, but that we also stretch the limits of our approach to that knowledge. What we know about how to study the trauma of the Holocaust can help and guide us in the study of other genocides, but it can also become a hindrance because that story often remains a frame of reference from which we cannot escape. Since "never again" has happened time and again, we must listen to the voices of survivors of new episodes of mass violence, discern and convey what is similar and what is different, and learn.

February 2008

Notes

1.   Martin Broszat, Saul Friendländer, "A Controversy about the Historicization of National Socialism," in: *Yad Vashem Studies*, 19 (1988): 1-47. Saul Friedländer, *Nazi Germany and the Jews 1939-1945, The Years of Extermination* (New York: Harper Collins, 2007). Saul Friedländer, "History, Memory and the Historian: Dilemmas and Responsibilities," in: *New German Critique*, 80, 2000.

2.   Richard A. Wilson, "The Historical Record of the International Criminal Tribunal for the Former Yugoslavia," in: *Human Rights Quarterly*, 27, 3 (2005): 908-942; Dominique LaCapra, *Writing History, Writing Trauma* (Baltimore, London: The John Hopkins University Press, 2001), 91; Samuel Totten, William S. Parsons, and Israel W. Charny, eds. *Century of Genocide: Eyewitness Accounts and Critical Views* (New York: Routledge, 1997).

3.　See Richard Crownshaw, Selma Leydesdorff, "On Silence and Revision: The Language and the Words of the Victims," in: *Memory of Totalitarianism*, ed. Luisa Passerini, (New Brunswick and London: Transaction Publishers, 2005); Nanci Adler, *The Gulag Survivor, Beyond the Soviet System* (New Brunswick: Transaction Publishers, 2004); Anne Applebaum, *Gulag: A History,* (New York: Doubleday, 2003).

4.　Nancy Wood, *Vectors of Memory, Legacies of Trauma in Postwar Europe* (Oxford, New York: Berg, 1999).

5.　An excellent example is Katherine R. Jolluck, *Exile and Identity, Polish Women in the Soviet Union during World War II* (Pittsburgh: University of Pittsburgh Press, 2002).

6.　For instance Gideon Greif's impressive account of the Sonderkommandos: Gideon Greif, *We Wept without Tears, Testimonies of the Jewish Sonderkommando from Auschwitz* (New Haven and London: Yale University Press, 2005).

7.　A good example is Graham Dawson, *Making Peace with the Past: Memory, Trauma and the Irish Troubles* (Manchester: Manchester University Press, 2007).

8.　Henry Roudiger, James Wertsch "Creating a New Discipline of Memory Studies," in: *Memory Studies* 1(1): 9-22, 2008.

9.　See also Susannah Radstone and Kate Hodgkin, "Regimes of Memory: An Introduction," in *Memory Cultures, Memory, Subjectivity and Recognition,* eds. Susannah Radstone and Kate Hodgkin (New Brunswick: Transaction Publishers, 2006), pp. 1-23.

10.　See for instance: Ben Kiernan, ed., *The Specter of Genocide, Mass Murder in Historical Perspective* (Cambridge: Cambridge University Press, 2003); Samuel Totten, William S. Parsons, and Israel W. Charny, eds., *Eyewitness Accounts and Critical Views* (New York: Routledge, 1997); Ervin Staub, *Becoming Evil. The Origins of Genocide and Other Group Violence* (Cambridge: Cambridge University Press, 1989); Alex. L. Hinton, ed., *Annihilating Difference, The Anthropology of Genocide* (Berkeley: University of California Press, 2002); Christina Howard, "Repression in Retrospect: Constructing History in the 'Memory Debate,'" in: *History of the Human Sciences*, 15 (3): 65-93; Joshua A. Fogel, ed., *The Nanjing Massacre in History and Historiography* (Berkeley: University of California Press, 2000); See, for instance, the journals *Genocide Studies and Prevention*, and *Journal of Genocide Research, Holocaust and Genocide Studies*.

11.　Alessandro Portelli, *The Order Has Been Carried Out, History, Memory, and the Meaning of a Nazi Massacre in Rome* (New York: Palgrave, 2003).

12.　Shoshana Felman, Dori Laub, *Testimony, Crises of Witnessing in Literature, Psychoanalysis and History* (New York, London: Routledge, 1992); Gadi Benezer, *The Migration Journey: The Ethiopian Jewish Exodus* (New Brunswick: Transaction Publishers, 2005).

13.　Kim Lacy Rogers, Selma Leydesdorff, Graham Dawson, eds., *Trauma: Life Stories of Survivors* (New Brunswick: Transaction Publishers, 2004).

14.　Herbert M. Adler, "The History of the Present Illness: Who's Listening, and Why Does It Matter?" *Journal of the American Board of Family Practice* 10, 1 (January-February 1997). The interview with victims can, of course, have negative consequences for the interviewer. Iris Chang, interviewer and author of, among others, *The Rape of Nanking: the Forgotten Holocaust of WWII* (New York: Basic Books, 1997), committed suicide.

15.　Onno Van der Hart, Ellert R.S. Nijenenhuis, Kathy Steele, *The Haunted Self: Structural Dissociation and the Treatment of Chronic Traumatization* (New York, Norton, 2007).

16. See, for example, Irina Sherbakova, "The Gulag in Memory," in L. Passerini, ed., op. cit, pp. 103-115; Nanci Adler, *The Gulag Survivor,* op. cit. pp. 38-42.

17. Francoise Davoine, Jean Max Gaudiellière, *History beyond Trauma* (New York; Other Press, 2004); Dori Laub, "From Speechlessness to Narrative: The Cases of Holocaust Historians, and Psychiatrically Hospitalized Survivors," in: *Literature and Medicine* 24(2): 253-265.

18. Jay Winter, *Sites of Mourning: The Great War in European Cultural History* (Cambridge: Cambridge University Press, 1998); Aleida Assmann, *Der lange Schatten der Vergangenheit, Erinnerungskultur und Geschichtspolitik,* (München: C.H. Beck, 2006).

19. See Passerini note 3, Radstone and Hodgkin, note 9, Lacy, Rogers, Leydesdorff, Dawson note 13, Benezer note 12; Timothy G. Ashplant, Graham Dawson, Michael Roper, *Commemorating War* (New Brunswick: Transaction Publishers, 2004); Barbara Miller, *Narratives of Guilt and Compliance in Unified Germany: Stasi Informers and their Impact on Society* (London: Routledge, 2000); Kate Hodgkin, Susannah Radstone, *Contested Pasts: The Politics of Memory* (New Brunswick: Transaction Publishers, 2005).

20. Norman Naimark, *Fires of Hatred, Ethnic Cleansing in Twentieth-Century Europe* (Cambridge: Harvard University Press, 2002).

21. See also Anne Heimo, Ulla-Maija Peltonen, "Memories and Histories, Public and Private: The Finnish Civil War in 1918," in *Memory, History, Nation. Studies in Memory and Narrative*, Kate Hodgkin, Susannah Radstone, eds. (New Brunswick: Transaction Publishers, 2006), pp. 42-56 [2003].

22. Varlam Shamalov, *Kolyma Tales* (New York: Penguin, 1995).

23. See also: Jan K. Coetzee (with Lynda Gilfillan, L. and Otakar Hulec) *Fallen Walls. Prisoners of Conscience in South Africa and Czechoslovakia* (New Brunswick: Transaction Publishers, 2004); Jan K. Coetzee. *Plain Tales from Robben Island*, (Pretoria: Van Schaik Publishers, 2000).

24. Jean Hatzfeld, *Machete Season: The Killers in Rwanda Speak* (New York: Picador, 2006); *Life Laid Bare: The Survivors in Rwanda Speak* (New York: Other Press, 2007); *Into the Quick of Life: The Rwandan Genocide—The Survivors Speak* (Philadelphia: Transatlantic Publications, 2005).

25. See for instance: Dalila Kerchouche, *Mon père, ce harki* (Paris: Seuil, 2004).

26. Joshua M. Greene, Shiva Kumar, *Witness, Voices from the Holocaust* (New York: Free Press, 1999).

27. See for instance: *Studies on the Audio-Visual Testimony of Victims of the Nazi Crimes and Genocides,* published annually in Brussels.

28. Luisa Passerini, *Fascism in Popular Memory. The Cultural Experience of the Turin Working Class* (Cambridge, Cambridge University Press, 1987); see also: Luisa Passerini, ed., *Memory and Totalitarianism* (New Brunswick: Transaction Publishers, 2005).

29. Alessandro Portelli, *The Order Has Been Carried Out, History, Memory and Meaning of a Nazi Massacre in Rome* (New York: Palgrave Macmillan, 2003).

30. See Fogel, op. cit, where in several articles the dominance of the patterns derived from the study of the Shoah is visible.

31. T. Hassan Sharif, *Resistance and Remembrance: History-Telling of the Iraqi Shi'ite Arab Refugee Women and Their Families in The Netherlands,* Ph.D., University of Amsterdam, 2004.

Part I

Truth-Seeking and Memory Failure in Stories of Chaos and Misery

Srebrenica in the History of Genocide: A Prologue

Norman M. Naimark

On July 2, 1995, the commander of the Drina Corps of the Bosnian Serbian army gave the orders for what became known as Operation Krivaja-95. This operation outlined a plan to attack the U.N. designated "Safe Area" of Srebrenica and eliminate the Bosnian Muslim enclave.[1] Accompanied by police and paramilitary units from both sides of the Drina, as well as Greek and Russian volunteers, the Bosnian Serb army attacked various points on the southern periphery of the enclave on July 6. The safe area was under the protection of "Dutchbat," a contingent of 570 lightly armed Dutch soldiers under the flag of UNPROFOR, the United Nations protection force. The Srebrenica Muslims had been formally disarmed already in 1993, as part of the agreement for the establishment of safe zones. The best-armed and professionally led units of the Bosnian Muslim army withdrew from the enclave. The remaining several thousand scattered soldiers of the Army of Bosnia-Herzegovina could offer little or no resistance to the Serbs.

Heavy shelling from the Serb units forced the Dutch to abandon a series of observation posts in the south of the Srebrenica area. Some Bosnian Muslim soldiers desperately tried to block the Dutch withdrawal, by taking Dutch hostages, and, in one tragic case, killing a Dutch soldier when a grenade was thrown at his retreating APC.[2] Meanwhile, the Muslim population fled northward towards the town of Srebrenica, already overcrowded with frightened and hungry refugees. The officers of "Dutchbat," a "barely operational unit" in the words of the Dutch defense minister Joris Voorhoeve, determined that they could offer no resistance to the Serbian advance.[3] Their repeated requests for air strikes over the next week were shuffled between U.N., NATO, and Dutch-government circles, without any serious consequences. The prejudiced attitudes of some of the Dutch officers and men toward the beleaguered Bosnian Muslim population did not bolster their interest in defending them.[4]

With no resistance of note, the Drina Corps mercilessly pounded the small formerly mining town of Srebrenica with artillery on July 9 and 10, taking control of it on July 11. The city had been packed with refugees; over 60,000 people were crammed into a town that had a prewar population of only 9,000. Thousands of refugees from Srebrenica had already begun to flee several miles northwards to the village of Potočari, where the Dutch had their headquarters in a huge former battery factory complex built by the communists. Thousands of others, led by Bosnian Muslim soldiers, took their chances with Serb shelling and dangerous minefields to try to reach Bosnian-held territory thirty miles to the west. The long-awaited NATO planes showed up from Italy on midday of July 11, desultorily dropping a few bombs, one of which hit a Serbian tank, and withdrew. This is what was called as a "pin-prick" attack.

Later in the afternoon of July 11, General Ratko Mladic, commander of the Bosnian Serbian Army, arrogantly walked the streets of Srebrenica with his Drina Corps generals, posturing for the television cameras and proclaiming that the city had been returned forever to the Serbs, in revenge of its loss to the Turks. Lieutenant Colonel Thomas Karremans, commander of Dutchbat, drank a toast with Mladic that was duly filmed for Serbian television. "Off camera," writes Samantha Power, "Mladic warned that if NATO planes reappeared, the Serbs would shell the U.N. compound in Potočari, where the refugees had gathered."[5] Meanwhile, some 20,000 refugees from all over the Srebrenica region converged on Potočari. Several thousand were able to push their way into the Dutchbat base through holes some were able to cut in the imposing wire and steel fence. Others were scattered in the surrounding fields and hills. Conditions were awful. Already, large numbers of people were sick and dying because of the lack of food, water, decent sanitation, and shelter.

The scene on the morning of July 12 was ominous. Chuck Sudetic writes:

> Serb soldiers began arriving in the field at about noon, just five or six at first, then dozens more. They were mostly clean-shaven men, middle-aged or younger. They wore army and police uniforms. Dutch troops formed a cordon around the Muslims, but after Serb soldiers threatened to use force, the gates to the UN base were opened and the Dutch troops allowed the Serbs to take their weapons and roam freely.... Women cried. Soldiers drunk on plum brandy belched out songs with crude lyrics. They fired bullets into the air and began leading the menfolk away.[6]

David Rohde adds to the scene:

Abject fear enveloped Potočari. It consumed the 15,000 Muslims in Potočari's parking lots and factory buildings, hysterical, hungry, beyond exhaustion. It paralyzed the Dutch, who tentatively patrolled the area close to their base or hid inside the compound. And it intoxicated the predators among the Serb soldiers and police.[7]

Vicious rapes and beatings went on at the same time.[8] General Mladic appeared in Potočari on the afternoon of July 12, once again accompanied by his chief officers and Serbian television. He "negotiated" with the Dutch about the transfer of the Bosnian Muslims to his control, promising safe passage out of Srebrenica for the refugees. He insisted that the Bosnian men be separated from the women and thoroughly checked to make sure there were no alleged war criminals among them. The Dutch helped in separating the males from the females. Meanwhile, on July 12 and 13, Mladic's troops and police—some on horseback, others employing fierce German shepherd dogs—were already rounding up Bosnian Muslim men and women for deportation. This was far from a peaceful process. Some were beaten, tortured, and killed on the spot; women were raped; the men and boys who had been taken away for "verification" purposes were massacred in place or trucked off to other locations, where they would eventually be killed. Rumors circulated that Mladic had recruited militia from both sides of the Drina to take out their anti-Muslim hatreds on the population of Srebrenica.[9] Officially, the Dutch supervised the transfer to Mladic's control of the refugees who had sought shelter in their compound. They stood by as the men and boys between the ages of 14 and 70 were separated from the women and children. They formed cordons along with the Serbian police to control the crowds of desperate refugees trying to board buses and trucks that had arrived to transport the women and children out of Potočari. Getting aboard a bus did not mean safe passage to Bosnian-held territory. Periodically, Bosnian Serb militiamen and paramilitaries stopped the buses, brutally harassed the women and girls while looking for money and jewelry, and sometimes removed the older boys.

Between July 12 and July 15, Bosnian Serbian military and paramilitary units successfully cut off columns of refugees trying to flee from Srebrenica. The largest column consisted of 10,000-15,000 people. Some 6,000 or so were soldiers, of whom, it is said, approximately 1,500 were armed. These were placed at the front and rear of the column.[10] The rest were mostly unarmed boys and old men, as well as some women and girls. Bombarded with artillery and subjected to the small-arms fire of snipers, they surrendered to the Serbs, some of whom employed the ruse of appearing in UNPROFOR uniforms and vehicles. Thousands of the refugees were transferred to detention centers, the largest of which were in Zvornik and Bratunac. From there, the men and boys were transported to various locations outside these towns and "liquidated," sometimes after fearful beatings and torture. Bosnian Serb Army units were deployed throughout the region to cut off the escape of smaller groups of refugees who tried to find their way through the forested hills · to Tuzla. The genocidal intent of the entire operation was underlined by the unwillingness of the Bosnian Serbs to allow the refugees to leave the enclave without interference.

Once the operation had been completed, the Bosnian Serbian Army and Ministry of Interior cooperated in a cover-up scheme to disperse the corpses. Part of their problem was that Madeline Albright had waived aerial photographs of the sites of the mass graves at a U.N. Security Council meeting on August 11. The Bosnian Serbs then dug up the mass graves of the Bosnian Muslim men and boys and reburied the bodies in dozens of sites around eastern Bosnia, with no particular relationship to the locations where the executions took place. Many of the bodies still had blindfolds, and the arms were bound behind their backs. With bulldozers and trucks, the Serbs scattered bodies and body parts in the mass graves, some of which have still not been found. Thus the difficulty both in knowing exactly how many were killed (most estimates are between 7,000 and 8,000) and in finding the identifiable remains of loved ones. So far, seventy mass graves have been located.

The Meaning of Srebrenica

With these events in mind, let me proceed to an overview of the role of Srebrenica in the history of genocide. First of all, it is important to discuss the term ethnic cleansing and its relationship to genocide, as exemplified by Srebrenica. Second, we should think about Srebrenica as a critical event in the international system during the post-Cold War world of the 1990s and the new century. What does Srebrenica mean to us and to the world more than a decade later? Third, we should try to come to terms with the effects of Srebrenica on the people of Bosnia, Muslims and Serbs, and on their future in the heart of the Balkans.

Ethnic Cleansing and Genocide

In my 2001 book, *Fires of Hatred*, I argued that the term "ethnic cleansing"—as it was applied during the war in Bosnia and later to talk about ethnic conflict throughout the region and the world—is useful for understanding other similar cataclysmic events in the course of the twentieth century.[11] New concepts are constantly being invented to describe, classify, and arrange events of the past in order to understand them in the present. In this sense, "ethnic cleansing," which was used with increasing frequency after the spring of 1992, is little different from the term "genocide," which derived its meaning from Raphael Lemkin's writings during World War II to describe what was happening to the victims of Nazism. True, Lemkin's term was his own, and he developed it with quite specific purposes in mind, while ethnic cleansing seemed to fit the needs of journalists and policy-makers to describe events on the ground in wartime Yugoslavia. Ethnic cleansing is presently taking on a juridical meaning through the war crimes courts in The Hague, just as genocide was originally defined by Article II of the United Nations Convention on the Prevention and Punishment of the Crime of Genocide of December 9, 1948, but is presently being expanded and interpreted in the international tribunals in The Hague, for former Yugoslavia, and in Arusha, for Rwanda.

There is a legitimate analytical distinction to be made between ethnic cleansing and genocide that involves intentionality, not unlike determining first-degree murder. Genocide (in German, *Völkermord*) is the intentional killing off of part or all of an ethnic, religious, or national group; the murder of a people or peoples is the objective. The intention of ethnic cleansing is to remove a people and often all traces of them from a concrete piece of territory. The goal, in other words, is to get rid of the "alien" nationality, ethnic, or religious groups and to seize control of the territory they had formerly inhabited. At one extreme of this spectrum, ethnic cleansing is closer to forced deportation or what has been called "population transfer"; the idea is to get people to move, and the means are meant to be legal and semi-legal. At the other extreme, however, ethnic cleansing and genocide are distinguishable only by the ultimate intent. Here, both literally and figuratively, ethnic cleansing bleeds into genocide, as mass murder is committed in order to rid the land of a people. This is clearly the case of Srebrenica.

Further complicating the distinctions between ethnic cleansing and genocide is the fact that forced deportation seldom takes place without violence, often murderous violence. People do not leave their homes on their own. They hold on to their land and their culture, which are interconnected. They resist deportation orders; they cling to their domiciles and their possessions; they find every possible way to avoid abandoning the place where their families have roots and their ancestors are buried. The result is that forced deportation often becomes genocidal, as people are violently ripped from their native towns and villages and killed when they try to stay.

Even when forced deportation is not genocidal in its intent, as recently found in the U.N. report about the events in Darfur, it is often genocidal in its effects.[12] Millions of people in this century have been marched in hungry columns across huge expanses of land and crowded into freight cars, buses, or holds of ships for journeys in which thousands, even tens of thousands, become sick, starve, and die. Even those refugees who survive forced deportation and life-threatening transport out of their homelands must deal with hunger, disease, and the sheer sorrow of living in refugee camps, begging for food, and seeking shelter in new lands out of reach of their persecutors. Even without the blatant case of mass murder in Srebrenica, the devastation of ethnic cleansing in Bosnia was severe enough to warrant international intervention.

The Role of Srebrenica in the History of Genocide

As often noted, Srebrenica was the largest incidence of mass killing in European history since the Second World War. It was also the first European case of genocide since World War II. It demonstrated that the slogan of "Never Again!" which emerged in the late 1960s as a consequence of the growing preoccupation with the Holocaust in the West, was exactly that, a slogan. Despite the revelations of the Holocaust and despite the U.N. Genocide Convention of 1948, the international community did little either to prevent the persecution and murder of the Bosniaks (Muslims) in campaigns of ethnic cleansing or to stop genocide, as it was perpetrated in Srebrenica. Srebrenica in this context was also a warning for the future. Genocide would and could happen unless the international community, and by this one generally meant its organizational representatives, the U.N., NATO, the European Union, the CSCE, and others, took direct action to prevent it. The launching of "Operation Deliberate Force" by NATO on August 30, 1995, which finally brought a peace accord to Bosnia-Herzegovina, the Dayton Agreement signed in Paris on December 14, should be seen as a response in good measure to the genocide in Srebrenica. Of course, there were other factors as well: the successful Croatian military campaign against the Bosnian Serbs, new divisions within the Bosnian Serbian government, the shelling of the Markale market place in Sarajevo on August 28, the decision of NATO to use its Rapid Reaction Force on the ground in Bosnia, and the determination of Slobodan Milosevic to reign in the Bosnian Serbs.[13] But more than anything else, it was Srebrenica that captured the imagination of Western public opinion and caused enormous embarrassment to the White House and other Western governments. Indeed, the resolute military response of the United States government and NATO to Serbian ethnic cleansing in Kosovo in the fall and winter of 1998-1999 also can be traced to the shock waves in the West about the depredations of General Ratko Mladic and the Army of the Serbian Republic in Srebrenica. If ethnic cleansing could lead to genocide in Bosnia, the same was possible in Kosovo. It would not be stretching the evidence to argue as well that prompt and resolute NATO and European Union efforts to stem the growing tensions between Macedonian Slavs and Albanians in 2001 grew out of the understanding that Slav-Albanian violence could lead to ethnic cleansing and much worse.

Changing Norms

Srebrenica also contributed to changing norms about intervention in stopping mass killing. The failure of the international community to take action in Rwanda in 1994, which may well have cost the lives of 800,000 Africans, also had a significant impact on the way people thought about intervention. The success of the spring 1999 NATO air attacks on Serbian positions in Kosovo and Serbia proper in forcing Belgrade to withdraw from Kosovo served as a model for the potential of humanitarian military intervention. Neither during the Armenian genocide, which was well known to the Western powers and public opinion, nor during the Holocaust, the extent of which was also clearly understood by Germany's opponents and their leaders, was military action taken to stop the mass murder of innocent victims. Such intervention was thought to be both unworthy of the practice of diplomacy and untenable under international law.

After Kosovo, prominent international lawyers, academics, and policymakers issued a series of reports that called for the setting of a threshold of severe human rights violations and international conditions, whereby the United Nations would be obliged to intervene with force. The government of Canada sponsored an International Commission on Intervention and State Sovereignty that issued the most influential of these documents in 2001.[14] The authors, led by the Director of the International Crisis Group and former Australian Foreign Minister Gareth Evans, emphasized what they called "The Responsibility to Protect." In short, states were responsible to protect their citizens against violations of their human rights that could and sometimes did lead to genocide. Ideas about state sovereignty were still important, but if states did not protect their citizens, then the humanitarian norms of the international community could and should trump sovereignty.

The gathering consensus in the West about the importance of setting up institutions that could respond militarily to violations of human rights norms was diverted—as was the international system as a whole—by the events of September 11 and declaration of a war against terrorism by the American president, George W. Bush. At the same time, the actions of the United States in Iraq, though condemned by many governments around the world, nevertheless confirmed the idea that norms of sovereignty could legitimately be subsumed to other, more pressing international concerns. The American administration increasingly cited crimes against humanity and genocide perpetrated by Saddam Hussein and his regime as the justification for intervention. Most recently, the U.N. Secretary-General's 2004 High Level Panel on the future role of the United Nations also highlighted the principle of "the responsibility to protect." I quote in full from the secretary general's report to the General Assembly:

> There is a growing recognition that the issue is not the 'right to intervene' of any State, but the 'responsibility to protect' of every State when it comes to people suffering from avoidable catastrophe – mass murder and rape, ethnic cleansing by forcible expulsion and terror, and deliberate starvation and exposure to disease. And there is a growing acceptance that while sovereign Governments have the primary responsibility to protect their own citizens from such catastrophes, when they are unable or unwilling to do so that responsibility should be taken up by the wider international community—with it spanning a continuum involving prevention, response to violence, if necessary, and rebuilding shattered societies. The primary focus should be on assisting the cessation of violence through mediation and other tools and the protection of people through such measures as the dispatch of humanitarian, human rights, and police missions. Force, if it needs to be used, should be deployed as the last resort.[15]

The "responsibility to protect" in this formulation was endorsed by the member states of the General Assembly in September 2005.[16] The problem with the High Level Panel's prescription is that if force is designated as the last resort, instead of as one of a menu of possible policy options, then circumstances tend to militate against its use, as Srebrenica demonstrates. In fact, the test of "last resort" is very high: "Has every non-military option for meeting the threat in question been explored, with reasonable grounds for believing that other measures will not succeed?"[17] Mass killing scenarios tend to develop quickly and unpredictably. Though planned by its perpetrators, the massacre in Srebrenica was such a case. Moreover, in situations where a multi-national effort is needed to engage in military activity, as was the case in Srebrenica, problems of intelligence, coordination, decision-making, and operational readiness are often too daunting for effective action to be taken.

Michael Ignatieff points out that there is an increasing gap between worldwide human rights standards, as they have developed since Rwanda and Srebrenica, and the "risk-averse means" that we have developed to defend them. He suggests a more robust use of force in the defense of human rights: "Failure to do this systematically in Rwanda and Bosnia undermined the credibility of human rights values in zones of danger around the world."[18] The questions remain, however, precisely at what point force can and should be used to deter or stop genocide, and what military formation(s) will carry out the intervention? Srebrenica highlighted both of these issues. The Dutch government resigned in 2002 as a consequence of a mildly critical report about Dutchbat's inaction in the Srebrenica safe area. What if Dutch soldiers had attempted to resist the Bosnian Serb invasion of Srebrenica? What if they had rejected Mladic's ultimatum at Potočari to turn over the Bosnian Muslim refugees in and around their compound? Did they show unconscionably more concern about their own welfare than that of the Bosnian Muslims in their care? The controversy in the Netherlands goes on, as new evidence paints a portrait of Dutch embarrassing indifference, complacency, and even cowardice in face of genocide.[19]

Ignatieff's pessimism has considerable justification in the subsequent handling by the international community of the depredations in Darfur. First of all, there has been an unnecessary and even unconscionable argument over whether the terrible mass killings, rapes, and forced deportation constituted genocide. As the Darfur crisis deepened, Colin Powell called it genocide as did President Bush. Recently, Jendai Frazier, a deputy secretary of state for Africa, indicated that the events were no longer genocide. Again, as in Rwanda, discussions about the dreaded "G-Word" dominate policy discussions about Darfur rather than the initiation of concrete measures to stop the Janjaweed murderous excesses against the Fur and other so-called "Black African" peoples of the region. Contrary to popular belief, the Genocide Convention of 1948 does not oblige its signatories to intervene. The only obligation of states is to stop genocide in their own territory, not elsewhere.[20] In assessing how to act in Darfur, Srebrenica should be kept in clear view. If initially the aggression in Sudan, like that in Bosnia, did not constitute intentional mass murder, but rather the violent expulsion of peoples from their land, Bosnia demonstrates how quickly ethnic cleansing can turn into genocide.

In Darfur already, as many as 70,000 people have been killed; more than 1.65 million have been internally displaced, while there are more than 200,000 destitute refugees from Darfur in neighboring Chad. Only the concerted pressure of the U.N., NATO, the European Union, and the United States on Khartoum can prevent further horrors. The soldiers of the African Union cannot handle the situation. Military intervention by NATO may well be required.

The Report of the International Commission of Inquiry on Darfur to the U.N. Secretary General (January 25, 2005) has been much criticized by the international human rights community for not condemning the actions of the Sudanese government as genocide.[21] But, in fact, the report leaves the question of genocide to the courts, in particular to the International Criminal Court, which will consider indictments of genocide against alleged Sudanese perpetrators. In addition, the report clearly states that "international offences such as the crimes against humanity and war crimes that have been committed in Darfur may be no less serious and heinous than genocide."[22] In the end, international intervention in Darfur should not be dependent on whether or not the crime involved is judged to be genocide. In retrospect, one could very well have said the same about intervention in Bosnia.

The Definition of Genocide

Srebrenica plays a central part in the evolving international juridical understanding of what constitutes genocide. After all, the precedents in international law for the crime of genocide have been very sparse indeed. The Nuremberg Trials are of limited help for setting such precedents; they were primarily about condemning aggressive war, not about putting Nazis on trial for mass murder. The Genocide Convention of 1948 was based, more than anything else, on concepts of genocide that emerged out of the work of Raphael Lemkin on the Nazi occupation in Europe and the horrors of World War II. Those who authored the convention, the members of the Sixth Committee of the General Assembly, were more interested in condemning and preventing the reemergence of Nazi-like crimes than they were in providing a broad palate for understanding the potentialities of mass killing. The Soviets and Poles—as well as other member nations—made sure that language about the mass murder of political groups was left out of the convention.[23] In short, the International Criminal Tribunal for the Former Yugoslavia (ICTY) in The Hague had to start pretty much from scratch.

Seen in this context, Srebrenica is the crucial event in the ICTY's mandate to prosecute war criminals and to sentence them for crimes against humanity. Srebrenica is also central to the indictments of genocide that have been entered at the ICTY in The Hague. Most significantly, the ICTY judged the massacre at Srebrenica to have been a case of genocide. According to the court in the case against General Radislav Krstic, by physically destroying the community of Bosniaks in Srebrenica, the Army of the Republic of Serbia committed an intentional act of mass murder against the entire Bosnian Muslim community, in the words of the Genocide Convention, "as such." More than 7,500 men and boys were executed; 30,000 women, children, and elderly were forcibly deported. The purpose, in the words of the President of the Serbian Republic, Radovan Karadzic, was "to create an unbearable situation of total insecurity with no hope of further survival or life for the inhabitants of Srebrenica."[24]

Krstic was initially convicted of the crime of genocide. But, after a successful appeal, this charge was dropped and he was sentenced to 35 years in prison for the lesser crime of "aiding and abetting genocide." His deputy, Dragan Obrenovic, received 17 years for war crimes. A number of figures known to have been involved in the Srebrenica genocide have still not been brought to trial. Milosevic also faced indictment for genocide, among other crimes, but died before sentencing. Mladic and Karadzic have similarly been indicted for genocide due to their roles in Srebrenica. Karadzic was finally turned over to the court in July 2008; Mladic remains at large. For the indictments to be successful, the prosecution will need to demonstrate intent on the part of the defendants to engage in mass murder. So far, the lawyers for the prosecution have been unsuccessful in doing so. But, quite remarkably, they have convinced the court that the mass murder of 7,500 human beings constitutes genocide, a judgment that will have implications far beyond the war in Yugoslavia. Unlike most of the recognized historical cases of genocide, there were no women or small children killed by the mass executioners in Srebrenica, and the numbers were in the thousands, not hundreds of thousands and millions.

The appellate court's arguments about Krstic's role in the genocide in Srebrenica are both interesting and consequential.[25] In upholding the original judgment of the Trial Chamber of August 2, 2001, that genocide was committed at Srebrenica, the court made it clear that the intentional killing of "part" of the Bosnian Muslim group had to be a "substantial part" of the group as established in earlier case law. But the court ruled that it could be a substantial part of "Srebrenica Bosnian Muslims." In other words, the intentional mass murder of a substantial part of a "group within a territory," even if it was exclusively men and boys, constitutes genocide. That the Bosnian Serbs forcibly deported the women and children also contributed to genocide, since that ensured that the Srebrenica Muslim community would be destroyed. The defense's argument that the victims were killed not to destroy a community and thus commit genocide but to eliminate potential military opposition of Bosnian Muslims was countered with evidence that the Bosnian Serbs killed infirm and mentally incapable old men, as well as young boys, who could not have been reasonable military opponents.

The court suggested that the Bosnian Serbs let the women and children go because of their "sensitivity to public opinion," not because they did not intend to commit mass murder. Moreover, the special quality of the Srebrenica territory, the fact that it was a U.N.-protected area, contributed to the impact of the killing and deportation of Srebrenica's population. The judge summarized:

> I consider that the alleged requirement for proof of intent to destroy the group physically or biologically was met by the disastrous consequences for the family structures on which the Srebrenica part of the Bosnian Muslim group was based. The Trial Chamber was correct in finding that the Bosnian Serb forces knew that their activities 'would inevitably result in the physical disappearance of the Bosnian Muslim population at Srebrenica'.[26]

The following taped recording of a conversation between Krstic and Obrenovic was played in court but disallowed as evidence on technical grounds. Still, it points to the essentials of the genocide conviction—intentionality, forethought, and a plan to kill all members of the national, religious or ethnic group within a particular entity.

Krstic: Are you working down there?
Obrenovic: Of course we're working.
Krstic: Good.
Obrenovic: We've managed to catch a few more, either by gunpoint or in mines [mine fields].
Krstic: Kill them all, Goddamn it!
Obrenovic: Everything is going according to plan.
Krstic: Single one must not be left alive. [Not a single one must be left alive.]
Obrenovic: Everything is going according to plan. Everything.
Krstic: Way to go, chief. The Turks [derogatory term for Bosniaks] are probably listening to us. Let them listen, the motherfuckers.[27]

Conclusions: Memory and History

The final and concluding problem that I would like to broach here has to do with memory and history. Some have suggested that one needs to learn how to forget painful historical events rather than to remember: that in the modern world—and especially in the Balkans—there is a surfeit of historical memory rather than a dearth of it. But the issue of collective memory is not really one of choice; the question is, really, how will the participants remember and how will we remember. In this connection, the courts have their job to do—to indict and prosecute the guilty in order that the victims, their relatives, and their societies can say to themselves that justice has been done. They must establish the chain of command and tie together the threads of responsibility for war crimes, crimes against humanity, and genocide. Despite the legitimate complaints about the ICTY, the interminable length of the trial against Milosevic among them, on balance it has performed these tasks admirably. Scholars also have their job to do. They have to try to understand how terrible massacres like Srebrenica happen, how a viable and dynamic multi-national society broke down, and how political leadership failed the respective peoples involved. Writers, artists, journalists, film-makers and others also have their tasks in helping societies understand what happened to themselves and how to digest these awful crimes. None of these tasks involve forgetting.[28] They are about remembering, documenting, understanding, and absorbing the past. They are about developing perspective and understanding. If we have learned any lessons from the Armenian genocide, which remains a highly sensitive historical bone of contention between Turks and Armenians, or the Holocaust, which required forty years of intense debate, research, investigation, reflection, and discussion among Jews and Germans before a Jewish Museum could be constructed in Berlin and the Holocaust Memorial could be built near the Brandenburg Gate, it is that perpetrators and victims can come to some kind of peaceful accommodation only when the past is explored openly and honestly, with full participation of survivors and scholars alike.

As these examples demonstrate, the process of coming to terms with genocide does not happen quickly or painlessly. In July 2005 a conference dedicated to the 10th anniversary of the massacre in Srebrenica was held in Sarajevo. The conference was sponsored by the city of Sarajevo, the University of Sarajevo and the University of North Carolina, Charlotte. The proceedings opened not in Sarajevo, but in Potočari, with speeches, formalities and the burial of six hundred and ten newly identified Muslims. The conference began the next day, 12 July, and was organized around one theme and one theme only: the genocide against the Muslim people of Bosnia-Herzegovina. Speaker after speaker rose to reinforce this nomenclature. One very able French social psychologist and expert on the history of genocide by the name of Jacques Semelin tried to make the argument that perhaps Srebrenica should not be considered genocide, but rather a form of ethnic cleansing or of massacre. His very sensible interpellation caused a stir of outrage among the Bosnians. He was denounced as a genocide denier. Charles Ingrao, head of the Scholars' Initiative project on the history of the war, gave an interview with a local paper that incorrectly reported that he, too, questioned the use of genocide to describe the events in Srebrenica. That also caused quite a stir. It is fair to say that this was not an academic conference at all, at least not the way we understand the idea. The proceedings were organized to enshrine the Srebrenica events in historical understanding as a case of genocide.

The Sarajevo conference on the 10th anniversary of Srebrenica was nothing more or less than an attempt to engrave the genocide into the new shrine of Bosnian national consciousness. Like the Jews in Israel and the Armenians in the Diaspora, the Bosnians understand the genocide as an integral piece, even the missing piece, of their historical narrative. Before the war, Bosnians—like the Jews and Armenians—were a relatively well-educated and cosmopolitan people, attached, to be sure, to their Muslim heritage, but ready and able to live in multi-national communities within a larger Yugoslavia.[29] The genocide changed all that. Now they consider themselves Bosniaks, and like the Serbs and Croats, they seek to build their own national institutions and culture, based primarily on their identity as victims. At the same time, they call for a united, democratic, and multi-national Bosnia-Herzegovina. This would mean, of course, an end to Bosnia's dysfunctional component parts inherited from Dayton, the Republika Srpska and the Croat-Muslim federation. The question remains, however, how do the Bosnians perpetuate the myths of victimhood at the hands of the Serbs, when they seek, at the same time, to incorporate a substantial Serbian population into the new Bosnia-Herzegovina. (There are similar, but less vital questions about the Croats.)

Meanwhile, the Serbs complain that no one remembers their losses at the hand of the Bosnians. Both Muslims and Serbs appeal to the international community for confirmation of their victim status. Combined with the traditional Serbian cultural understanding of their historical victimhood, this new Serbian martyr complex makes for a powerful and dangerous political force in the contemporary Balkans. Getting the Serbs to recognize the full scope of their complicity in genocide and ethnic cleansing in the Balkans has proven as difficult as finding a way for the Turks to accept their responsibility for the Armenian genocide, and for many of the same reasons. Neither Serbs nor Turks are ready to accept the perceived insult to their national dignity that recognition of genocide against others implies.

For many Bosnians, Srebrenica is not just a particularly nasty incident in the history of the war, 1992-1995. Like Auschwitz for the Jews, it has become a sacred site for worship, a slogan rather than a place where horrible crimes were committed, and a plaint for international recognition of suffering. On February 27, 2006, the Bosnian government convinced the International Court of Justice in The Hague to take up its civil suit against the government of Serbia-Montenegro. Attempts by the Serbs to settle out of court have come to naught. Although the chief Bosnian lawyer, Sahib Softic, says that the goal of the plaintiffs is "to heal past wounds in the region," this can hardly be the result of an attempt to recover damages of up to 100 billion U.S. dollars. Where he comes closer to the truth is his claim that the essence of the suit is "moral, not material…. It is more important for us that it establishes that genocide has taken place."[30] It is noteworthy that the suit does not confine genocide to Srebrenica and instead insists that it was part and parcel of the entire war from 1992-1995. In a similar spirit, the Bosnian legal scholar Smail Cekic, the chief organizer of the conference on the 10th Anniversary of Srebrenica described above, protested against the report on "ethnic cleansing" authored by the "Scholars' Initiative." In his letter of February 9, 2006, to Charles Ingrao, head of the project, he writes: "The crime of genocide in Bosnia-Herzegovina is unique, including its intent in relation to the complete territory of Bosnia-Herzegovina." He adds: "the term 'ethnic cleansing' implies genocide in all its forms."[31]

It is now more than ten years since the war and the signing of the Dayton Accords. Despite the efforts made by the U.N., NATO, the European Union, and a host of other international institutions, Bosnia is an economic and political mess. There is plenty of blame to go around. The Dayton agreement has left Bosnia hamstrung by an inoperable governmental system. There may have been no choice, but there is certainly nothing to be proud of in the disastrous ethnically-based institutional arrangements that Dayton bequeathed to the Bosnians. If the economy of Bosnia-Herzegovina has improved by fits and starts over the years as a result of the notable presence of foreign NGOs, relief missions, militaries, and other organizations in the country, the resentments, corruption, and social problems bred by the "internationals" undermine domestic stability and sense of common purpose. In the end, though, the European Union has every reason to stay the course and apply its vast resources to solving Bosnia's economic and infrastructural problems. Bosnia-Herzegovina, just like Croatia and Serbian-Montenegro, has every reason to pursue the "association and stabilization" agreements with the European Union. The real problem that lies at the heart of the Bosnian misery is that of identity. If the genocide is at the core of national consciousness, then it is hard to imagine a multi-national state can succeed in the future. But there are no workable alternatives.

Notes

1. Srebrenica had been designated a U.N. "safe area" on April 16, 1993, according to Security Council Resolution 819. For historical narratives of the Srebrenica massacre, see, among others: Jay Willem Honig and Norbert Both, *Srebrenica: Record of a War Crime* (New York: Penguin, 1997); David Rohde, *End Game: The Betrayal and Fall of Srebrenica: Europe's Worst Massacre since World War II* (Farrar, Straus and Giroux, 1997): Samantha Power, *"A Problem from Hell": America and the Age of Genocide* (New York: Basic Books, 2002), 391-421; "Report of the Secretary-General pursuant to General Assembly Resolution 53/35 (1998), 'Srebrenica Report', 15 November 1999, in Smail Cekic, et al. eds. *Genocide in Srebrenica. United Nations "Safe Area," in July 1995* (Sarajevo: "CPU", 2001); and Chuck Sudetic, *Blood and Vengeance: One Family's Story of a War in Bosnia* (New York: W.W. Norton, 1998).
2. See the accounts of the shooting and hostage-taking by David Rohde, *Endgame*, 35-36, 49, 65.
3. Honig and Both, *Srebrenica*, 184.
4. Guido Snel, "Holandski nacionalizam gori je od balkanskog," *Dani*, 421 (July 8, 2005): 21-26.
5. Power, 400.
6. Sudetic, 292-293.
7. Rohde, 229.
8. Ibid.
9. Ibid., 296.
10. Charles Ingrao, "Research Team 6: The Safe Areas," 23. Ingrao is the author of this team report. He is also the organizer of the remarkable, multi-national on-line project, "The Scholars' Initiative," of which it is a part. These reports, most of which are in draft forms, are available at: www.cla.purdue.edu/si.
11. Norman M. Naimark, *Fires of Hatred: Ethnic Cleansing in Twentieth-Century Europe* (Cambridge, Mass.: Harvard University Press, 2001), 2-5. Another recent book that talks about the importance of distinguishing ethnic cleansing and genocide is Michael Mann, *The Dark Side of Democracy: Explaining Ethnic Cleansing* (Cambridge: Cambridge University Press, 2005), 10-18.
12. *Report on the International Commission of Inquiry on Darfur to the United Nations Secretary-General*, Pursuant to Security Council Resolution 1564 of September 18, 2004. (Geneva, January 25, 2005).

13. In a new book on the Dayton Accord, Derek Chollet mentions a number of factors that brought peace to Bosnia-Herzegovina. See his analysis, Derek Chollet, *The Road to the Dayton Accords: A Study of American Statecraft* (New York: Palgrave Macmillan, 2005), 184, and that of Ivo H. Daalder, *Getting to Dayton: The Making of America's Bosnia Policy* (Washington D.C.: Brookings, 2000), 162-166. Both authors emphasize the importance of Srebrenica to the shift in American and NATO policy. Chollet is rather too entranced by the miracle-working of Richard Holbrooke, and forgets, as does Holbrooke himself, that the war was brought to an end because of the bombing, not because of Dayton. See Richard Holbrooke, *The End a War* (New York: Random House, 1999).

14. International Commission on Intervention and State Sovereignty, Gareth Evans, Mohamed Sahnoun, et al., *The Responsibility to Protect*, December 2001.

15. United Nations General Assembly. 59th Session, "Follow-up to the outcome of the Millennium Summit," Note by the Secretary General, December 2, 2004, A/59/65, pp. 56-57.

16. United Nations General Assembly. 60th Session. Resolution adopted by the General Assembly (September 16, 2005), October 24, 2005, p.p. 30-3l. It is important to note that while the use of force is not excluded in this rendition of the "responsibility to protect," it is also not specifically mentioned.

17. Ibid., 58.

18. Michael Ignatieff, *Human Rights as Politics* (Princeton, N.J.: Princeton University Press, 2001), 43-45.

19. The publication of the 2002 report by the Netherlands Institute of War Documentation prompted the government to resign. A number of Dutch scholars, including Mient Jan Faber and Selma Leydesdorff, have continued to investigate the behavior of Dutchbat in the Srebrenica massacre. For the report, see: Netherlands Institute for War Information, *Srebrenica: Reconstruction, Background, Consequences and Analysis of the Fall of a Safe Area* (http://194.134.65.21).

20. Article 1 of the Genocide Convention states that its signatories "undertake to prevent and to punish" the crime of genocide, but Article 6 indicates that this obligation only applies to genocide committed within one's own state. Article 8 reinforces this conclusion by noting that states can call on the Security Council to take actions against genocide, but that they have no need to do so themselves unless it takes place within their own borders. William A. Schabas, *Genocide in International Law* (Cambridge: Cambridge University Press, 2000), 491-502.

21. In a recent draft article to be published in the University of Chicago Law Review, David Luban, an international human rights lawyer, criticizes the report on a number of counts: 1) that it incorrectly assesses the genocidal essence of the mass killing in Darfur; 2) that it denies genocide the status of being "the crime of crimes," and 3) that it serves politicians as a "cover for inaction." David Luban, "Calling Genocide by Its Rightful Name: Lemkin's Word, Darfur, and the U.N. Report," draft article, 2006.

22. *Report of the International Commission of Inquiry on Darfur*, 4.

23. "Political groups," the Soviets insisted, "were entirely out of place in a scientific definition of genocide and their inclusion would weaken the convention and hinder the fight against genocide." *UN Third Session*, Sixth Committee (of the General Assembly). Sixty-fourth Meeting, October 1, 1948, "Continuation of the consideration of the draft convention on genocide," 12-19.

24. Prosecutor v. Radislav Krstic [2004] ICTY 7 (April 19, 2004), 56.

25. Prosecutor v. Krstic, April 10, 2004, 65-75.

26. Prosecutor v. Krstic, April 19, 2004, 67.

27.   Cited in Slavenka Drakulic, *They Would Never Hurt a Fly: War Criminals on Trial in the Hague* (New York: Viking, 2005), 102-103.

28.   This may be an exaggeration, as one of my former students, Emira Tufo, now a Bosnian U.N. official, pointed out to me after having read an earlier draft of this paper. She thought many Bosnians would just as soon forget the war and have no serious relationship to the genocide in Srebrenica. Bosnian literature in translation about the war backs up her observation. Some of it, to be sure, is bitter and angry about what happened. See especially Dubravka Ugresic, *The Culture of Lies: Antipolitical Essays* (University Park, Pennsylvania: Penn State Press, 1998). But much of the literature is almost whimsical and otherworldly about the improbability of the actual events. See Aleksandar Hemon, *The Question of Bruno* (New York: Vintage, 2000), and Miljenko Jergovic, *Sarajevo Marlboro*, transl. Stela Tomasevic (New York: Archipelago Books, 2004).

29.   On the history of Bosnian national consciousness, see Muhamed Filipovic, *Bosnjacka Politika: Politicki razvoj u Bosni u 10. i 20. Stoljecu* (Sarajevo: Svjetlost, 1996).

30.   *RFE/RL Newsline*, part II, vol. 10, no. 35 (February 24, 2006).

31.   Emphasis in the original. Prof. Dr. Smail Cekic, University of Sarajevo, to Prof. Charles Ingrao, Purdue University, February 9, 2006. I thank Prof. Ingrao for sharing the letter with me.

1

When Communities Fell Apart and Neighbors Became Enemies: Stories of Bewilderment in Srebrenica

Selma Leydesdorff

No one knows why the Srebrenica massacre happened. Europe's worst mass killing since the Second World War remains an enigma, largely because of the unanswered questions surrounding the international political game that led up to the event.[1] Srebrenica stands for atrocity. It is no longer even necessary to say "massacre"—simply uttering the town's name is enough to evoke images of the horrors committed there. During the Bosnian war, so-called "safe areas" were created, territories protected by the United Nations where Muslims could take refuge. Srebrenica was declared such a "safe area" in 1993, protected by the Dutch army under United Nations command, until July 1995 when it fell into Serb hands. The Serbs massacred thousands of civilians. Exactly how many is unknown, but the reported figures range from 7,000 to 10,000. Before the massacre began, women, children and older men were herded into the U.N. compound of Potočari where they expected to be given shelter. Many younger men had chosen to risk fleeing through the woods to territory controlled by the Bosnian army. Few made it to safety, however. They were killed in the woods, and those men who went to Potočari perished in the massacre. Srebrenica is the place where thousands did not have time to say goodbye, where people saw their loved ones for the last time and where people lost the will to live because the pain of separation had become unbearable.[2]

Ten years after the Bosnian war, its history is being written. A memorial culture is being created in which the narratives of the "facts of war," such as the defense of Sarajevo, the role of the political leadership, the military strategies and the reaction of the international community, form part of the founding myths of a new nation. Together, the memories of war form a polyphonic text that frequently manifests itself as a bitter lament or an indictment.[3] There are often conflicting versions of events, their meaning and their importance. Within this memorial culture, scant attention is paid to the thousands of women who survived, in many cases with children. The public debate focuses on questions such as "Who was responsible for the fall of the safe area?" But questions along the lines of "How did you manage to survive?," "Can you go on living after what you have seen?," and "Are you only capable of hatred or do you see any chance for redemption?" are not posed.

On the rare occasions when the survivors of Srebrenica are heard, their voices are spoken through the language of political polemics, or through the juridical language of the writ of summons the survivors have presented to the Netherlands and the United Nations. In both cases, the survivors' pain, grief, and bewilderment have been transformed. Even at the annual public commemoration of the massacre, there is no space for the deep and intense mourning of the survivors. Those who wish to pay their respects to loved ones must do so with hundreds of cameras looking on. The survivors receive even less attention in the writing or, rather, rewriting of history. In this chapter I will attempt to show how indispensable the survivors' voices are in any serious history of Srebrenica and how stories can contribute to and modify our understanding of what happened in the fateful days after the fall of the enclave. As in all histories of war—and of genocide in particular—we must include the stories of the survivors if we are to obtain an honest and fair historical record.[4]

The Importance of Survivors' Voices

For the last five years I have listened to the women who survived "Srebrenica." They live in villages, refugee camps and small towns, with little access to the centers of power. Many of them are still uprooted; few have found a place they can call home. A growing number of them want to return home because life as a refugee is so harsh. Today, Srebrenica is a desolate place offering few facilities and even less employment. Many of the surrounding villages are still in ruins, but one occasionally meets women there, living with children in what were once houses (before the villages were shelled). The returnees have had a hard time putting together the bits and pieces of their lives. Material conditions are appalling, and to make matters worse for the Muslims who return, Srebrenica is now "enemy" territory. According to some estimates, 6,000 people have not found a permanent place to settle. These displaced people obviously want their economic conditions improved, but they find it even more important to know why their husbands, fathers and sons were killed. They also want to know what happened elsewhere during the war. They wonder what took place on the international stage and whether the fate of their town was negotiated in exchange for raising the siege of Sarajevo. In short, they want to preserve the memory of what so many seem to want to forget. And they wait for news.[5] Even those who know that their men are dead are waiting for the deaths to be confirmed and the bodies found.

The memories of these genocide survivors contrast sharply with the reports and analyses through which the political debate is conducted, documents which rarely mention the survivors and are for the most part commissioned by national governments. It is vital to the survivors that their voices be heard in the public domain. They want their ordeal to be known. The history of the war should include their own stories of betrayal, survival, and loneliness. It should reflect their own recollections of the mass murder and their efforts to come to terms with it. Their memories of the war have led them to accuse the international community and the Dutch army of "betraying" them—and I have chosen deliberately to phrase this in the same way they do.

In my research I have dealt with many themes, including the destruction of cultural patterns, emptiness, endless waiting and hoping, and bewilderment at the dramatic social changes which have taken place with far-reaching consequences for the women's daily lives. The outbreak of the Bosnian war led to the destruction of a pluralistic culture.[6] A society that was once multicultural, albeit created and held together by strong authoritarian government, today no longer exists. The breakdown of safety and security has left a legacy of fragmented and traumatized lives, and hence traumatized stories. Researchers have debated at length about how they should interpret the memories of survivors, which are inherently volatile, sad and full of unspeakable horror. Yet despite these potential difficulties, there is now a strong consensus that no serious history of genocide can ignore the voices of survivors.[7] Their stories, however, are not straightforward accounts of "what happened." Like all memories, they are based on perceptions of the present. They are deeply moving accounts that shift back and forth between frozen memories of atrocities and the later reconstruction and interpretation of the hostilities they suffered.[8] The stories, in turn, give meaning to the present and constitute the survivors' longings and musings about the future world they would like to live in. The accounts are emotional and subjective, at times bitter—but not always.

As early as 1978 the American historian Hayden White questioned "the fictions of factual representation,"[9] that is, the Western notion that empiricism was the only entrance to a so-called "reality." He argued that this prejudice prevents us from grasping experiences that do not fit into the traditional historical mold based on the criticism of written sources, in which emotions are chiefly regarded as disruptive, and introducing bias and error. In Nancy Wood's *Vectors of Memory*, the Holocaust survivor Jean Amery admitted that his memories were embedded in what Nietzsche called "resentment."[10] In Wood's view, however, this resentment acts as an impetus for critical and moral reflection, just as it does in the writings of Primo Levi. Wood contends that such "resentment" represents "a trenchant rebuke of the moral dereliction of societies in whom victims placed their trust." Moreover, she continues, "these reflections on memory-as-resentment still speak to us today, not because the genocides to which we are witness are analogous to the Holocaust," but because, like Amery, "victims have experienced their fate as one of abandonment by the outside world."[11] It follows that in the writing of the history of genocide—and this includes Srebrenica—"emotional" memory and "objective" historical research are interwoven and inseparable. This is inevitable. It is as much the historian's task to decipher witness accounts, including charged emotional language, as it is to interpret whatever "traditional" written sources are available. This is the only way in which we can hope to arrive at a truly historical account of what happened.

A few years ago the historian Omer Bartov, arguing in favor of microhistories of genocide at a local level, wrote: "he devil is in the local," for it is there that we can see the mechanics of mass violence. These microhistories enrich our understanding of the mass killings of our century, events that usually deal not only with perpetrators and victims, but also with a variety of bystanders, collaborators and resisters. He argued for the use of new disciplinary methods, pointing out that "much of what we have been unable to grasp when looking at the 'big picture' can be much better understood when seen at the local level."[12] Anthropological research into how people survive can help us comprehend how people cope with history at a personal level and negotiate the gap between their new and former lives.[13] Such "negotiation" certainly has an impact on how history is remembered. But in studying the microhistories from my own interviews, I have concluded that the main problem is not how memories are constructed versus "reality." The main problem is what *cannot* be remembered and put into words. To begin with, the women I have interviewed were reluctant to talk about the atrocities and the pain they had gone through. At a deeper level, the survivors either did not wish to remember or, more frequently, certain episodes were too difficult to recall in the light of their present lives. I am referring not to the trauma, but to their past of peaceful co-existence with those who eventually betrayed them. This past can hardly be understood now. The betrayal they witnessed, the participation of friends, neighbors and loved ones in murder and genocide, also prevents them from developing any vision of the future, for such a vision can only be based on feelings about what was perceived as "good" in the past.

In the interviews I have conducted, memories often manifest themselves as bitterness and angry accusations of betrayal by the Dutch army in particular. The women I have spoken to recount the arrival of the Serb soldiers (known as the Chetniks), the disruption of previously good relations between the ethnic groups and the mass murder. They also describe how they have tried to give meaning to what happened to them, how they have resumed their lives, and how they have attempted to incorporate their experiences into their life stories. These are traumatized fragments that reflect the women's truth about their subjective experience. "Truth" in this case is consistent with what psychoanalyst Shoshana Felman calls a truth more profound than legal truth—which she saw as institutionalized and culturally channeled—and more complex than judgment and ordeal.[14] The stories show us the microhistories of genocide; they are diverse and profoundly human.

Narratives Out of Order

When the survivors talked to me, one meta-narrative I encountered was fury about the betrayal. However, the narratives were usually more complicated. They defied any (semi-) official explanation that posited the events that took place as inevitable. They decried the silence that greeted the question "Why did history take the course it did?" By taking this critical stance, the narratives placed themselves outside of ordered reality. Often these stories were indeed chaotic—as traumatized stories tend to be. The women who told them shared a desire to explain that they were abandoned and betrayed by the world, and that no one seemed to care. In my view, their stories asked the world questions about moral accountability. Until now, the world had closed its ears to such painful suggestions.

The stories I have been told showed all the characteristics of trauma narratives. They were always highly personal accounts of survival. They often contained several messages. And they borrowed heavily from genres of disasters and loss they heard elsewhere that provide them with the phrases, words and descriptions that allowed them to bear witness to a fate that was difficult to express. How could victims/survivors find words for the horror that unfolded before their eyes? Where should they begin their story, and what words could describe the feeling that came up and grabbed them by the throat when they started to talk? What should they say and what should they omit? Was it not better to be silent since the task of remembering and speaking was so horrendous? Some historians argue that a trauma has not truly been witnessed until the traumatized has testified. If this is true, then the eyewitness account is essential.

Fazila Speaks

> I do not hate anybody. Why should I hate? Why? I could hate, if I knew who had taken him away. I would like him to have the same terrible fate, but I could not kill him. I could not kill, I could not kill. Let God judge him. I could never kill a child, anybody's child. Whatever he may be, he is a child, and he has a soul. And I love people, I love animals. I have a cat, a hen, and two lambs. I returned here to be able to have animals. What could I do in Sarajevo, in a flat, or somewhere? I love nature and I live with nature. I know when it is spring, autumn and winter.

Fazila has returned to live in her village of Potočari, five kilometers from Srebrenica. Sitting with me in her poorly heated house, she spoke for hours. She told me about her life as a survivor of the Srebrenica massacre. I could see from the way she covered her hair with a headscarf that she was a religious woman. Since the first time I interviewed her, she has opened a small market stall near the enormous graveyard at Potočari where she sells books and flowers to those who visit the graves. She gave me a ballpoint pen with the words "Potočari Memorial" written on it. It was the first opportunity to give someone a present, she said.

She came from a well-to-do family, but the war was severe and serious threat forced them to flee in 1992. She eventually managed to return home during the war and it was from there that she left for the compound where the crowds were herded together in 1995. She lost her husband and her son. She told me about the circumstances under which she departed:

> There was a terrible shelling at dawn. I was sleeping in one room and my husband in another. We did not sleep in one room because of the shelling. We thought that if one of us got killed, the other would stay alive. But I was very frightened so I went to his room. I asked if this was the end. But he told me that it was something special, but there had never been so much shelling. It was Wednesday or Thursday, and our children were in Srebrenica. I was terribly worried about my children. My Hamed [her husband, *S.L.*] told me not to worry because our children were clever. He thought that

Fejzo would go with his pals across the woods. However, my Fejzo arrived on foot from Srebrenica. He'd walked through all those shells, and wasn't hit by any of them. It was Friday. Nirha came in an UN car, the one they used to transport dead people. … So they both came on Friday. I was glad to see them, but I was also overwhelmed with worry, not knowing what to do with them, where we could go. You see, I can talk a lot, I can talk about everything, but when I remember the moments when I was leaving my house, when I departed.… My husband was sitting there and did not let me do anything. He told me not to panic, that Srebrenica would not fall. One of my neighbors came in that evening and told me that everybody had left and asked me what I was waiting for. I took a bag and put some underwear in it, nothing else. And I squeezed a coat in it too, I simply did not think that there might be a moment when I would not have anything, crazy woman that I was. But panic does not allow you to reason properly. I made myself a rucksack. My Fejzo told me not to make a big one, 40 by 60 cm would be enough. I grabbed a kind of a curtain from the window, left the house and said good-bye to him. I went down and saw a huge line of people going from Srebrenica towards the Dutch compound. I returned to see my son once again. He came with me to the bridge. His chin was trembling and he told me: "Mum, do not cry, the more you cry, the worse I feel." However strong I was, I could not endure all that, Of course I was traumatized. I could not, I could not. He was not guilty of anything, he did not owe anything to anybody. And I do not know even where his bones are. I curse them, Oh God, my God.

At this point—like in all my interviews—we had to stop and rest until this sudden wave of sorrow had ebbed. Such moments always occurred when interviewees talked about the way they embraced someone for the last time or how they said goodbye, when mothers talk about being separated from their sons while protesting that they were too young to be killed. Or, as in this case, when a young man left for the woods and both knew it might be the last goodbye. With some effort, Fazila continued. She told me how she arrived with thousands of other displaced people at the spot where the men were eventually separated from the women to be killed. When Fazila and Nirha got to the compound, they did not understand what was happening. They heard people crying, and knew quite soon that women had been raped, babies murdered, and men mutilated and taken away for "interrogation." She continued:

So I went with Nirha. They let us enter [the compound], four by four. … I lay, I sat on the concrete. I had only one towel, which I had brought along for when I changed my underwear. Well, that towel became my quilt, my pillow, my mattress, everything. It was like that for two days and two nights. And I was not hungry at all. I only felt cold and frightened. Mind you, it was July and very hot, but I felt a terrible cold. I felt the freezing cold along my back.

Like all women, she was evacuated and ended up in the capital, Sarajevo, which was crowded with refugees, people who often met them with contempt because they were considered backwards. She waited for news. It was not immediately clear that her husband and son had been murdered. It was obvious that many men had been killed, but it was believed that many more might still be alive in camps in Kosovo or elsewhere in Serbia. Since then such hopes have faded and the waiting has been replaced by a wish to give the men a decent funeral.[15] At present, their deaths are marked by an annual July 11th commemoration at an immense graveyard in Potočari.

Fazila's husband and son were among the missing. She said: "My husband's remains were found in a secondary grave at Jadar.[16] They buried him without his head. They found the head later on, so there will be another burial. Again. Apart from all that, I have to live and work, to run the house, to see people, to... What? What am I like? What am I made of?"

Again we had to stop the interview. She tried to explain that she cannot bear the sadness, but that she knows she has to because life goes on. To bury her husband was part of her struggle against inhumanity. A decent funeral becomes a personal way of assigning meaning to a life that must go on. Her refusal to hate is another aspect of her sense of self, of the way she dealt with the past. She also acknowledged her friendship with some of the "others" who have been demonized over the years.

Before the war, she told me, she never cared whether someone was a Serb or a Muslim:

I did not care at all. It was important whether somebody was human, good. I never thought that there could be a war, that we would fight one another. I thought that somebody would attack us. I had a school friend, Zora, she is still working. I shared a bed with her in Tuzla [the provincial town where both studied, *S.L.*]. I was a witness at her wedding. I loved her like... Always together. She came to my house, I went to hers.

Was she Serb?

Yes, she is. I did not mind, my parents did not mind. I used to spend a week with her family, she used to come and spend a week with my family. I did not eat pork and she never offered me any food containing pork, she respected that.

Do you still see her?

Yes, of course. I saw her for the first time as soon as I came to Srebrenica and we both cried very much. I took it very hard. Now, whenever I go to Srebrenica I must go to the shop where she works. She is working, she was lucky, her children stayed alive. She was in Bratunac [another small town 10 km from Srebrenica; it is now nearly exclusively populated by Serbs, though lately Muslims have resettled into a hostile world there, S.L.] I never felt she was to blame because the Serbs had killed my child. Those people were murderers. I cannot say that I hate her because she is a

Serb. I cannot hate her or any other Serbs just because the Serb criminals, soldiers, tortured and did God knows what with my child and my husband. What can I do? I am sad because of all the things that happened to us.

Fazila has become more religious since the war. She said that gave her life meaning. Like many women I interviewed, she felt it was her destiny to survive:

I do not practice my religion as much as I should, but, The Mighty be praised, if it had not been for my religion, if I had not turned to God, everything would have been more difficult. I have found consolation. Before the war I trusted people, I believed in them more than I did in myself or God. Now I believe more in God than in people, because people change. Sometimes you think that somebody is your friend, that he is a good man. But when he loses control, when nobody can control him, he becomes a beast. Then you see that they are your friends out of self-interest. (…) If, God forbid, the same thing happened again, I would choose to go through the same. I have matured and I have learned things you cannot learn from books or stories. And that would not have happened if I had not been in Srebrenica. And I was not killed, I am alive! There was hunger, there were many things. A war is not only killing. Immorality, prostitution, hunger, everything bad, everything that is the worst comes to the surface.

A Past Too Painful

Fazila's kindheartedness is an exception. Though many realized that neighbors would one day be neighbors again, they were so thoroughly shocked by the hostility and betrayal that they could no longer summon up trust. Sevda was a poor, elderly lady I interviewed in the provincial town of Tuzla. She told me she was among the thousands crowded into Potočari:

We thought they would help us and that they would help our people who went through the woods. Srebrenica had been conquered, that was a fact. We were prepared to leave and if necessary there would be an exchange of territory … But when I meet them now I ask them "Why didn't you help, at least my brother. He was also your brother, … we all loved each other didn't we?" … but they say: "We did not dare. There were orders from Serbia, from someone, we don't know who." But I think a neighbor can always help a neighbor.

Sevda still meets these former neighbors in the street and talks to them, "but my feeling is that there is blood on their hands, there is iron wire, they might bind me and slit my throat."[17]

Neither Fazila nor Sevda had realized the war was coming closer, though they knew the fighting was going on elsewhere. They had not noticed how, for some time previously, the Serb population of the region had been creating the concept of "the other" in their language, thoughts and feelings. Or how in a similar fashion the Muslims had been cutting themselves off from anyone who was not "one of them." For several years, ethnic hatred had been rekindled by a Serbian hate narrative that ultimately primed the Serb population to take part in the killing.[18] Historian Ben Liebermann has described this "cognitive dissonance" between the long-term national history of hatred and the short-term daily history of co-existence, friendship and love [19]—a dissonance that could inhabit the same person. The process of alienation was visible at a microcosmic level, for instance in the way Muslim boys no longer "hung out" in the streets with the "others" but congregated in separate groups instead. It was also noticeable in the schools, where children became increasingly segregated. But no one expected this process to culminate in such extreme violence and betrayal.

Muska fled to the Netherlands where she slowly tried to find some peace. She came from Srebrenica and was interviewed in the spring of 2006. She described the separation and told how she suddenly felt she was no longer welcome in the bars she had frequented in the past.

> You feel the atmosphere, you leave as soon as you can, everyone knows you. It is such a small region ... everything was changing. I noticed it in the attitude of my friends at school. You arrived at school and they told you there was a warning on television to be watchful. Some told me this land belonged to the Serbs, and when you heard that you got very silent and scared. You didn't want to be conspicuous. ... You knew that your next door neighbor was going to do something bad, even though you weren't from another Republic or country. No, I am talking about my neighbor. That was so scary. You did not know what would happen next.[20]

These good memories of co-existence with "the other" have become problematic. It is easier not to talk about them, to deny past feelings and replace them with stronger emotions of hatred and disappointment. Maybe these are not emotions at all, but merely genres people employ so they can talk about the past and present without needing to think too deeply. Memories of their previous lives have been eclipsed by feelings of loss. This is why the women I interviewed can hardly imagine positive feelings when they think about the past. Everything that was normal has been disrupted. The moment of disruption is clearly grafted in their memory, but it is precisely that moment which also conceals all positive feelings about the time before. Cruelty is present in abundance, however.

Nura lives in a refugee camp, where conditions are very bad. It was winter when I arrived and there was snow and mud everywhere. Women carried barrels with water since many of the houses have no water supply. Often they slipped in the snow. Nura is a widow though her husband was not killed in Potočari. He managed to escape into the woods. Then he was caught and Serb soldiers slit his throat, but even this he survived. He crawled his way to safe territory and ended up in a hospital where he was treated. But after he had returned to his wife Nura and their children, he died. When I spoke with Nura, two of her three children were sitting in the room. Nura seemed emotionally absent, and I wondered if it was not too painful for the children to listen. She insisted that she wanted them there. We tried to speak about the period before the war. But she had forgotten nearly everything about that time and did not know how to talk about it. She knew she was on good terms with her Serb neighbors, but she can hardly imagine that now.

Nura was born in 1965. When she got married, she told me, life was beautiful. Her husband worked in the mine and in a local shop. But at some point employees were laid off and the signs of ethnic division began to appear. A man from the village disappeared and many moved away. The family no longer felt safe and started to sleep in the open. Then the war came and they fled to the mountains, only to end up as refugees in Srebrenica.

> When we arrived there, we stayed alive somehow, trying to find food. Everything was alright, but there was shelling every day.... We had a cellar next to our house. Our house was very old, like a ruin. But next to it there was a new house with a new cellar dug out in the ground and we all hid in there. Everyone who lived near the house found shelter there. Children could not go out much. They did not dare to play outside. ... There was a little well behind the house where we took the laundry to be washed. And one day we were told that Srebrenica would fall. We went up into the hills, to a village called Pusmulići, and stayed there for the night'. But nothing happened, so they returned.

She went on to tell me how she tried to fetch food rations dropped from the air. When she managed to get hold of some, they were stolen by stronger people. When the enclave fell she ended up in Potočari. She did not want to talk about her time there. "All kinds of things happened in Potočari ... hanged people ... we found a man hanging from a piece of iron wire in a toilet. When we went to fetch water, we found five people with their throats slit, under a tree. ... There were many things. On the way to Potočari we heard them shouting. ... We watched houses burn down, we heard them shouting." The people she met there told her stories of rape and abuse. She was scared.[21]

As hard as it was for Nura to talk about this, Potočari was not her worst trauma. After several months she was contacted by the people who had been taking care of her dying husband. The couple were reunited. He came to live with her in the camp where she still lives today. She took care of him for several months, but he went back to the hospital and died on the first of October. Despite their unlikely survival, she ended up a single mother in a miserable refugee camp. Memories of those last weeks, when she knew he would die, still haunted her. It was such a slow and painful death. This was the story she wanted to tell: the story of how her husband made it back to her, of how much strength he had shown and how they had managed to be together again.

In a way, I was more saddened by Nura's story than by many others because the fate of her husband had been so cruel. Her present life was very sad and poor. It was clear the children could no longer stand to hear the story and I did not dare ask any more questions. I could only listen while looking at their faces. How can children listen to the story of their father's throat being slit? I had got used to the ways people talk about the pain of saying farewell when their husbands went off into the woods or when they were separated by the Serbs. One example of this was the story I heard from Timka, who lives in a small village with her sister-in-law. She still has a strong memory of that moment of separation:

> I cannot describe what it was to separate. We had discussed the possibility, because the situation was getting too dangerous. They fooled us, you know. We were told to go to the compound, that it would be safer there. We were told we would survive. It was not true. None of those men who went to Potočari are here now, but then neither are those who went through the woods. My son's last words were "mother we are going now, take care of the children." Then they left and I have not heard anything since.

She does not want to talk about her three days in Potočari. In fact she does not even want to remember them: "Please don't ask me too much," she begged.[22]

I had first met Timka when I interviewed her sister-in-law. She had interrupted that interview several times by audibly losing her breath. It is a behavior that I call silent crying. Now, however, she was calmer. On the day of Timka's interview, my interpreter and I stayed with her a full day, drinking coffee with her and trying to put her at ease. She complained about loneliness. To her, the past and present merged, short distances become long and long ones short. Somewhere there was a non-temporal no-man's land where stories were told, where chronology was absent and where she was confused most of the time. But it was the emptiness of her present existence that shocked me most, the lack of any context. While Nura kept living in the emptiness of a crowded refugee camp, sometimes managing to find work, there was nothing for Timka: no story, just numbness. And the complaint that life was empty.

Empty Lives

There were so many who complained about emptiness, so different and yet so similar.[23] I met Ajkuna in 2004. She lived in a deserted school with her daughter-in-law and many other refugees. There was one main room that provided shelter for her, her daughter-in-law and three grand-daughters. When I came to the door she welcomed me and expressed how the world had been turned on its head:

> There is no man to come and help you, to cut a tree branch, no. There are no pensions, either. We are bound to pay a debt for this house.... But, by God, we have no money, we have been reduced ... to nothing. I swear by God. My child, we have to.... But, there is no one, no one to come... You have to pay even to have a knife sharpened. There is no one. With due respect to you, only you. Nobody else came to see me, to visit me, to say....

Really?

> Nobody except you. Nobody. I have lost all my children, my husband, son-in-law, cousins, nieces. I have no one. I am so happy you came. You are the only visitor I ever had. ... Bayram comes, Bayram goes, the New Year comes. I am alone in my room and I cry. No one comes to the door, no one comes to ask: "Where are you granny? Where are you mother?" Nobody.

Were you born into a large family?

> Yes. It was a large family. My mother had six of us. And all of my family died. Mother, brothers, father, everybody, everybody. Nobody stayed. Nobody.[24]

Ajkuna was starting to forget her past, which she blamed on her age. She did not mind, for it brought relief. But perhaps she simply had too many chaotic memories.

Maybe this was what afflicted many of the women. Still, years are going by and some of the women know very well that the insanity of hatred has to stop. Of course, they initially felt chaos and hatred too, but they also knew that hatred was not a permanent solution. This charitability was astounding given the fact that all of them underwent the same fate, though in different ways. They lost husbands, sons, fathers and brothers, and their lives will never return to what they once were.

When emptiness replaces memory, it also replaces connectedness, context and a place in society. There is no positive memory or positive future. It is indeed better to forget. Remembering the past requires the survivor to explore positive feelings that are bound to resurface, feelings that disrupt the paradigm of emptiness. Few survivors can summon the emotional strength to do this. One woman who lost twenty-two members of her family, including her husband and three sons, managed to tell me about the positive feelings she had towards her former Serb friend. While she spoke, the pain was clearly visible on her face.

> I dreamed about her, and I was amazed to hear that her sons had served in the army, a special unit. When I returned to my village and went to her mother's house she wanted to embrace me and kiss me. But I told her "We are not what we were before." She started to cry and told me that her sons had not killed my son. But I told her "They didn't do anything to save him either." Deep inside I still love her, though I would never admit it. I don't want to forgive her.[25]

That would only further complicate a bond already confused by the love she still feels.

An Accumulation of Traumas

The fall of Srebrenica and the horrors of Potočari haunt people like a nightmare. Potočari was the culmination of endless suffering, of years of hunger and destitution. The great massacre overshadowed the slow death of a city on which the world had turned its back. Many reports have been written by the United Nations and other international bodies about the extreme conditions people were living in. Comparisons have been drawn with the ghettos of the Second World War.[26] People arrived in the town after fleeing from the surrounding villages, bringing with them all they could carry. Some had wandered for weeks through the snow, trying to avoid enemy ambushes. The town had no food until airplanes started dropping relief rations. Later on, when the fighting got extreme, rations of food and medical supplies no longer got through. There were many shocking accounts of mothers wandering through the countryside, struggling to feed their babies and small children. These stories help explain how such deep hatred was sown.

"They told us to go to Srebrenica" Jasmina told me on the doorstep of her house, for inside, there was hardly any room. It is eleven years after the war. Her daughter was very small then, "I started crying, Enisa [her daughter, *S.L.*] was not much older than a year, and I had to carry her. I picked her up with one arm and I took my rucksack. I followed the Bosnian army." I had visited Jasmina in the camp where she lives with her daughter, in a room 2 by 2.5 meters in size. This was where they slept and lived. The camp was in the mountains, far from any villages or towns. However primitive the conditions, her suffering was much greater in 1992, when she was chased from her village and fled to Srebrenica, three years before the massacre.

I walked for two days and two nights. I went with other people through the woods. We got to Potočari, to the school. Soldiers helped us. They saw I had a little baby, so they gave me a plate of beans to feed the child. There was no bread, only beans. I fed the child and we stayed there for the night. In the morning, the soldiers told us that we had to run to Srebrenica, because the enemy might see us from the Zvijezda hills in Bratunac, and start firing on us. We set off for Srebrenica. I think it was about 7 or 8 kilometers, on foot. I had to carry my Enisa and a rucksack with her clothes. When we got to Srebrenica, there were so many people, I cannot describe it. In one spot somebody made a fire, somebody was trying to warm up, in another place there was a dead man, and so on. I slept with Enisa in the snow, for four days. Nobody wanted to give us shelter.

Where did you find accommodation?

In the school. I was in the school. I had no place else to go, everything was full. There were many other people too, not just us. There were people from all over the place, from eight municipalities. We went to a classroom. There were eighty of us in that classroom. We did not even have a foam mattress, only a blanket which I had brought with me. I spread it on the floor so that my child could lie down. I really suffered, suffered much.

How many people slept outside?

Oh, thousands. Terrible.

In the snow?

Yes. People made a fire, and they let you warm yourself, if you brought some wood. But I had never been to Srebrenica, how could I bring wood? I could not leave Enisa, I had no one. Later the Red Cross moved us to a city café where they put up some dividing walls. ... I lived there for five months. Not only me, there were other people as well. There were some metal wardrobes, and there were walls. Then we got foam mattresses. Later on, we received aid, when Morillon [the UN general whom the women prevented from leaving town since they felt if he left, protection would be gone. He promised to help them in March 1993, *S.L.*] was there. We kept him in the school so that he could not escape. He was our only consolation, our hope. He came to Bratunac to negotiate. Then we received aid. We got foam mattresses, blankets, food started coming in, cleaning agents, soap, shampoos, so conditions improved.

But before then, how did you clean, how did you change your child?

Well we made a fire outside. We put two pieces of rock and a plate over them. If we did not have a plate, we used one from an old stove. Then we boiled the laundry. I got up at three o'clock in the morning to bring water in jerry cans. So I boiled her clothes and then mine. That is how we washed, we made a fire outside, we did not have anything in the classroom. So I coped.

She, too, ended up in Potočari[27] again in 1995, earlier in the chapter I mentioned she had arrived there in 1992.

Loss of Context

While many survivors felt that July the 11th was the low point of the war, for Jasmina that moment in the snow was far worse. She had gone from living in a protected house in a village where she socialized with her Serb neighbors to being a woman totally alone, in the snow. It seems impossible to deal with betrayal by people who were once so close. Later on, the confusion only got worse when the Muslims were betrayed once again, this time by the international community. All normal relations fell prey to chaos. The whole context of normalcy was lost.

The survivors wished to understand how a normal life, with its daily ups and downs, could be so radically disturbed. How life could descend into such complete chaos that one can no longer bear to recall happy pre-war memories like weddings or the birth of a child. Such events can only be remembered and retold in the knowledge that some who figured in these stories as friends later became enemies. How can survivors evaluate their society if it is the same society that created such evil?

It took a long time for me to realize that the life stories of the survivors of Srebrenica were not only fragmented by trauma but also by the impossibility of the story itself. Since any narrative of the past is interwoven with a vision of the future, the confusion is aggravated. The women do remember the multicultural society they originally came from and they still think it is important to live together. They were raised on a brand of communism that suppressed any expression of cultural difference, but at the same time they internalized positive feelings towards the members of the other ethnic group. Despite the current nationalist myth that the region has always been rife with war and hostility, even the most illiterate women are able to describe the alliance between nationalism and state politics that was the origin of all the destruction and bloodshed. They describe, as Fazila did, how some Serbs were "our Serbs," and that no one believed they would ever harm their fellow villagers. On the contrary, they trusted some of them until the bitter end. And they give examples of their "good" behavior. But trauma seems to obstruct memories of such positive feelings. Talking about the normality of the pre-war days can actually increase the chaos in memory because it underscores the contradictions in the significance of old friendships. The loss of friendships mingles with a fundamental loss of trust in the world and the loss of loved ones. The survivors are left with the unsettling forces of grief, mourning and conflicting emotions with no stable sense of normality to provide counterbalance.

Still, survivors sometimes emphasized that not everyone has always been the enemy. But suddenly, their "visions of normal existence" narrowed into hostile feelings. Such stories enable us to grasp the survivors' feelings about killings, whether these were carried out by strangers, fellow villagers, schoolmates, or even former friends. As an outsider I listened with bewilderment and wonder at how relations could have changed so rapidly. Why did neighbors become murderers?

Reconnecting to the Future

The stories I have been told paint a picture that does not appear in any official report. They add another dimension to what we know about the genocide. We learn to look at what happened through the eyes of survivors. Once the survivors have recalled and retold the past, they can also talk about the future and how they want to live. Few of the women who reached this point believed that hatred was, and still is, permanently entrenched in their country. They longed for a pristine world in which nationalities and cultures exist side by side. We might call it a world of diversity, but they would use the word "multicultural." They once had a society where people lived side by side; and although Tito's method of denying difference was less than ideal, at least life was good. To return to that world is a loftier aim than hatred; it is the only model for calm and security, for a life worth living. And that is where the women have taken the initiative and have behaved differently from what one might expect. While such an undisturbed life may be unattainable, it was still a desirable goal that gave shape to the survivors' stories. This is what I have learned from what I call "anthropologies of survival."

On one level, these stories are an impetus for moral reflection. They are also the personal truths of victims who are trying to express something beyond their previous experience, for which they have neither language nor concepts. But they are more. We cannot understand war without knowing human suffering. All these women have been muted. In speaking to me, their voices are being heard for the first time. It is my firm belief that their stories are essential to history. No history can be written without knowing and accounting for such historical "facts" at an empirical and a theoretical level. In order to do so, we must transcend the traditional methodology of history and acknowledge the value of memory as an essential component of historiography. History must take into account the way memory is shaped and ignored by historical research, otherwise it will never answer key political and moral questions, such as: "Why do we write?" and "Why are we hesitant to look at the unimaginable?." Any history that shies away from these issues allows us to shirk our responsibilities.

Notes

1. Research is done in the international network created by Charles Ingrao called the Scholars Initiative. See: http://www.cla.purdue.edu/academic /history/facstaff/ Ingrao/si/scholars.htm.; NIOD, *Srebrenica, een 'veilig gebied:. Reconstructie, achtergronden, gevolgen en analyses van de val van een Safe Area.* (Amsterdam: Boom, 2002); Rapport d'information de MM. René André et Francois Lamy,.3413, deposé le 22 novembre 2001, en application de l'article 145 du réglement. (l'Assemblée Nationale, Paris 2002); Republika Srpska, *The events in an around Srebrenica between 10th and 19th July 1995* (Banja Luka) June 2004 with appendix October 2004;

    Jan W. Honing, Norbert, Both, *Srebrenica: Record of a War Crime* (London: Penguin, 1996); Hasan Nuhanovic, *The Role of International Factors in Srebrenica. Chronology, Comments and Analysis of Events,* (unpublished) Pod zastavom UN-a, Međunarodna zajednica i zločin u Srebrenici (Sarajevo: Preporod, 2005). Major research and major historical descriptions have mainly been made by journalists. I mention some of the excellent work:

    David Rhode, *Endgame: The Betrayal and Fall of Srebrenica. Europe's Worst Massacre since World War II* (Boulder: Westview Press, 1997); Roy Gutman, *A Witness to Genocide* (New York: Macmillan, 1993); Sylvie Matton, *Srebrenica, Un Génocide annoncé* (Flammarion: Paris, 2005); and Mark Danner with his inspiring publications like "Great Betrayal" *New York Review of Books*, March 26, 1998; "Bosnia: Breaking the Machine," *New York Review of Books*, February 19, 1998. "Bosnia: The Turning Point," *New York Review of Books*, February 5, 1998. There are also very good documentaries like *A Cry from the Grave* by Leslie Woodhead in 1997. A beautiful novel written by someone who knows the region is Chuck Sudetić, *Blood and Vengeance, One Family's Story of War in Bosnia* (Harmondsworth: Penguin, 1998). An impressive survivor story is Emir Suljagić, *Postcards from the Grave* (London: Sage Books, 2005).

2. See also Selma Leydesdorff, "Stories from No Land: The Women of Srebrenica Speak Out," in: *Human Rights Review* 8 (3): 187-199; Selma Leydesdorff, "Oral Histories and Their Challenge to Collective Memory: The Case of Srebrenica," in *Bios, Zeitschrift fuer Biographieforschung, Oral History und Lebensverlaufanalysen,* Sonderheft 2007, 113-120.

3. Ger Duijzings, "Commemorating Srebrenica: histories of Violence and the Politics of Memory in Eastern Bosnia," in *The New Bosnian Mosaic, Identities, Memories and Moral Claims in a Post-War Society,* eds. Xavier Bougarel, Elissa Helms, Ger Duijzings, (Aldershot, Burlington: Ashgate, 2007), 141-167.

4. There is a vast array of sources for describing the suffering of genocide. See for instance. Dominique LaCapra *Writing History, Writing Trauma* (Baltimore, London 2001); Donals E. Miller and Lorna T. Miller, *Survivors: An Oral History of the Armenian Genocide* (Berkeley 1993) and Gadi BenEzer "Trauma Signals in Life Stories," in *Life Stories of Survivors, Trauma,* ed. Kim Lacy Rogers, Selma Leydesdorff (New Brunswick 2005, reprint of 1996), 29-45; Samuel Totten, William S. Parsons, and Israel W. Charny, eds. *A Century of Genocide: Eyewitness Accounts and Critical Views* (Routledge: New York and London, 1997).

5. It is common also in the stories of the women who survived the Rwanda genocide, though the genocide was far less gendered there see Esther Mujawayo, *Survivantes, Rwanda, dix ans après le genocide* (Paris: L'Aube, 2004).

6. Ruzmir. Mahmutćehajić, *Bosnia the Good, Tolerance and Tradition* (Budapest: Central European University Press, 2000, translated from Bosnian).

7. Richard Crownshaw, Selma Leydesdorff, "On Silence and the Words of the Victims," in *Memory of Totalitarianism*, ed. Luisa Passerini (London, New Brunswick: Transaction Publishers, 2005), vii-xiii.
   Marina Calloni, ed., *Violenza senza Legge, Genocidi e crimini di Guerra nell'età globale* (De Agostini Scuola: Novarra, 2006).

8. Dori Laub, "Oral History in the Making. Pittfalls and Breakthroughs—or the Unconsciousness in Action," in *Bios*, op. cit., 106-113; Dori Laub, Nuri C. Auerhahn, "Knowing and Not Knowing Massive Psychic Trauma: Forms of Traumatic Memory," in *The International Journal of Psychoanalysis*, 74 (1993): 287-302.

9. Hayden White, *Tropics of Discourse, Essays in Cultural Criticism* (Baltimore, London: The John Hopkins University Press, 1978), 121.

10. Nancy Wood, *Vectors of Memory: Legacies of Trauma in Postwar Europe* (Oxford, New York: Berg, 1999), 61-79.

11. Wood, op. cit., 8.

12. Omer Bartov, "Seeking the Roots of Modern Genocide: On the Macro- and Microhistory of Mass Murder," in *The Specter of Genocide, Mass Murder in Historical Perspective,* ed. Ron Gellathy, Ben Kiernan, (Cambridge: Cambridge University Press, 2003), 87.

13. Ivana Maček, "Imitation of Life, Negotiating Normality in Sarajevo under Siege," in ed. Xavier Bougarel, Elissa Helms, Ger Duijzings, op. cit., 39-59.

14. Shoshana Felman, "Education in Crisis, or the Vicissitudes of Teaching," in *Testimony, Crises of Witnessing in Literature, Psychoanalysis and History*, ed. Shoshana Felman, Dori Laub (Routledge: London, New York, 1992), 1-57.

15. Craig Evan Pollack, "Returning to a Safe Area? The Importance of Burial for Return to Srebrenica," *Journal of Refugee Studies*, XVI, 2 (2003): 186-201;

16. To evade accusations of genocide, the Serb killers exhumed graves and reburied the corpses. This made it difficult to determine where the corpses came from. Identification depended on analysis of the soil and dust surrounding the corpses. Such graves are called secondary. If the corpses are disinterred again, the graves are called tertiary.

17. Interview Sevda H in Tuzla, 2005.

18. Paul Miller, "Contested Memories: The Bosnian Genocide in Serb and Muslim Minds," *Journal of Genocide Research*, VIII, 3 (2006): 311-324.

19. Ben Lieberman, "Nationalist Narratives, Violence between Neighbours and Ethnic Cleansing in Bosnia Hercegovina: A case of cognitive dissonance," *Journal of Genocide Research*, VIII, 3 (2006): 295-309.

20. Interview with Muska, refugee to the Netherlands, conducted by Anna Albers in 2006.

21. Interview with Nura Duraković, 2005.

22. Interview with Timka M. Sase, 2004.

23. This corresponds with what has been written by Peter Read in *Returning to Nothing, The Meaning of Lost Places* (Melbourne: Cambridge University Press, 1996).

24. Interview with Ajkuna K., 2004.

25. Anonymous interviewee, 2005.

26. The situation in the town is best described in eyewitness accounts given to the International Tribunal for former Yugoslavia. The best placed are descriptions by eyewitnesses at the lawsuit against Naser Orić the Bosniak, who was accused of war crimes against the Serb population in villages surrounding Srebrenica. The defense argued that people had no other possibility than to plunder since they were starving. Orić was sentenced to two years and immediately released.

27. Interview with Jasmina L. Ježevać, 2004.

2

Localizing the Rwandan Genocide: The Story of Runda

Jacob R. Boersema

Introduction

More then ten years after the Rwandan genocide that started in April 1994, there is a consensus in the literature that the killing campaign on the national level was organized by a small group of hardliners both in the military and in the government. Most of them had ties to Rwanda's ruling party. Their success in spreading the killing nationwide depended largely on their ability to mobilize civilian administrators, loyal military units, political party networks, and the media to execute their order to kill and to incite others to commit violence.[1] This explanation leaves un-examined how these hardliners were able to mobilize local accomplices and how this process unfolded at the community level.

This chapter reconstructs the national-local dynamic of one community by retelling the oral history of the commune of Runda in the central province of Gitarama, from the start of the civil war in 1990 and the introduction of democracy in 1991, until the genocide of April 1994. The chapter thereby picks up the recent call to re-evaluate the explanatory power of local level studies.[2] It maps the dynamic of social and political relations between (and in between) the actors on the local level, both during and in the years prior to the genocide, while also paying attention to the links to the events on the national level. This perspective helps to expand the theoretical explanation that focuses on the cleavage of ethnicity in Rwanda as an explanation for the violence.[3]

While the differences between Hutu and Tutsi were central during the genocide, prior to the violence there were socio-economic and political developments that fundamentally reshaped relations both between and in-between ethnic groups in the countryside and between the local and the national level. The few studies of pre-genocide local communities in Rwanda show rising inequality in the countryside in the eighties and early nineties.[4] As a consequence socio-economic relationships, particularly between the small group of elites and the peasants, and between the youth and the elders, were strained. Cleavages in the division of power, land, and social outlook formed the basis for rising tensions and conflicts. This chapter will show how these were exacerbated by the civil war and particularly by the democratization process in the early nineties.[5] The story of Runda exemplifies how the national political power struggle in Rwanda between 1990 and 1994 was mirrored by an equally vicious local battle for power in the countryside. It shows how the two were connected and this political struggle could take a catastrophic turn, and end with genocide on the Tutsi population.

Methodology

Ideally, both oral history and archival research should be used to reconstruct the history of the genocide in the local community, but due to the unavailability of archive sources, this history is based on oral sources; recollections of past events by individuals who live, or have lived, in the community.[6] Interviews for this research were focused on gathering facts about the history of the whole community. But naturally, such general facts are recounted as part of intimate personal histories. The openness of communities and their individual members to talk about the traumatic events of the genocide varies widely across Rwanda. Predominantly this depends on the number of perpetrators originating from the community, those still at large and living in the community, and the number of surviving Tutsis and their positions in the community.

Individual memory is strongly influenced by public memory in the community.[7] In communities where there is an open debate about the past a strong collective narrative can develop that can dominate people's own recollections and experiences. Where there is no open debate, individuals might feel pressured to remain silent. Doing oral history and reconstructing the collective history therefore involves paying attention to the connection between the collective and the individual narratives, the common and individual language, the moment of interviewing, the informant's place in the community now and in the past, and the interaction between interviewer and interviewee.[8] Despite the individuality of memories, there were patterns in the various narratives told, and regularities in the way particular groups remember the past.[9] Here, there is only space to make a few short remarks pertaining to two of the main interviewed groups: survivors and perpetrators.

There is a difference between the testimonies of a survivor and an eyewitness. The survivor's picture of the genocide is limited by how they survived and how possible it was to observe or place what was happening to them and to others. Genocide survivor testimonies vary widely depending on the impact of the traumatic event.[10] The relationship between trauma and the reliability of victims' memory, memorization, and recollections is unclear, making broad generalizations on the nature and truth content of testimonies of traumatized witnesses difficult.[11] Survivors were found to be both highly aware observers of the events they underwent, as well as suffering from memory failure.

Perpetrator testimonies were, in a different way, selective and incoherent, and the same was often true for testimonies of their family members. The reliability of self-report varies according to the behavior being reported—or asked after—and the social approval associated with that behavior.[12] During the research there were many instances where witnesses, particular (suspected) perpetrators or people who were socially connected to them, would be vague, or seemed to suffer from, or fake, amnesia, repression, or confusion.[13] Vagueness protected the speaker from probing questions about individual responsibility and knowledge, and inhibited speaking about socially sensitive issues. As a consequence, perpetrators, even those who confessed and were sentenced, would not report on the acts they committed.[14] But denial, lying or presenting (obvious) errors does not make an interview completely meaningless. In his portrait of a group of killers, the French journalist Hatzfeld convincingly showed how perpetrators lied in many ways, but still disclosed parts of the truth.[15] Tonkin in a similar vein noted:

> The finding of error in an account ... does not necessarily invalidate the account, or the medium through which it is purveyed. It may also be very revealing. In what purports to be reminiscence, it is well known that all sorts of errors, foreshortenings and forgettings occur which need not mean that key information is absent.[16]

Civil War and Democracy

The invasion of the Rwandan Patriotic Front (RPF) in 1990 surprised and frightened many people in Rwanda, including the people of Runda community. The initial attack of the RPF lasted no longer than a month, was militarily unsuccessful, but the signal to the public was clear. A member of the local authorities remembered:

> We did experience signs from the war, people were afraid, and people's activities decreased. They thought: "Why should I work in the field when I maybe have to run tomorrow?" Instead of going into the field, people were talking among each other about the war. Some people also stopped their building activities. Not because of the money, but they did not want to build anything that would soon be destroyed.[17]

The civil war erupted at a time when most Hutus were already dissatisfied with Habyarimana's repressive, corrupt and elitist regime. But the rebel army of the RPF was not the type of opposition they had envisioned. It was filled predominantly with the children of Tutsis that had fled Rwanda after independence in the early 1960s. Only a few important positions in the rebel army were filled with Hutus who were opposed to the regime. The fear that was spread by the news of the attack, reinforced by misleading reports in the media, and the repressive reactions of the authorities, proved fruitful ground for new anti-Tutsi racism. Extremists presented the attack as an effort to re-install the Tutsis' dominance over the Hutu majority and held the Tutsis inside Rwanda responsible for the attack.

The introduction of democracy proved to be another explosive issue in the countryside. Traditionally the local elite had gathered around the government party MRND, the *Mouvement Révolutionaire National pour le Développement* (National Revolutionary Movement for Development). They had reigned for almost twenty years. Now, there was space for opposition, and long-buried grievances surfaced, ventilated through new political parties. Local elites, who dominated political life, started to compete for power, support, and privilege, turning communities into political battlegrounds. Gitarama, where Runda is located, had been the heartland of Kayibanda's Parmahutu-MDR party, the *Mouvement Démocratique Rwandais* (the Rwandan Democratic Movement) who had ruled after independence. This party was quickly reconstructed after 1991, followed by several smaller other political parties, all building on twenty years of resentment of regional discrimination by the Habyarimana regime. The opposition quickly gained ground and challenged the old elite with their vested interests in the MRND.

Claver Kamana was by far the most prominent MRND member in Runda, if not Gitarama. He had a prominent position in the national MRND, was vice-president of the party in Gitarama and the party president in Runda. Kamana had been born in 1935 as the oldest son of a Tutsi mother and a Hutu father. In the late 1960s, with the help of

Dutch development workers, he started his company: *Entreprise Kamana Claver, Hydrolique et Construction*. Around the same time he also obtained his first political post as *conseiller* in his own community. By the end of the 1980s his company had become one of the largest construction companies in the country, employing hundreds of people from Runda. He was the dominant figure in economic, social, political and religious life, with good contacts with the national MRND elite.

After the MDR was erected, he quickly became the focus of their criticism. At the beginning, the MDR was united with other parties in their opposition to the MRND regime. Meetings and protests were held, and the rhetoric was characterized by strong anti-Habyarimana pleas, and calls to halt the regional discrimination.[18] Because of Kamana's strong dependence on the state for commissions, he chose to stay in the MRND, aware of the critical importance of a MRND victory for his business. Yet many of his former friends were lured by the MDR and its promises of change and an end to inequality. Kamana was losing friends and influence, but using patronage and bribes managed to keep some of his friends and local bureaucratic contacts in the MRND.[19] Kamana's commitment to the MRND went, however, beyond economic opportunism. It was also ideological, as evidenced by his early and dedicated involvement in the JRND (also known as Interahamwe), the youth wing of the MRND. Kamana had always had good contact with the youth. He was a long time supporter of the local football club "Runda Sport" which largely depended on his support.[20]

In the early 1990s his acquaintance with these young men became the ideal setting for political recruitment. The team had always been ethnically mixed, but this changed when Kamana got more politically involved. A family member of one of the Tutsi football players remembers what happened after the matches in the season of 1992:

> After the match, Kamana would talk about politics with the football players, about MRND and if they wanted to become a member. He said that publicly, he was not secret about it. If someone wanted to become a member himself, he went to Kamana secretly after the meeting. For anybody with some intelligence, it was obvious what Kamana was doing. Some wanted to, others did not.[21]

Half of the football team became avid Interahamwe members. Outside the football club Kamana also assembled young people from the community to talk with them about politics and the MRND, often using local leaders who he employed as intermediaries.[22]

In 1992 the power struggle became more intense, both nationally and locally. The practice of *Kubuhoza* (to be liberated), originally introduced by the MDR, was adopted by the MRND. People were pressured (sometimes violently) to become members of the party or to stay in the party. Although *Kubuhoza* was practiced mostly "on" men, women were also made members. As a Hutu woman recalls:

> They went to your house with a group and took your hat or your membership card and burnt it. When someone resisted, they were sometimes beaten very hard. It was in your interest to accept. Girls were also members, especially educated ones.[23]

Enforcing participation was also used at political meetings, especially by the MRND. Through this political competition youth parties became increasingly radical. The MRND had been the first to erect a youth wing but in response the MDR decided to erect their own youth group, the JDR, which soon challenged in popularity and activity the JRND.

The youth groups were in charge of the "rounding up" for the meetings. A Tutsi remembers:

> Sometimes the *responsable* asked us to participate in meetings from the MRND. If someone refused to come to a meeting, the *responsable* would come after the meeting, together with some young members of the MRND. They would dance and sing: *Munda hario akaremereye* (In the stomach there is a heavy thing). It meant that someone was angry with you. It was a common song in 1992 by the members of the MRND. Party members would come during the day, inside the compound, and they always asked the head of the household to come outside and dance with them.[24]

Political discussions more and more spilled over into public slander and bar fights.

Nationally, the MDR had made considerable progress by 1992. They became members of the interim government and forced Habyarimana to start negotiating with the RPF. At the local level at the height of the political power struggle between the MRND and the MDR there were rallies and gatherings almost every week.[25] Being on the defensive, most incidents of violent political behavior were reported from the MRND. As a Hutu remembers:

> In July 1992 the MRND had a meeting in Gihara sector. After the meeting MRND members threw stones at some members of the other political party. They hit someone who had to go to the hospital. A prominent MDR member was also hit. After they hit him, they even chased him all the way down to his house, but he managed to escape.[26]

MDR supporters in turn targeted Kamana personally, throwing rocks at his house and flattening his car tires.

As a countermeasure Kamana bribed a number of MDR members to inform him on plans to boycott and harass him or his allies. For this he increasingly relied on new friends he had made within the Interahamwe in Kigali. One of them, Josef Setiba, became Kamana's political right hand. Setiba, a medicine man by training, had made a quick career in the Interahamwe. He had originally been invited by his Tutsi neighbor, who was a deputy in parliament for the MRND, to become a member of the MRND.[27] Setiba had never been politically active but had become well-to-do through his medical practice and people respected him in the community. Setiba says he always had felt "a strong sense of obligation towards the government."

In April 1992 he got to know by accident a prominent MRND figure, the national president of the Interahamwe, Robert Kajuga who asked him to get involved in the JRND, the Interahamwe in his sector and invited him to the first national meeting of Interahamwe leaders. Setiba liked what he heard at this meeting:

I firmly agreed with the explanation that all other parties were cooperating with the RPF. I had never liked them. They seemed to want to govern the country like they did before in 1959. And how could I like a party that came to kill? I enjoyed the group I became part of. I was suddenly part of something big. We were united, and had the same objective.

In December 1992 Setiba was selected president of the Interahamwe of the commune. He was good at fund raising and could draw on a stable support group who consisted of, among others, Silas Kubwimana, a master builder from Taba and Claver Kamana. In June 1993 Setiba was elected president of the JRND in Kigali Rural. As head of Kigali Rural, he became a member of the central Interahamwe committee in Kigali Town, and responsible for discipline, which entailed punishing the members that did not stick to "the mission."[28]

As Kamana's right-hand man Setiba would meet with people from Runda in Kigali to gather information on the MDR.[29] He would inform Kamana on the whereabouts of MDR members, the financial problems and the political infighting. Kamana's tactic was to divide and rule. Still, Kamana felt increasingly threatened and had grown accustomed to bringing a band of about ten Interahamwe members to accompany and protect him.[30] In the summer of 1992 the power struggle reached a violent peak. It started with an MRND meeting on 13th of July. A Hutu recalls:

That day Kamana lead a meeting at the football field in Runda. Afterwards Kamana and many MRND members came in minibuses and trucks to one of his bars. People thought that they were all Interahamwe.[31]

The arrival of a large group of MRND supporters and Interahamwe sowed unrest in Runda among members of MDR and the Tutsi part of the population. As a Hutu remembers: "As we heard the singing of the Interahamwe, we became very afraid."[32] A Tutsi recalls:

The rumor had it that they would hunt down Tutsis. They said that Tutsis had been killed in other areas of Rwanda. Many Tutsis did not dare to sleep in their houses and that night many went into the fields when it became dark.[33]

Others saw Kamana's arrival as an opportunity. The MDR leadership in Runda, knowing people's fears, anticipated unrest after the MRND meeting and considered it a good opportunity to overtake the community leadership. Their aim seems to have been the death of Kamana.[34]

More then 200 people had gathered, armed with stones and bows and arrows. As a Tutsi remembers:

> Everyone was crying and shouting. We shouted aloud, so many people came for help. We had blocked the road. It was already dark when we saw the Interahamwe at night, saw them closing the door of the bar.[35]

Masejeschu and Karega were leading the operation. In Kamana's bar about thirty Interahamwe from Kigali had gathered, and ten local Interahamwe who had joined them. When the Interahamwe saw the crowd outside, they started to throw stones. The MDR supporters retaliated. The fight did not last long. Seeing the numerical superiority of the MDR the Interahamwe fled.[36] After the attack on the bar the crowd was directed to Kamana's house, but he had escaped.[37] Kamana himself had phoned the prefect of Gitarama from the bar to report the attack, but he did nothing, seeing him as a threat to his authority and the main cause of the spread of political violence into his prefecture. He appeared only the next day, together with several military when the violence had ceded.[38] Kamana had managed to escape to Kigali, but four Interahamwe were arrested and brought to the communal prison of Runda.[39]

The ousting of Kamana brings to an end a period of political turmoil in Runda. As a symbol of the supreme rule of the MDR its members put up a tree with a flag from the party on the square in the center of Gihara.[40] After this it remained relatively quiet until the summer of 1993. Then the RPF resumed their attack. The new radio station RTLM had given political extremists from MRND a new outlet for their radical thoughts. They suggested that all Tutsis were RPF accomplices. Specifically PL-members, a mostly Tutsi party, were linked with the RPF and labeled *Inyenzi*, (cockroaches). This message spread across Rwanda and infected ethnic relations. The strategy of president Habyarimana after the Arusha Peace Accord was to play the ethnic card, split the MDR into a moderate fraction who supported the Accord, and an extremist fraction going by the name of MDR Power. In Runda, and probably the whole of Gitarama, the MDR had ruled almost supreme for the previous year. The split of the national leadership on Arusha caused unrest. Some local MDR leaders chose to support the power factions, while others were more ambivalent. As one MDR supporter formulated it: "At the national level, the power ideology created unity among the Hutu, but at the local level it brought division."[41]

The turning point was the infamous power speech at a meeting in Kigali, on October 23, transmitted live on RTLM. During his speech Karamira, the second vice-president of the MDR talked for the first time of MDR-Power and Hutu power, arguing that all Hutus must unite. He suggested Twagiramungu was a traitor, cuddling up to the RPF, forcing a split in the MDR. In Runda, many people followed the speech on the radio, including the MDR political leadership who did not have to think long about which side to choose. The son of a former prominent MDR-member recalls:

> The local leadership was united on this point. There were a lot of discussions about power, but we all supported Karamira. We thought Twagiramungu was a thief, a traitor with no personality. He had been a friend of Habyarimana. He was a man that could not be trusted. In Gihara nobody could openly support Twagiramungu. Karamira wanted an MDR that was like the original Parmahutu party. But Twagiramungu wanted to do some modifications, but only in his own interests.[42]

But most MDR members in Gitarama supported Twagiramungu and his moderate fraction, including the Prefect. Together with other important MDR party members in Gitarama the Prefect wrote a letter to the national MDR bureau telling them they disagreed with the Hutu power movement.[43] Runda in that sense was an exception. The choice for the power movement cleared the road for a new alliance with Kamana. During his year in Kigali he had become increasingly caught up in radical activities. He was heavily involved in the training of the Interahamwe and he had also stepped up the recruitment of new Interahamwe in Runda. The Interahamwe underwent a critical development in the fall of 1993 as from October onwards both the leadership of the Interahamwe and its members received military training.[44] They were preparing for a war.

In October Kamana organized a big MRND meeting on the football field of Runda. There were several local and national speakers. The content of their speeches was not directly anti-Tutsi but strongly suggestive. As a Hutu remembers: "They did not speak openly against Tutsis nor of power, but they talked about 'to fight the common enemy that had attacked us, we have to fight and unite.'"[45] The meeting was a big success. The singer Simon Bikindi, known for his infamous anti-Tutsi songs, and popular among the youth,[46] performed together with a group of dancers. After his ousting, Kamana had been a *persona non grata* for more then a year, but now he returned to Runda without any problems. The meeting symbolized the rise of a MRND/MDR power block in Runda, replacing the political battle from before. What had been a political fight between Hutus slowly turned into an ethnic conflict, but only gradually and without many noticing its possible consequences.

The Tutsis in Runda were aware of most of these developments.[47] When the president of Burundi was killed in November 1993, many Hutus expressed their anger about his death and connected it to the attacks of the RPF. However, no real or open anti-Tutsi actions were ever reported in Runda before April 1994. As a Tutsi said: "There had never been open anti-Tutsi actions. I still drank with my Hutu friends everyday. We have been surprised."[48]

The 6th of April

The first week in April was a school holiday. On Wednesday 6 April the president's plane crashed. The next day, people gathered on the square and at the bars to discuss the situation.[49] Nobody knew what was happening, but all feared what was to come.[50] Tutsis expected the worst[51] and most tried to keep a low profile.[52] A Tutsi remembers: "People gathered in the streets and talked with each other, both Hutus and Tutsis. Although I must say, we Tutsis talked also among ourselves, what would happen to us."[53] Tutsis who worked in the fields during the day did not dare to return to their houses at night, returning only in the morning to check up on their abandoned properties and milk the cows.[54]

The local authorities, led by the *bourgmestre* (mayor), the *conseillers* and the *responsables*[55] all worked together to calm the situation. In the afternoon of April 7 several Hutu extremists attacked a Tutsi in Kigese, but the bourgmestre together with four policemen intervened and imprisoned three of them. Many believed the bourgmestre was able to control the situation. Hutus and Tutsis slept at or near the communal office for their safety. The events in Kigali alerted the prefect of Gitarama. On April 8 he called for a meeting with all the bourgmestres of Gitarama. They discussed the security situation in Gitarama and concluded that the situation in all communes was still calm. The prefect instructed them not to put up any roadblocks, to forbid others from doing so, and to let all refugees through.[56] In an effort to restore order the bourgmestre of Runda talked to the MDR leadership, Karega and Masejeschu. He remained worried about the situation, according to a friend: "In the evening he passed by my shop. I was there, and he asked me how I assessed the situation in Runda. I told him it was okay. The bourgmestre told me that he thought he would be killed."[57]

One of the problems for the bourgmestre was the arrival into the community of the Interahamwe led by Setiba who was inciting people to "go to work"—the infamous euphemism to start killing Tutsis. The bourgmestre made a call to the prefect to ask for his assistance. As the prefect of Gitarama recounts:

> On the 8th Setiba had come with little trucks full of Interahamwe. The bourgmestre called me to say that the Interahamwe tried to attack. I asked eight soldiers to go but when the soldiers arrived in Runda, Setiba had returned after pillaging some goods. The bourgmestre called for help, but he seemed to do nothing himself.[58]

Despite the bourgmestre's efforts, Setiba again took his jeep on the 9th, picked up six Interahamwe and drove to Runda.[59] Arriving at the commune office, he did not wait for the bourgmestre to appear. He walked in and dragged the bourgmestre from the back of the building to the front, where a large crowd had gathered. He screamed at him: "Are you a Tutsi? Are you one of them? Are you? You stop the ones that went to work?"[60] He hit the bourgmestre in the face and ordered him to open the prison gates and free the prisoners.[61] He said to the prisoners: "You have to do your work." Then he addressed the crowd and explained his mission in clear terms: "When we come back, we want to see all Tutsis being killed."[62] Setiba and his gang then pillaged several shops of well-known Tutsis. Everywhere he passed, he shouted at the population: "Why don't I see a body of a dead Tutsi? Why don't you start doing your work?" In the afternoon, Setiba returned to Kigali and took the bourgmestre with him. He did not return until late in the afternoon.[63]

The incident happened early in the morning, but many people saw what happened, among them the Tutsis that had taken shelter in the commune office. Setiba's overpowering the bourgmestre in front of his constituency sent a strong signal to the community that he was no longer in charge and in control, and that the Interahamwe could do as it pleased. For Tutsis, it was clear that they could not expect protection from the authorities anymore. As a Tutsi remembers: "In the evening the bourgmestre was back from Kigali and promised to continue to protect us. But we left however to Muganza, and spent the night there in the woods."[64] As agreed during the meeting of the April 8, the prefect visited Runda to ask the people to stay calm, and to send the refugees to Gitarama-ville. But when he arrived in the afternoon of the April 9, he saw that only fifty people were around.[65] He concluded the bourgmestre had given up.

In Kigali the events quickly evolved. After the presidential plane was shot down, fighting flared up, provoked by the RPF attack on Kigali. They occupied Gatsata, a large neighborhood in the north of Kigali. The international community quickly abandoned the country and what had seemed like political killings quickly slid into full-scale genocide. From the April 8 and 9 onwards, the Interahamwe deliberately attacked safe havens where Tutsis had gathered. As Kigali was surrounded by the RPF in the north and the east, the main escape route for its inhabitants was to the south, the road to Gitarama and Butare crossing through Runda. Many sought refuge in the countryside.

The commune of Runda destabilized rapidly. Its location, only ten minutes by minibus from Kigali—hardly an hour's walk—made it a place of first resort for refugees to escape Kigali. By Saturday April 9 their numbers had increased significantly.[66] Most of the refugees were women and children,[67] and were a burden on the population, requiring food and housing.[68] The bourgmestre opened the primary school. Some found a place with family or acquaintances, but many also camped by the roadside or in the fields.[69] The sheer numbers and the absence of an allocation policy destroyed the harvest and agricultural fields.[70] The refugee wave continued to grow for the next few days.

With the refugees came the stories. Most were Hutus fleeing and they had all seen what happened in Kigali. As a Tutsi woman testified:

> The atmosphere deteriorated by the hour. Many of the refugees brought along their hatred and racism to Runda. Some of the people from Kigali, a majority being Hutu, came with machetes. They said: "Hey, it stinks here, it smells like snake."[71]

The Tutsi refugees that arrived in Runda, having escaped the horrors in Kigali, sowed fear among the Tutsis of Runda. A Tutsi woman remembers how a woman showed up at their door:

> She told us that her husband had been killed. She had been hidden by a neighbor in Kigali, but was in total shock when she arrived in Runda. She told of all the Tutsis that were killed and of all the bodies that were littering the street in her neighborhood in Kigali.[72]

On Sunday, April 10 a large column of "big cars with white people" passed through Runda on their way to the Rwanda-Burundi border, escorted by a number of U.N. military vehicles. The United States had arranged a U.N.-protected caravan to Burundi by car. People remembered the huge column of cars, and, as a Tutsi woman summarized: "It made us fear for the worst."[73] It was a defining moment. "All Tutsis knew what was going to happen," an old Tutsi man remembered.[74] Rwanda's violent history played its part as they recalled 1958 and 1973.[75] As an old Tutsi woman said: "By the time the refugees had come, all Tutsis were afraid. Some already ran away, others were hiding."[76]

The Catholic priest remembers how the bourgmestre was pressured to cooperate with the new genocidal regime. As he recalls:

> Just before the genocide I saw the bourgmestre with "Beniga," the sous-prefect at Munini, in the south, a known extremist. He came one day and asked me: "Are you going to leave?" "Yes," I said, and he replied: "In ten or fifteen days it is going to be calm again!"[77]

On the 11 April there was a second meeting at the prefect office. The bourgmestre of Taba, Akayesu, told the attendees that Claver Kamana, Silas Kubwimana, and others were organizing the local Interahamwe and telling them to be vigilant and ready. The group decided that the prefect would visit all the communes to talk to the population and to support the bourgmestres.[78] However, the prefect increasingly lost control over the prefecture as everywhere local bands of Interahamwe put up roadblocks, encouraged by local leaders who challenged the local authorities and supported the violence against Tutsis.

Initiating Genocide

Claver Kamana was in Kigali when the president's plane president crashed. Like many, he was initially confused as to what was happening. He and his family hid in the Hotel de Mille Collin.[79] Soon, however, Kamana learned that his MRND "friends" were in control of the situation and his help would be appreciated. The Interahamwe leadership met in the morning of the 7 April at the prefecture office in Kigali. Both the leadership cadres at the prefecture and commune level attended the meeting, members of the JDR power fraction were also present, as were Setiba, Claver Kamana, and Silas Kubwimana. The prefect of Kigaliville, Colonel Tharcisse Renzaho, led the meeting. The main point of discussion was the availability of weapons in the different sectors. It was decided they would be distributed immediately to the various groups of Interahamwe.

The next day there was a second meeting that included the national leaders of the Interahamwe, the prefect, and the military leadership. Kamana was present as the representative from the commune of Runda, and as a funder of the Interahamwe, together with Silas Kubwimana. Setiba was also present. The decision was made to attack the churches, and other places where Tutsis had gathered and to distribute guns to the local Interahamwe, to enable them to participate in large-scale attacks. It was decided that if necessary, soldiers would support them in these attacks.[80]

After the meeting Kamana and Kubwimana left with the Interahamwe leadership for another private meeting at its headquarters, *Etamajore.* There, Kamana and Kubwimana suggested pushing the genocide into Gitarama with an attack on Runda and Taba. Kajuga and Ngurampatse, the leaders of the Interahamwe, agreed and when Kamana left the meeting, he ordered Setiba to lead the mission to Runda. Kubwimana would be in charge of the expedition to Taba. Setiba would be given weapons.[81] The attack group from Interahamwe from Runda that had been trained in Kigali would be assisted by a small number of Runda insiders that would operate from the community. Preparatory meetings were organized in Runda on the night of the 12th to explain how to do "the work," a euphemism used those days for killing.[82]

In the early morning of the 13 April a large convoy of Interahamwe and some local people from Runda left from Kigali to Runda. As a former Interahamwe remembers:

> We left from the prefecture office in Kigali around 10 a.m. There was one convoy travelling to Runda, led by Setiba, and one to Taba. We brought guns to distribute to the local Interahamwe, and to the JDR power faction. Power was a Hutu—we said. Both groups went into one big bus, the weapons were put in two little lorries. The bus drove first to Setiba's house in Kitiginy, on the way to Runda, to pick up more Interahamwe. Then the bus drove to the bridge, where it was stopped.[83]

Rumor had spread that the Interahamwe would come from Kigali and moderate MDR members had gathered at the bridge over the Nyabarongo. The bourgmestre was also present, leading the gendarmerie from Gitarama.[84] When the bus with Interahamwe arrived at the bridge it stopped in front of the roadblock. Setiba realized they could not go through without using force and returned to Kigali where they armed themselves with a rocket-launcher.[85] On returning, they threatened to use it against the gendarmerie who gathered—they disappeared with their cars.[86] Part of the Interahamwe got out of the bus and mixed with the refugees from Gatsata walking up the hill. It was a frightening sight, according to an old Tutsi man: " They showed people their weapons. They had clubs with metal objects in it, swords, and machetes. They wore banana leaves and had their faces painted. Some wore masks so as not to be recognized."[87]

They started to knock on people's doors to check if they were Tutsi or not. The bus continued with the others to Runda where guns and grenades were distributed.[88] Setiba, who carried all the ammunition and food in his car, drove on to supply other communes.[89] Soon the first grenade was used to open the door of the house of a Tutsi:

> I was cooking with my grandmother when I heard the sound of a grenade, I thought it exploded in the house of Calixte Karimuabo. We got up and left the house and joined my uncle who was already out. In the chaos I lost sight of my grandmother.[90]

To all Tutsis the signal was alarming and clear. As one remembers: "We saw the houses burning in Kigese and Sheri, we saw fire and smoke. Some Tutsis were running and we got very scared."[91] Many Hutus also heard the explosions and were equally unsure what was going on. As one of them said: "We heard the grenades and other guns at Kigese. We wondered if the war had started."[92]

It was not the war that had started. It was a carefully set up military operation to murder the Tutsis of Runda. The plan consisted of two groups of attackers: the first was assigned to go from house to house to search for Tutsis and to bring them to the river. They had received hand grenades from Setiba.[93] A Hutu remembered how he was rounded up:

> In the morning of the first day of the genocide, Jean Paul Ruberanki'ko, Boudain, and Sankara came to me and asked: "Why don't you go to work? Come with us." They already had weapons. They told everybody where to go. Jean-Paul and Boudain gave orders. I think Setiba, and also Sankara led them. Jean-Paul was the main chief of my group.[94]

Another group, led by Jean Marie Hakizimana did the identification of the Tutsis. Sankara assisted Jean Marie. He was a longtime friend of Setiba and the community *agronome*. He knew who was who in the community.

In the beginning the Interahamwe and the former soldiers, who were leading the killing bands, killed some Tutsis with bullets. But after a while the groups went from house to house to kill the Tutsis with machetes. The leaders would walk in front, followed by a growing group of local Hutus. As a Hutu participant explains: "In the beginning the group was small and had about twenty civilians. But as we were walking, the group just became bigger and bigger."[95]

If they found a Tutsi, the leaders would ask for his or her identity card. If a Tutsi, they ordered the Hutus to kill him. Sometimes the Interahamwe came to a house and entered it by force. They would talk to the head of the household and if he were a Hutu they would ask him to follow them, forcing him to take a weapon.[96] Sometimes the group split up and small groups were assigned to go after particular Tutsis. At the beginning, numerous rumors went around about resistance and the whereabouts of Tutsis. One Hutu for instance heard that two people had found a list with Hutus that should have been killed by the RPF sympathizers.[97] The Bourgmestre supervised the whole operation, although it is unclear to what extent he was really in charge. People that refused to participate were locked up in the *cachot*, the small commune prison.[98]

At the school in the center of the community many Tutsis, both local and from other regions, were trying to hide among the crowd. But soon they were separated from the Hutus. According to a Tutsi:

> The local people separated us Tutsis from the Hutus. The people from Kigali were judges on their appearance. They gathered the local women and children on the square at the school. Some Interahamwe and people that collaborated with them brought some green beans. They held them in front of our noses and said "too bad you can not eat it." They wanted to pester us about our hungriness. When they had gathered us all on the square the Interahamwe asked their chiefs what to do with us. They said: "Bring them back to where they come from: Abyssinia."[99]

When the male and female Tutsis were separated, most of the men were killed immediately and thrown in the toilet holes of the church and school. Some of the men were killed only after they were thrown in the toilet holes.[100] The women and children were ordered to walk on foot to the river. One Tutsi estimates the number at about a hundred.[101] The Tutsis were guarded by a group of about fifty people, both Interahamwe and local people. According to a Hutu, one group had received instructions to bring the Tutsis to the river. A second group was instructed in the "procedures" to do the drowning.[102] A Tutsi who survived the massacre at the river recounts what happened down at the bridge at the Nyabarongo River:

> When we arrived at the river, we could see other people had drowned there. It was 10.a.m. when we arrived at the river. When the group of Interahamwe met the other group that was already at the river they told them not to drown them at once because there might be some Hutus left in the group. The Interahamwe checked everybody again, but there was no Hutu in our group. One by one we were ordered to jump into the river. At that moment, my fear had disappeared. I was ready to die. It felt like life was over. They cut the young boys in the neck and sometimes tied their hands, because they might be able to swim. Some women were also cut. I estimate there were about 200 Tutsis. Most of us could not swim, but if you could, you still did not have a chance. The Interahamwe stood on both sides of the river to keep pushing you back in, or kill you with their machetes.[103]

Conclusions

The genocide in Runda found its roots in the intense political battle between members of the local elite supporting MDR and MRND. This battle emerged out of attempts of the dissatisfied local elite to break the decade long hegemonic community leadership of Claver Kamana and the MRND. His aggressive pro-MRND stand and politics can be partly explained by his economic dependence on the state but his early involvement in the Interahamwe shows he was also ideologically motivated. His radicalization was key to the developments leading up to the genocide. The local and prefectural authorities played an ambivalent role on the political scene. They failed to uphold public order, even providing tacit support for particular violent actions with the ousting of Kamana as the most evident example. After his ousting it was the introduction of the power ideology that provided Kamana with a new opportunity to gain the upper hand in the political battle. What had been a political cleavage in the community was thereby remade into an ethnic one. The genocide that was unleashed by a small group of hardliners in Kigali was pushed into Gitarama on behalf of the Interahamwe leadership. But they acted on personal demands from two of their main financers, Kamana and Kubwimana, who saw genocidal violence as a legitimate means to regain control of their own communities. Setiba's effective leadership of the operation is not surprising given his role as Kamana's right hand man. His affiliation with the MDR elite and the authorities in Runda assured a smooth execution of a well-organized mass-murder campaign that killed all but few of the Tutsis in Runda.

Notes

1. The research for this chapter would not have been possible without the kind help and supervision of Dr. Philip Verwimp, my field supervisor and Prof. Dr. Johannes Houwink ten Cate, my university supervisor. The chapter would not have been written without the encouragement of Dr. Nanci Adler and Prof. Dr. Selma Leydesdorff.
    Scott Straus, *The Order of Genocide: Race, Power and War in Rwanda* (Ithaca: Cornell University Press, 2006), 11.

2. See for instance: Omer Bartov, "Seeking the Roots of Modern Genocide: On the Macro- and Microhistory of Mass Murder," in *The Spectre of Genocide. Mass Murder in Historical Perspective,* ed. Robert Gellately and Ben Kiernan (Cambridge: Cambridge University Press, 2003); Stathis Kalyvas, *The Logic of Violence in Civil War* (Cambridge: Cambridge University Press, 2006); Charles Tilly, *The Politics of Collective Violence* (Cambridge: Cambridge University Press, 2003).

3. See: Stathis Kalyvas, "The Ontology of Political Violence: Action and Identity in Civil Wars," *Perspectives on Politics,* 1,3, (2003) 475-494.

4. Danielle De Lame, *A Hill Among a Thousand. Transformations and Ruptures in Rural Rwanda* (Madison: The University of Wisconsin Press, 2005). See also: David Newbury and Catherine Newbury, "Bringing the Peasants Back In. Agrarian Themes in the Construction and Corrosion of Statist Historiography in Rwanda.

A Review Essay," *The American Historical Review*, 105, 3, (2000): 874. Villia Jefremovas, *Brickyards to Graveyards* (New York: SUNY Press, 2002). Villia Jefremovas, "Loose Women, Virtuous Wives, and Timid Virgins: Gender and the Control of Resources in Rwanda," *Canadian Journal of African Studies*. 25, 3, (1992): 378-395. André C. and Jean-Philippe Platteau, "Land Relations under Unbearable Stress: Rwanda Caught in the Malthusian Trap," *Journal of Economic Behaviour and Organisation* 34 (1998): 1-47.

5.   For the best overview of this political process leading up to the genocide, see: Alison Des Forges. *Leave None to Tell the Story. Genocide in Rwanda.* (New York: Human Right Watch, 1999). For other accounts of the local political power struggle, see: Timothy Longman, "Genocide and Socio-political Change: Massacres in Two Rwandan Villages," *Issue: A Journal of Opinion*, Summer, (1995): 18-21. Michel Wagner, "All the Bourgmestre's Men: Making Sense of Genocide in Rwanda," *Africa Today* 45, no.1 (1998): 25-36.

6.   Charles Mironko, "Igitero: Means and Motive in the Rwandan genocide. *Journal of Genocide Research*, 6, no. 1, March, (2004): 47-60.

7.   Jean Hatzfeld, *Dans Le Nu de la Vie. Récits des Marais Rwandais* (Paris: Editions du Seuil, 2000). Stef Janssen, "The Violence of Memories Local Narratives of the Past After Ethnic Cleansing in Croatia," *Rethinking History* 6, 1 (2002): 77-94. Elizabeth Tonkin, *Narrating Our Pasts: The Social Construction of Oral History* (Cambridge: Cambridge University Press, 1992), 10.

8.   Stephan Caunce, *Oral History and the Local Historian* (New York: Longman Group, 1994). Paul Thompson, *The Voice of the Past: Oral history,* (Oxford: University Press, 1988) Selma Leydesdorff, *De mensen en de Woorden,* (Amsterdam: Meulenhoff, 2004).

9.   In the footnotes of the story of Runda I have therefore indicated whether the source was a Tutsi or a Hutu. While not every Hutu interviewed was a perpetrator, all of the Tutsis were survivors.

10.   Hatzfeld in Selma Leydesdorff, *De mensen en de Woorden,* (Amsterdam: Meulenhoff, 2004), 112.

11.   For an overview see: M.P. Koss et al., "Traumatic Memory Characteristics: a Cross Validated Mediational Model of Response to Rape among Employed Women," *Journal of Abnormal Psychology*, 105 (1996): 421-432 and W.A. Wagenaar and J. Groeneweg, "The Memory of Concentration Camp Survivors," *Applied Cognitive Psychology,* 4, (1990): 77-87.

12.   Stephan N. Haynes, *Principles of Behavioral Assessment,* (New York: Gardner, 1978).

13.   The realization that memories are contradictory and internally inconsistent does not stop people from believing and enacting them. See: Barbara Myerhoff, "Life Not Death in Venice: Its Second Life," in *The Anthropology of Experience,* edited by Victor Turner and Edward M. Bruner (Urbana, IL: University of Illinois Press, 1986), 261-86.

14.   Vagueness is a crucial instrument of self-protection among perpetrators, as is selective amnesia. See: Gresham, M., Sykes, G., and David Matza, "Techniques of Neutralization; A Theory of Delinquency," *American Sociological Review,* (1957): 664-670. And also: John Muncie, Eugene McLaughlin, and Marie Langan, *Criminological Perspectives. A Reader* (London: Sage Publications, 1995). And for a recent example how that works in a community context: Steff Janssen, "The Violence of Memories: Local Narratives of the Past after Ethnic Cleansing in Croatia. *Rethinking History* 6, no. 1, (2002): 77-94.

15.   Jean Hatzfeld, *Une Saison des Machetes* (Paris: Editions du Seuil, 2003).

16. Elizabeth Tonkin, *Narrating Our Pasts: The Social Construction of Oral History* (Cambridge: Cambridge University Press, 1992), 114.
17. Interview 8, Hutu. Interviews conducted in August and September 2004.
18. Interview 33,Tutsi.
19. Interview 41b, Tutsi.
20. Interviews 2, Hutu; 10, Hutu.
21. Interview 39, Tutsi.
22. Interview 33, Tutsi.
23. Interview 25, Hutu.
24. Interview 41b, Tutsi.
25. Interview 41b, Tutsi.
26. Interview 42, Hutu.
27. Interviews 56; 68, Hutu.
28. Interviews 55, Hutu; 68, Hutu; 66, Hutu.
29. Interview 68, Hutu.
30. Interview 55, Hutu.
31. Interview 41a, Hutu.
32. Interview 7, Hutu.
33. Interview 27, Tutsi.
34. Interview 48, Hutu.
35. Interview 22, Tutsi.
36. Interview 47, Hutu.
37. Interview 41a.
38. Interview 47.
39. Interview 30, Hutu.
40. Interview 30, Hutu.
41. He concluded: "Only during the genocide it brought unity, maybe…" Interview 48, Hutu.
42. Interview 54, Hutu.
43. Interview 55, Hutu.
44. Interview 66, Hutu.
45. Interviews 27, Tutsi; 48, Hutu.
46. Interview 39, Tutsi.
47. Interviews 55, Tutsi; 58, Hutu.
48. Interview 48, Hutu.
49. Interview 51, Tutsi.
50. Interview 38, Hutu.
51. Interview 51, Tutsi.
52. Interview 41b, Tutsi
53. Interview 57, Tutsi.
54. Interview 55, Tutsi.
55. There are no direct translations for these terms. They are heads of lower administrative units, then the commune. A *conseiller* heads every sector (around 600 people), while a *responsable* heads every cellule (around 100 people).
56. Interview 55. See also: Alison Des Forges. *Leave None to Tell The Story. Genocide in Rwanda.* (New York: Human Right Watch, 1999), 270.
57. Interview 63, Hutu.
58. Interview 55, Hutu.
59. Interview 68, Hutu.
60. Interviews 63, Hutu; 5, Hutu; 51, Tutsi.
61. Interview 63, Hutu.

62.   Interviews 39, Tutsi; 33, Tutsi; 41b, Tutsi.
63.   Interviews 22, Tutsi; 43, Tutsi.
64.   Interview 43, Tutsi.
65.   Interview 55, Tutsi.
66.   Interviews 15, Hutu; 1, Hutu 43; Tutsi.
67.   Interview 68, Hutu.
68.   Interview 10, Hutu.
69.   Interview 6, Hutu.
70.   Interview 10, Hutu.
71.   Interview 22, Tutsi.
72.   Interview 22, Tutsi.
73.   Interview 28, Tutsi.
74.   Interview 33, Tutsi.
75.   Interview 38, Hutu.
76.   Interview 22.
77.   Interview 37, Spanish priest.
78.   Interview 55, Hutu.
79.   Interview 7, Hutu.
80.   Interview 66, Hutu.
81.   Interview 66, Hutu
82.   Interview 69, Hutu, 53, Hutu.
83.   Interview 66, Hutu
84.   Interviews 29, Tutsi and 38, Hutu.
85.   Interviews 43, Tutsi; 33, Tutsi; 35, Hutu; 68, Hutu.
86.   Interview 55, Hutu.
87.   Interview 33, Tutsi.
88.   Interview 66, Hutu.
89.   Interview 68.
90.   Interview 39, Tutsi.
91.   Interview 43, Tutsi.
92.   Interview 66, Hutu.
93.   Interview 53, Hutu.
94.   Interview 66, Hutu.
95.   Interview 44, Hutu.
96.   Interview 44.
97.   Interview 6, Hutu.
98.   Interview 69, Hutu.
99.   Interview 41b, Tutsi.
100.   Interview 41b.Tutsi.
101.   Interview 55, Tutsi.
102.   Interviews 66, Hutu; 41b, Tutsi.
103.   Interview 41b, Tutsi.

3

Memories and Silences: On the Narrative of an Ingrian Gulag Survivor

Ulla-Maija Peltonen

The focus of my research is an Ingrian man born in 1922, Tauno, and his story relating to his personal experiences in Stalin's labor camps in the then Soviet Union from 1939-1950.[1] Due to the sensitive nature of the information contained in his story and interviews, I shall refer to him by his first name only. The idea of recording his account came initially from Tauno himself, who now lives in Finland, or more specifically from a neighbor, who encouraged him to tell his story to a researcher. In the early spring of 2001, I received a telephone call at the Finnish Literature Society. Tauno's Finnish neighbor told me about the Ingrian man's experiences and about his eagerness to tell his story to a researcher. I immediately resolved to meet the man, because what I had heard bore a striking similarity to the accounts from the Finnish Civil War of 1918 that I have researched at length.[2]

Our first meeting took place in October 2001. The neighbor acted as our intermediary and told me: "If there is to be trust between you, it will happen in an instant. And if he trusts you, he will tell you his story." Thus began a collaboration that was to last several years. Between 2001 and 2002 I met Tauno five times. I transcribed our tape-recorded conversations and Tauno checked them and made additions as necessary.[3]

Macro and Micro-Dimensions of the Account

Finns have lived in Ingria, the area near present-day St. Petersburg, for over 400 years. Migration to Russia in the east and back to Finland has depended largely on the shifting political situation. During the 1920s and 1930s, Ingrians were the largest group of Finns in the Soviet Union.[4] Because of their ethnic background, Finns living in the Soviet Union became one of the targets of Stalin's nationalist policies. In the area around present-day St. Petersburg, the collectivization of farmsteads, the establishment of cooperatives, and the series of forced migration, deportation, imprisonment, disappearances and deaths fall into three phases: 1929-1931, 1935-1936 and 1937-1938. During the latter period the order was given to shoot about 4,000 Ingrians in the area around St. Petersburg and to deport over 10,000 to prison camps. Ingrian Finns were deported to the Kola Peninsula, Siberia, Asia, and the Sakhalin Island off the coast of Japan. For the Ingrians, the Second World War was a period of absolute disintegration.[5] The Ingrians' national awakening began as a result of *perestroika* towards the end of the 1980s and their remigration to Finland began in the 1990s.[6]

My interviewee, Tauno, was born in 1922 in the village of Koivukylä near St. Petersburg. There were four children in the family. Tauno's father worked as a driving instructor in St. Petersburg while his mother remained at home to care for the four children. His father and uncle were imprisoned and lost their lives during the third wave of Stalin's purges between 1937-1938. When, in our first interview, I asked Tauno about his life, this is how he began his account:

> The year of my birth, 1921, and my name were both false. In prison you had to lie. I was a political prisoner. Koivukylä was destroyed after the war. It's only 17 km from St. Petersburg. My childhood home was in Koivukylä.
>
> What about your parents?
>
> My father, Matti Matinpoika, worked in St. Petersburg as a driving instructor. He was imprisoned in 1937.
>
> What happened then?
>
> One night there came a knock at the door, a black dog started barking. My brother and I were asleep. They produced a document stating that they had the authority to take him prisoner. They took my father away and we never saw him or heard of him after that. My mother went to St. Petersburg many times looking for him at the Communist party headquarters, a place the Finns and Ingrians called the black or the green house—no, it was the grey house. They always lied and told her that he had been sent to Siberia or some other place. Then in 1965 we found out that he had received the death sentence and had been executed in March 1938.[7]

Well aware of the situation, in 1939 the seventeen-year-old Tauno decided to flee to Finland, where one of his father's brothers lived. The young man, who had studied as a lathe operator in St. Petersburg, planned to cross the Finnish border in secret, but he was caught and eventually sent to prison in December 1939. His mother tried to have him freed, but to no avail. The inhabitants of Koivukylä, including Tauno's mother and three siblings, were deported to Yakutia in Siberia. The family scattered. Tauno was sent to a labor camp. He attempted to escape three times and was caught each time. When he was caught for the second time, he changed his Ingrian name, assuming a Russian one instead, and changed his age by one year. He had taken his new identity—his name, year of birth, and crime—from a grave he had seen in a cemetery. This is how he recalls the event:

> I set off along the Pechuro River running by the edge of the forest; there was lots of black currant bushes and I ate lots of currants. A man in military uniform had spotted me and he arrested me. The previous day I had visited a cemetery with no crosses. Each grave bore the name of the deceased, their sentence and date of birth. I happened to notice the information of a 21-year-old boy. He had been sentenced to three years imprisonment under article 162D: theft. I remembered his name and number in case I was ever recaptured.[8]

Tauno decided that he would not remain in the prison camp but would try to escape any time an opportunity presented itself. His tenure in prison—in a total of seventeen different camps—lasted ten years. He survived the notorious gold mines in Kolyma and Magadan, where it was widely believed that nobody came out alive.

In our final interview, I asked Tauno about if he wanted to say anything more about conditions in the prison camps. He said:

> The conditions were terrible; they weren't fit for humans. Animals had better conditions than people in those camps. For instance, in some camps there wasn't a refectory, only a field kitchen. There was a field kitchen in Pechuro, and they managed to bring food in from somewhere. They would cook somewhere, but there were no dishes, no spoons [laughs], nothing to pick up the food with. You used whatever you could find—wood, piece of birch bark, your own galoshes, if you had a leather hat you'd use that, or an old tin. You'd often borrowed a tin from someone that had one. You were rich if you had a tin. There were no spoons at all, so we had to drink the food. It's incredible, not even the old folk were given spoons in the camps.

> Was the food warm?

> They brought us warm food. First we'd get breadcrumbs; we were even given wheat flour. We mixed the flour with water and drank it. There was no talk of fat or vegetables [laughs]. The old camps, like the one in Birobidzhan in the Jewish autonomous area, all had a refectory with proper dishes. That was my last camp. It was 1950 and I'd been in various camps for almost ten years. You didn't work in that camp. It was for punishment only; discipline was strict.[9]

Tauno was finally released from the prison camps in 1950. However, it was not until 1951 that he was reunited with his relatives. When I asked

Tauno how he received information about his family and his mother, he replied:

> I found out in 1951. I looked for my brother in what is now Novo Altai. Armas was at the university in Petroskoy (Petrozavodsk, the capital of the Republic of Karelia, Russia), I found out after sending a letter. He visited me in Altai during the summer and informed me that our mother had died in Trofimovsk, Siberia. He told me about the funeral. Armas placed a small cross at the site of the grave, but when he went back the next day the cross was gone. Back then there was a terrible shortage of firewood; people burned everything they could find because it was so cold. The site was on the banks of the Lena River; it was a steep bank, the river rose and wore away the soil. My brother said that the river had probably already swept the grave away.[10]

His brother informed him that their mother had died of hunger in Yakutia in 1943. After his release, Tauno ended up in the industrial town of Novo Altai, where he soon married and had two children. When I asked Tauno how the change of name had affected his life, he replied:

> It was easier to live as a Russian. I spoke perfect Russian, and even today I probably speak it better than Finnish [laughs]. Nobody knew I was Finnish. I had learned my new name and date of birth so well, that even if someone had asked me in my sleep I wouldn't have got it wrong.[11]

For over twenty years (1950-1970) he lived as a Russian engineer, until he decided to take back his Finnish name and move to Petroskoy. His Russian family did not accept his decision, nor did they accept the newly revealed details of his previous life, and the family split up. Tauno finally realized his childhood dream and moved to Finland at the end of the 1990s. He is one of the few male Ingrians to have survived the prison camps.

Tauno's account centers on life in the prison camps, his attempted escapes, and the interrogations. It includes numerous incidents and anecdotes, though he only spoke about his life on the outside when asked specifically. Tauno also gave me a handwritten account from 1978 of his attempt to cross the border into Finland and of his being captured just before the Winter War in 1939.[12]

At the primary focus of my research are questions relating to remembering and forgetting. Why did Tauno remain silent for almost forty years, and why in 2001 did he finally decide to share his story with a public archive? What is he telling us, and what does his story tell us? My second question relates to the war, the prison camps, suffering, and evil. How did Tauno possibly survive? In this chapter I shall concentrate on one theme in particular: the fine line between life and death that recurs throughout Tauno's account.

Social Constructivism and So-Called Other Knowledge

Oral history research, micro historical research and women's studies have all deepened our understanding of the past by demonstrating the many innovative ways of formulating new questions on familiar subjects. Giovanni Levi has stressed the fact that all social action—including narration—seems to result from continual negotiation and manipulation, the choices and decisions in the face of an individual's normative reality, which despite its apparently endless selection of options, does not offer much scope for personal interpretation or freedom.[13]

Narrators choose the particular form of expression that best suits their experiences. Associated with the narration of violence and terror is not only the idea of testimony, but a combination of the narrator's *witness statement*, their experiences, and the mode of presentation.[14] In court a witness will testify in support of a given claim and will provide a statement proving their testimony to be correct. The witness is also an eyewitness, who swears an oath thereby assuring the court that s/he is speaking the truth. On one level, the narrator of concentration camp experiences can be compared to an eyewitness, though on another level, this account differs significantly. Central to the witness statement is the compulsion to remember events correctly, and one could debate whether, as such, a witness statement is the fitting form for a narrative recalling experiences in the concentration camps. In a juridical sense, witness statements stress the importance of logical details, the names of people and places, times, seasons and years. The most important distinction from the juridical model is that life history gives the narrator the space to reflect, revisit memories and even argue against them.[15] Face-to-face conversation allows for both flexibility and control. In oral history the narrator presents an interpretation of what has happened to him/her, how and why it happened, who was involved, and an assessment of any repercussions. In an interview situation the challenges of interaction are associated with an attempt to express emotions. Reko Lundán has summed it up thus: "When someone tries to express to another person as precisely as possible what he feels and what is true for him, I believe this is the highest form of communication. Through words we can come closer to one another, sense one another's hopes, fears, beliefs, love...."[16]

By nature the witness statement is a deeply autobiographical form: it recounts in the first person events that happened to the subject, a secret divulged only in part to other people. It is an account of what happened to me, what only I experienced, saw, heard, and felt.[17] Researchers of the genocide during the Second World War have stressed the idea of the witness statement as a deed, not simply a presentation. Indeed, narratives and witness statements dealing with genocide in many ways recall medieval folk law. In medieval times a witness statement was not required to provide any information or understanding of an event, rather it was expected to express the ethical relationship of joint responsibility between the subject, the event in question, and others. Joint responsibility is not the theme of vernacular witness statements; it is the basis of their theoretical content.[18]

Andrea Frisch, who has researched medieval witness statements and testimony, points out that, in medieval times, testimony was often unable to provide the "facts" of an event, but served to uphold the testimony of either the witnesses themselves or the accused party, thus making it an *ethical testimony*. This manner of testimony demonstrated the coexistence of oral and written forms of expression, the transference of oral testimony into a written form, and its links to the judicial system of the Renaissance. The mode of giving testimony indicates that the weakening of the status of oral testimony did not mean that oral testimony was dismissed from juridical discourse altogether. Frisch shows that the shift from oral witness statements to the practice of written testimony caused many problems in courtrooms of the day.[19]

Carlo Ginzburg has considered in a most interesting light the reasons why courtrooms of the sixteenth century did not think one witness statement sufficient, and required several. He points out the fact that the epistemological foundations of (historical) research and jurisprudence do not stand alone, and that it is impossible to adapt juridicial principles for the purposes of research. Ginzburg makes a distinction between courtroom testimony and historical testimony.[20] Witness statements are hierarchical: an oral witness statement (or narrative) is a primary source; when it is written down it becomes a secondary source. Experiences can also be divided into primary, secondary, and tertiary experiences. As I see it, accounts of experiences in the concentration camps or the narratives of the losing side in the Finnish Civil War of 1918 fall into these same categories. Making the distinction between experience of an event and knowledge of an event is particularly fruitful. *Epistemological testimony*, based on knowledge, and *ethical testimony* contain different levels of information. In this context I understand the witness statement in the broader sense of *historical testimony*, which carries with it both an ethical dimension and the relationship of the discourse to other people.[21]

The narratives outlined above give us information that we would not normally have. Official information about wars often avoids moral standpoints and individual experiences. Instead it concentrates on facts and appeals to us to accept the necessity of violence in a war situation. However, those affected often hold knowledge which questions and challenges officially divulged information. By this I refer to other knowledge, a phenomenon that manifests itself in a number of different ways. Sakari Hänninen, Jouko Karjalainen and Tuukka Lahti, who have conducted research into poverty in Finland, understand other knowledge as falling into three categories: *silent knowledge, counter knowledge,* and *weak knowledge. Silent knowledge* refers to an experience that bears significance for people's everyday behavior, but that is difficult to explain or understand. *Counter knowledge* is by nature confrontational; it questions official knowledge and clears the way for other options, for ideas that have been forgotten or brushed aside. *Weak knowledge*, on the other hand, "does not close its eyes to the mysteries of history, but considers matters carefully, shares responsibility, and rethinks the fundamentals of human existence in difficult social situations. It is aware of the boundaries of knowledge and of the irrevocability of such considerations." Weak knowledge might be, for instance, recounting the story of one's personal experiences. This requires quiet and the ability to listen.[22]

Remembering, Silence, Forgetting

It is pertinent to ask which topics may be dealt with in public, which in private, and which may not be dealt with at all. Many who have researched the lasting trauma caused by the concentration camps of the Second World War have pointed out that listeners often find the very mention of the camps stirs confusing emotions, offense, shock, fear and terror.[23] It is hard to confront the feelings of guilt and responsibility caused by traumatic experiences. Silence and the attempt to forget these experiences can be viewed as an attempt to reconcile conflicting emotions and common sense, as remaining silent simplifies matters, shuts the trauma off, making it easier to get on with day-to-day life. Silence is an act of protection as much as it is a defense mechanism. It may also be the result of changes in the subject's personal relationships or political opinions. It represents an attempt to eschew responsibility, and in this way is bound up with the conflict and dialogue between political and cultural values. All memory is selective and informed by an inherent sense of value, and the irrefutable element of silence points to the idea of truth, which in turn is more closely allied with memory than it is with forgetting.

Freudian psychoanalytical terminology is often used spontaneously, as if these terms were clear to all. Among these commonly used terms are *trauma* and *denial*. In the traditional sense, denial refers to the mental process that prevents the conscious realization of a given experience, whereas *trauma* refers to a mental injury or defect. Violence always leaves trauma behind it. The concept of trauma as it affects the individual can, however, be broadened to include in its purview historical events, communities and nations, as Dominick LaCapra posits. The denial associated with trauma does not per se include anything "individual." The act of processing a historical trauma requires memory and a critical approach to that which initially caused the trauma. Methods of confronting historical traumas include *acting out* and *working through*. The process of working through—the fundamental reconciliation of a difficult memory—is significant, as merely acting out or talking about a matter can hinder grieving and clouds the basic question of remembering. The binary of memory and history is not an easy one.[24]

Memory can be seen as both *historical experience* (emotional memory) and *historical awareness* (deliberate memory). Although they are opposites, the two are interdependent, because they both manifest themselves in a social and cultural-historical context. Historical awareness is linked with ideology, historical experience with the deeper mental structures. Whereas historical experience identifies with individual, private memories, historical awareness identifies with collective, public memories. Historical awareness links memory to politics and the discovery of the other.[25]

Historical experience and historical awareness overlap notably in folklore and oral history. In the field of folklore, the term "collective tradition" has come to mean the commonly experienced and accepted tradition of all. It should not be understood as something fixed, but, as Seppo Knuuttila has pointed out, as a way of thinking that is comparative, negotiable, and reciprocal.[26] Collective concepts refer to the ways in which people interpret aspects of their own experience. In this manner both folklore and oral history provide information about historical experience as a subjective, individual memory, and historical awareness as a collective, public memory. What is important is what the group remembers collectively, and what aspects of the community's past form the focus of that memory. Integral to this is the notion that disputed matters engender alternative thought and debate.[27] Historical memory is central to narratives from the concentration camps and the civil war. They place emphasis on the cultural context of the narrative and the interpretational aspects of remembering, what is remembered from the past, what matters are recounted, and, indeed, what matters it is possible to recount. Social and collective memory links to the question: who remembers? For instance, communal rituals remind people what tradition they are taking part in.[28]

The social settings of memory are neither neutral nor natural. Oral history is dominated by two frames of reference. Firstly there is the referential, that relating to real life. Writing or speaking about real life is not simply reproducing life; it is constructed around the writer or speaker's own understanding of his of her life. Secondly there is a signifying relationship between writer and reader or between listener and speaker. In this relationship, the intentions of both parties are open to misunderstandings.[29]

Situation and Narration

There are a number of reasons behind the Ingrian man's silence. Chief among them may be that, until as late as the 1970s, talking about political prisoners and prison camps could cost someone their life.[30] Tauno confirmed this when I asked him if people ever spoke about the disappearances or the labor camps amongst themselves.

> I didn't speak about it; nobody did. Sometimes we would whisper that so-and-so had been in a prison camp. Those who had been in the prison camps rarely ever smiled. Everyone knew the people sent there were innocent. [We didn't talk about it, and if somebody tried, they disappeared without a trace.] [31]

Tauno clarified his earlier interview by annotating the transcript on 7/1/2003: "You could talk to friends, but in public places you had to be careful." Primary to this narrative are the changes in the political climate after Yeltsin came to power. *Perestroika* enabled the Russian human rights organization *Memorial* to challenge such hushed-up matters in the public eye. For instance, beginning in 1991, information about the victims of Stalin's purges was published in the magazine *Karelia* (formerly known as *Punalippu*, "the Red Flag"). These lists featured the person's name, date of birth, nationality, the time of their imprisonment, and information as to whether the person was still alive and when s/he had been rehabilitated. Tauno's father was rehabilitated in 1965, during the Khrushchev era, and Tauno himself in 1989.

Tauno recalled searching for information about his father. At the KGB office in Petroskoy, an official showed him the clause explaining why his father had been imprisoned, and he no longer needed to search further. This is how Tauno expressed his feelings upon hearing of his father's fate:

> I went to ask for information about my father. In Petroskoy there was a major and I asked him what exactly my father had been accused of. I asked for the documentation to be sent from St. Petersburg. He said that this would be pointless, that there would be nothing there. He took a folder from the shelf and showed it to me. It showed my father's name and surname and said that he had been sent to a camp, nothing else. Pointless, he said. My brother Armas managed to have the documents sent to Perm, where he was living at the time. He told me that our father was accused of being a spy, a terrorist and a traitor. In total he was charged on nine counts. The words "spy" and "traitor" were printed on the cover of the folder. When I later saw that document, my heart started racing and my eyes filled with tears. He [my brother Armas] read that, at first, our father had denied everything and said that he had done nothing wrong, that he was an honest worker, that he had no time for spying or anything like that. They didn't interview him again for a long time, but at the second interview he signed the confession. They probably beat him up the first time; he would have realized that denying the charges was pointless. I don't understand how he could admit to so much. I would have admitted far less. But everything was signed, even the certificate decreeing his death sentence was signed. Was he so weak and ill by this point that dying was an easier option? Or was he too ashamed to let his children see him in a state like that? What did they do to him? That's what I don't understand.[32]

Antti Eskola has considered the fundamental question of the methods we use to understand people. He stresses the importance of interaction in culture. Understanding is the answer that arises from the interrelationships between people. There are two distinct forms of understanding: understanding a given act, which requires a certain cultural awareness, and understanding motive, which requires explanation. Eskola states that "what gives our lives strength and meaning is something outside us, something towards which we strive, or task that we wish to fulfill."[33] For instance, the pivotal episode in *Man's Search for Meaning*, Viktor Frankl's recollection of experiences in Auschwitz, describes a deep-set desire to write things down inside the concentration camp. For Frankl, writing a book became the reason for carrying on. Writing the manuscript of this book became the action that gave life its meaning, and piece by piece the text began to take shape. Eskola points out, however, that some actions are not sufficient to give life meaning; these actions must be pleasant, they must have communal value.[34] In Frankl's case what was important were the imaginary readers for whom he wrote every day. In light of this, we can conclude that, for Tauno, what gave his life meaning were his planned escapes and his imagined life in Finland. During the course of our interviews, Tauno reiterated many times that he decided right from the outset that he would not stay in the prison camp. When I asked, "How do you keep your head clear in a situation like that?," he responded "I suppose I must have had guts and determination, I decided I wouldn't stay there, and I wouldn't die there."[35]

Elie Wiesel, a Jewish man who survived the Nazi concentration camps, wrote that if someone else had written his story, he would not have to do it. He said he was writing to bear witness to what happened. Nobody gives a witness statement for its own sake; they do so in order to assume responsibility.[36] A Jewish woman, Janina Bauman, kept her silence for forty years, and only after the death of her mother did she realize that she was now the only person who could tell the story of her family. She said that she felt indebted to the Poles who helped the Jews, and that it was her duty to leave behind her a written testimony.[37] The same could arguably apply to Tauno. His narrative is imbued with the ethical aspect of testimony; it is not merely a reportage of what happened in his life.

Social Coherence

The concepts, generalizations, and images included in this narrative only become understandable when they are linked to the real world, the physical reality that they describe. Tauno's account raises a number of questions. For example, in what context should it be considered?[38] And what significance can one account hold for the reconstruction of the history of the prison camps? How do life's micro- and macro-levels overlap? These questions relate to the substance of the narrative itself: the war, the prison camps, the brutalities, and the evil. Unanswered, but perhaps implicit, is also the question of how this man survived. Generally, we might ask, do stories of war feature acts that would account for survival? In narratives describing the evil and suffering of a generation, there are also references to acts of good. How can they be accounted for?

Here I understand the term "goodness" in the same manner as Charles Taylor, i.e., as a set of moral deeds, which give people the right to a life worth living. Goodness incorporates moral attitudes, respect, and responsibility for life and other people. Good deeds inherently display an assessment of what is right and what is wrong, and of what it means to be a human amongst other humans.[39]

Tzvetan Todorov has also pointed out that acts of good are this important yet, in times of need, all too rare a phenomenon. Using a number of different sources, Todorov reconstructs the goodness that appeared in the complex historical situation of Bulgaria in 1943. Aside from Denmark, Bulgaria was the only country in Nazi-controlled Europe that did not uphold the order to deport Jews from the country in 1943. Instead, Bulgaria sheltered them.[40] In times of social conflict, goodness is understood as deeds, which do not appear in official sources, but which exerted great influence on the final result of the conflict.

In focusing my attention on a factual account of life in the prison camps, I have attempted to uncover information, fragments, clues, symptoms, and even of acts of good. I have tried to reveal the significance of the narrative by employing the idea of *thick dialogue*. By this I mean the dialogue between listener and speaker, or between writer and reader. In "thick dialogue" of this nature, questions arise dialectically out of answers given, and vice versa.[41] By focusing on expressions referring to the reciprocity between narrator and listener, referential ways of speaking or writing and the rhetorical devices of narrator or writer, by paying attention to choices of words, recurring metaphors, the use of personal pronouns, references to literature, and the moment of narrating or writing, we can uncover concepts and emotions both subjective and commonly shared.[42] Oral history reveals the narrator's understanding of history. Luisa Passerini stresses the special importance of oral sources, as they widen the narrator's sphere of reality to include the everyday, experiences, the position of the oppressed and the displaced.[43] The dimensions of the narrative exist in relation to memory, ideology, and the subconscious. Oral history and folklore bring into question the traditional positivist notion of science as a reflection of objectivity dictated from the outside. In lieu of incontestable facts, one must search for knowledge useful from the perspective of one's research questions as a whole.[44]

One of the recurring themes in Tauno's narrative is the fine line between life and death, the moment when life and death are both valid options. Tauno himself does not place particular emphasis on such moments; rather they arise through the researcher's questions. How can a moment be encapsulated in the narrative? The length of the narrative reveals an interesting point. The narrator may give a long, expansive description of an experience that lasted only a moment, while an entire life can be passed over in a few words. Lingering on a particular episode may be the narrator's way of stressing its importance, but it may equally be a way of detracting attention from a more subtle emphasis elsewhere. The duration of the narrative may contain implicit meanings, and this is always a question of the relation between the speed of the narrative and the narrator's intentions, and how what is important is made implicit.[45]

The following example comes from my final interview with Tauno in summer 2002. This story began when I asked whether any deaths occurred at the labor camp. I shall now examine the following narrative from a forest labor camp between 1948-49, in which Tauno was seriously injured after a tree fell on top of him. What acts of good occur in the narrative? How significantly does the moment present itself within the context of the story?

In the interview Tauno first described the difficulty of the logging work, then the accident.

> I don't remember what happened; I broke my pelvis. I woke up and saw the bonfire burning; I noticed something had been placed underneath me. The first thing I did was ask for water. One of the prisoners filled a tin with snow, put it on the fire to melt, and gave me the water. I was sent back to the camp, but I couldn't feel my legs. The chief of the camp and his assistant appeared with an iron bar. They didn't hit me though. I was taken to a hospital, I was there for a week, and I didn't eat so much as a gram of bread. It looked as though a branch had gone through my stomach, I couldn't move at all. Then [laughs] the chief came back again, he was a former prisoner, who'd decided to stay on at the camp. He came over and asked me something, and I felt as though I wouldn't get through this, that I was going to die there and then. The guard then came over and asked my surname, what I was in for and all that. I didn't want to talk, and he said that if I didn't want to answer him they'd send another man to the hospital in my place. The patient was then left to die. Still they came and picked me up; I couldn't move, and when they started carrying me I shouted as loud as I could because the pain was so terrible. There was a railway station, and from there you were transported back to the camp, where the prisoners were kept behind bars [Camp No. 6]. You were allowed out to the logging sites, but after work they would put you in handcuffs and take you back to your cell. We were waiting for a freight train full of wood. The guards suggested that they lift me up on top of the logs. It crossed my mind that they might try and break my back altogether. I shouted loudly. [On the train there was a freight car. Its door opened and out came] a commander [in a soldier's uniform], I can't remember his military rank. He put a stop to my shouting and asked what was going on. The others said that they were trying to lift me on top of the logs. The commander asked, "Is he a man, a pig, or some other animal?" and said that they were not men if they treated me like that. Then they put me on the floor of the freight car, and one of the guards even lay his fur coat beneath me. I don't know how far we had traveled when they carried me into the hospital. [If they had managed to lift me on top of the logs, I wouldn't remember those times or events.] (The sections in square brackets are the narrator's amendments made on 7.1.2003).[46]

This first-person narrative may be classed as an eyewitness account, a witness statement, or the description of a firsthand experience. The scenes of the narrative are the logging site and the forecourt at the railway station named Bira near Birobidzhan, a town and the administrative center of Jewish Autonomous Oblast Russia, located on the Trans-Siberian railway. The people involved are the first-person narrator, Tauno, the other prisoners and guards inside the camp, and the guards and commander outside. The pivotal moment is the fragility of goodness, seen in the unknown commander's deed as he stepped into what was happening: "What is going on … is he a man, a pig, or some other animal?' and said that they were not men if they treated me like that." Temporally the narrative takes place on several levels: at the time of the event itself (1948-49), at the time of the narrative in summer 2002, and in January 2003 when Tauno made amendments to his narrative. At that point he added the following evaluation to his story: "If they had managed to lift me on top of the logs, I wouldn't remember those times or events." It is with this evaluation that the narrator asks us: what if?[47]

On Interpretation

In her research into sixteenth-century pardon tales, Natalie Zemon Davis draws attention to the fictional aspects of pardon tales told by those sentenced to death, and the manner in which the narrator's identity, wishes, crime, and its consequences are brought to the fore. In examining these tales, it is possible to uncover a probable, or at least a moral truth. Focusing solely on facts sidelines the significant point of what is real and what matters relate to the underlying questions of humanity. The question of truth is fundamental.[48]

How can we best attain information relevant to our questions? The fidelity of information is always culturally bound. Understanding ways of thinking and different meanings helps us form our own interpretation of events. As a result of what kind of process did Tauno survive? From his narrative we learn something basic about the totalitarian power hierarchy, based on control and the will to uphold rules. The narrative describes how other people in the same situation helped their fellow sufferer. But he was also helped by one upholding the power hierarchy, one whose moral code regarding the humane treatment of others had not broken.

This narrative is more than simply a report of an event, as it contains an ethical dimension. Through this narrative we glean information to which, without the narrative, we would not be privy. The silent knowledge in the example above, the reference to the fragility of goodness, resonates all the more strongly when it is seen in its wider context: the history of the prison camps and the stories of those who survived. The example serves as ethical proof that the system is not absolute, and that even in totalitarian systems individuals can influence events and make moral judgments.

In the context of social conflict, goodness is seen as deeds whose role in shaping the final outcome is decisive. Primo Levi, the Jewish chemist and writer who survived the concentration camps, emphasized in his 1947 book, *If This Is a Man* (Italian title *Se questo è un uomo*), that the purpose of writing a book about the concentration camps was not to seek out new accusations, but "at most to serve as source material for the calm research of the human mind." As such, the history of the concentration camps must serve as a warning example: if people can do this to the Jews, all people are therefore potential victims.[49]

In Levi's estimation, humans can be split into two groups that differ radically from one another: those who are saved and those who are destroyed. Other criteria, such as good and evil, wise and stupid, cowardly and brave, fortunate and misfortunate, are not as clear to him, as they incorporate too many different shades of meaning.[50] Many scholars who have conducted research into the genocide of the Second World War have noted that people react to their nightmares with either extreme noise or extreme silence; there is no "in between."[51] Tauno was silent for almost forty years, until he decided to tell his story, to bear witness to what happened.

Leona Toker, who has researched literary accounts of experiences in Stalin's prison camps, views these accounts as personal witness statements of the historical reality. Toker posits that, as a body of work, Gulag literature offers a unique insight into ethically oriented narratives from the prison camps. Gulag literature and Holocaust literature break the mold of other national literatures: for instance, Primo Levi's books are not representative of Italian literature; Elie Wiesel's short stories do not represent French literature; and the works of Aleksander Solzhenitsyn or Varlam Shalamov dealing with the prison camps do not represent Russian literature. They, and the works that followed them, process the heritage of the labor-camp lore.[52] The testimony of those who survived warns us to be wary of officially sanctioned information and statistics. Toker asserts that classifying all personal memories as biased, subjective, and self-perpetuating leads ultimately to a naïve faith in the truthfulness of official sources. Official sources are no less problematic than private ones.[53]

The accounts of Gulag survivors prove the significance of other knowledge. The idea of an ethical dimension in these narratives is linked to the memories of those who experienced the civil war and the prison camps, and to the need to impart this secondary knowledge because of its very sensitivity. It is also to do with being able to hear and listen to witness statements of dangers that form a permanent part of our *historical ozone layer*, through which memories of a destructive past are filtered, as Lawrence L. Langer puts it.[54]

In the field of oral history research, differing interpretations and meanings are increasingly constructed analytically from the available sources. Many different narratives are important. Literature—and oral history—

may serve as historical evidence, so long as the word "evidence" is not understood merely in juridical terms, but in a wider sense as an ethical dimension. It raises the question of the significance of memory. We can only remember if someone before us has remembered.[55] The challenge to research is in how we isolate from a variety of sources references to reality, knowledge, and the possible truth.[56]

Notes

1.   Soviet labor camps, i.e., the Gulag. See Nanci Adler, *The Gulag Survivor: Beyond the Soviet System* (New Brunswick: Transaction Publishers, 2002); Leona Toker, *Return from the Archipelago. Narratives of Gulag Survivors* (Bloomington: Indiana University Press, 2000); See also Irina Sherbakova, "The Gulag in Memory," in *Memory and Totalitarianism. International Yearbook of Oral History and Life Stories I*, ed. Luisa Passerini (Oxford, Oxford University Press 1992); and Ilkka Mäkinen, "Libraries in Hell: Cultural Activities in Soviet Prisons and Labour Camps from the 1930s to the 1950s," in *Libraries and Culture*, 28, 2 (Spring 1993).

2.   Ulla-Maija Peltonen, *Punakapinan muistot. Tutkimus työväen muistelukerronnan muotoutumisesta vuoden 1918 jälkeen* (Summary: Memories of the Civil War. A Study of the formation of the Finnish working-class narrative tradition after 1918) Finnish Literature Society Publication 657, Helsinki 1996; Ulla-Maija Peltonen, "The Return of the Narrator," in *Historical Perspectives on Memory*. ed. Anne Ollila Studia Historica 61. Finnish Literature Society, Helsinki 1999 and Ulla-Maija Peltonen, *Muistin paikat. Vuoden 1918 sisällissodan muistamisesta ja unohtamisesta.* (Summary: Sites of Memory. On Remembering and Forgetting the Finnish Civil War in 1918) (Helsinki: Finnish Literature Society Publication 894, 2003). For further information Anne Heimo & Ulla-Maija Peltonen, "Memories and Histories, Public and Private: After the Finnish Civil War," in *Memory, History, Nation. Contested Pasts*, ed. Katharine Hodgkin and Susannah Radstone (New Brunswick and London: Transaction Publishers, 2005), 42-56. [*Contested Pasts. The Politics of Memory*, eds. Katharine Hodgkin & Susannah Radstone (London and New York: Routledge, 2003].

3.   Our interviews about Tauno's experiences in the Gulag lasted 11 hours in total. The recordings are kept at the Sound Archives of the Finnish Literature Society. Due to the sensitive nature of the material I will not give any more specific reference for them.

4.   In 1917, 140,470 Ingrians are documented as living in the area. See Hannes Sihvo, "Inkeriläisten identiteetti muutosten paineissa," in *Inkeri, kansa ja kulttuuri* ed. Pekka Nevalainen and Hannes Sihvo (Helsinki: Suomalaisen kirjallisuuden seura 1999). In 1943 around 63,000 Ingrians were evacuated to Finland. See Helena Miettinen, *Menetetyt kodit, elämät, unelmat. Suomalaisuus paluumuuttajastatukseen oikeutettujen venäjänsuomalaisten narratiivisessa itsemäärittelyssä.* Sosiaalipsykologisia tutkimuksia 11. (Yliopistopaino, Helsinki: University of Helsinki, 2004), 26.

5.   Miettinen, Ibid., 2004, 25-26; Sihvo, Ibid., 1991, 343-355.

6.   Ibid., 2004, 25-26; Sihvo, Ibid., 1991, 343-355.

7.   Folklore Archives of the Finnish Literature Society. SKSÄ 219.2001. Ulla-Maija Peltonen 25.10.2001.

8.   Ibid., SKSÄ 222.2001. Ulla-Maija Peltonen 12.12. 2001.

9. Ibid., SKSÄ 229.2002. Ulla-Maija Peltonen 19.12.2002.

10. Ibid., SKSÄ 219.2001. Ulla-Maija Peltonen 25.10.2001.

11. Ibid., SKSÄ 227.2002. Ulla-Maija Peltonen 10.6.2002.

12. This hand-written account is 59 pages long. Tauno has also donated a number of other personal documents and photographs to the Folklore Archives of the Finnish Literature Society.

13. Giovanni Levi, "On microhistory," in *New Perspectives on Historical Writing*, ed. Peter Burke (Cambridge: Polity Press, 1991, 107; Tzwetan Todorov, *The Fragility of Goodness. Why Bulgaria's Jews Survived the Holocaust,* (London: Weidenfeld & Nicolson, 1999).

14. Vieda Skultans, *The Testimony of Lives. Narrative and Memory on Post-Soviet Latvia* (London and New York: Routledge, 1998), xii, 22.

15. Selma Leydesdorff, "A Shattered Silence. The Life Stories of Survivors of the Jewish Proletariat of Amsterdam," in *Memory and Totalitarianism.* International Yearbook of Oral History and Life Stories I, ed. Luisa Passerini (Oxford: Oxford University Press, 1992), 148.

16. Helsingin Sanomat 19.11.2006. In Memoriam Reko Lundán 1969–2006.

17. Jacques Derrida, *Demeure: Fiction and Testimony*, trans., Elizabeth Rottenberg (Stanford: Stanford University Press, 2000), 43.

18. Andrea Frisch, *The Invention of the Eyewitness. Witnessing & Testimony in Early Modern France.* North Carolina Studies in Romance Languages and Literatures Number 279 (North Carolina: University of North Carolina Press, 2004), 184-185.

19. Frisch, Ibid., 2004

20. Carlo Ginzburg, "Only One Witness". I have used the Finnish version, "Ainoa todistaja. Juutalaisten tuhoaminen ja todellisuuden periaate,"in *Johtolankoja. Kirjoituksia mikrohistoriasta ja historiallisesta metodista* (Transl. Aulikki Vuola) (Helsinki: Gaudeamus 1996), 127-128. Carlo Ginzburg, *The Judge and the Historian. Marginal Notes on a Late- Twentieth-Century Miscarriage of Justice* (London & New York: Verso, 1999), 51, 185-205.

21. Alessandro Portelli, *The Death of Luigi Trastulli and Other Stories* (Albany: State University of New York Press, 1991), 250, 256; Alessandro Portelli, *The Battle of Valle Giulia. Oral History and the Art of Dialogue* (Madison, Wisconsin: The University of Wisconsin Press, 1997); Frisch, 184.

22. Sakari, Hänninenand Jouko & Lahti, Tuukka Karjalainen, ed. *Toinen tieto. Kirjoituksia huono-osaisuuden tunnistamisesta.*(Helsinki: Sosiaali- ja terveysalan tutkimus- ja kehittämiskeskus, 2005), 5.

23. Dori Laub, "Bearing Witness, or the Vicissitudes of Listening," in Shoshana Felman and Dori Laub, *Testimony: Crises of Witnessing in Literature, Psychoanalysis, and History* (New York and London: Routledge 1992), 58; See Luisa Passerini, "Memories between Silence and Oblivion," in *Memory, History, Nation. Contested Pasts,* ed. Katharine Hodgkin and Susannah Radstone (New Brunswick and London: Transaction Publishers, 2005), 238-254.

24. Dominic LaCapra, "Revisiting the Historians' Debate. Mourning and Genocide," in *History & Memory,* (University of Tel Aviv, 1997), 80–112; Peltonen, Ibid., 2003.

25. See Lawrence L. Langer, *Holocaust Testimonies. The Ruins of Memory,* (New Haven and London: Yale University Press, 1991); Luisa Passerini, *Fascism in Popular Memory. The Cultural Experience of the Turin Working Class,* (Cambridge: Cambridge University Press, 1987); Luisa Passerini, "Introduction," in *Memory and Totalitarianism.* International Yearbook of Oral History and Life Stories, ed.

Luisa Passerini (Oxford: Oxford University Press, 1992), 12–13; Anton van den Braembussche, "History and Memory. Some Comments on Recent Developments," in: *Jäljillä. Kirjoituksia historian ongelmista*. Part 1. Festschrift to Jorma Kalela 12.11.2000 ed. Pauli Kettunen, Auli Kultanen, Timo Soikkanen (Turku: Turun yliopisto 2000), 77–84.

26.   Seppo Knuuttila, "Kansanomainen maailmankuva," in *Maailmankuva kulttuurin kokonaisuudessa. Aate- ja oppihistorian, kirjallisuustieteen ja kulttuuriantropologian näkökulmia.* Juha Manninen & Markku Envall & Seppo Knuuttila (Oulu: Pohjoinen, 1989), 119–120, 122–123, 125.

27.   Peltonen, Ibid., 1996, 30; Michael Billig, "Collective Memory, Ideology and the British Royal Family," in *Collective Remembering,* ed. David Middleton & Derek Edwards (London: Sage Publications 1991), 60.

28.   See Peltonen, Ibid., 1996, 23-31.

29.   Philippe Lejeune, *On Autobiography.* Katherine Leary, trans., Theory and History of Literature, vol. 52. (Minneapolis: University of Minnesota Press, 1989), 70–73; Portelli, Ibid., 1991, 20–21. Lejeune examines Sartre's autobiography "Les Mots" (1964) engl. "The Words" (1964). Many researchers have underlined the importance of examining the system of influence between reader and text.

30.   Langer, Ibid., 1991; Sherbakova, Ibid. 1992, 102–115.

31.   Ibid., SKSÄ 227.2002, 10.6.2002 Ulla-Maija Peltonen. The text in square brackets is the narrator's addition made in 2003.

32.   Ibid., SKSÄ 227.2002. Ulla-Maija Peltonen 10.6.2002.

33.   Antti Eskola *Jäähyväisluentoja*. Tammi, Helsinki, 1997, 111.

34.   Eskola ibid. 1997, 103, 112-113.

35.   Ibid.,SKSÄ 225.2001. Ulla-Maija Peltonen 12.12.2002.

36.   Shoshana Felman and Dori Laub, *Testimony: Crises of witnessing in Literature, Psychoanalysis, and History* (New York and London: Routledge, 1992), 3.

37.   Janina Bauman, Muisti ja mielikuvitus", in *Otteita kulttuurista. Kirjoituksia nykyajasta, tutkimuksesta ja elämäkerrallisuudesta* ed. Maaria Linko, Tuija Saresma, Erkki Vainikkala Katariina Eskolan juhlakirja. Nykykulttuurin tutkimusyksikön julkaisuja 65. Jyväskylän yliopisto, Jyväskylä, 2000, 336–337.

38.   Satu Apo, *Viinan voima. Näkökulmia suomalaisten kansanomaiseen alkoholiajatteluun ja –kulttuuriin*. Finnish Literature Society Publication 759, Helsinki, 2001, 20.

39.   Charles Taylor, *Sources of the Self. The Making of the Modern Identity* (Cambridge, Massachusetts: Harvard University Press1989), 92-94, 96.

40.   Tzwetan Todorov, *The Fragility of Goodness. Why Bulgaria's Jews Survived the Holocaust* (London: Weidenfeld and Nicolson, 1999), Todorov , 2001.

41.   Portelli, (1997, 9-13) discusses the notion of "thick dialogue." For more on the dialogue between official and unofficial culture cf. Mikhail Bakhtin, *Rabelais och skrattens historia. François Rabelais' verk och den folkliga kultur under medeltiden och renässansen* (Uddevalla: Antropos, 1986) 445-447.

42.   Gerard Genette, *Narrative Discourse Revisited,* trans., Jane A. Lewin (Ithaca: Cornell University Press, 1994); Jay Winter, *Sites of Memory, Sites of Mourning. The Great War in European Cultural History* (Cambridge: Cambridge University Press, 1997), 223-226. Peltonen, Ibid., 1996, 90-107, 296-297.

43.   Passerini, Ibid; 1987, 53-55.

44.   Jorma Kalela, *Historiantutkimus ja historia* (Helsinki: Hanki ja jää, 2000, 91).

45.   Portelli, Ibid., 1991 47-49; Anna-Leena Siikala, "Toisiinsa virtaavat maailmat," in *Kaukaa haettua. Kirjoituksia antropologisesta kenttätyöstä.* ed. Anna Maria Viljanen & Minna Lahti (Helsinki: Finnish Anthropological Society, 1997), 47;

Annikki Kaivola-Bregenhøj, "Kertomuksia inkerinsuomalaisten identiteetistä," in *Kaukaa haettua. Kirjoituksia antropologisesta kenttätyöstä* ed. Anna Maria Viljanen & Minna Lahti (Helsinki: Finnish Anthropological Society, 1997), 203-211.

46. Ibid., SKSÄ 226.2002 Peltonen 10.6.2002.
47. Anna-Leena Siikala, *Tarina ja tulkinta. Tutkimus kansankertojista.* Finnish Literature Society Publication 404, Helsinki, 1984, 35.
48. Natalie Zemon Davis, *Fiction in the Archives. Pardon Tales and Their Tellers in Sixteenth-Century France* (Cambridge: Polity Press 1987).
49. Primo Levi, *If This Is a Man* (London: Penguin Books, 1979); (Finnish transl. *Tällainenko on ihminen*, Tapio Hiisivaara, Tammi, Helsinki, 1962, 107).
50. Levi, Ibid., 1962, 220, 224.
51. Langer, Ibid., 1991; Felman and Laub, Ibid., 1992.
52. Toker, p. 9, quotation Sidra DeKoven Ezrahi 1980.
53. Toker, p. 3.
54. Langer, p. xv.
55. Toker, p. 123; Skultans, 1998.
56. Giovanni Levi, "Historians, Psychoanalysis and Truth," in *Between Sociology and History. Essays in Microhistory, Collective Action, and Nation-Building* Ed. Anna-Maija Castrén, Markku Lonkila and Matti Peltonen Studia Historica 70. (Finnish Literature Society, 2004), 83-86.

Part II

Aftermath: Trauma and Emotions

4

"My Entire Life I Have Shivered": Homecoming and New Persecution of Former Slave and Forced Laborers of Nazi Germany

Christoph Thonfeld

Research on the Aftermath of Nazi Forced Labor

This chapter is based on 180 life story interviews which were conducted with former forced laborers of Nazi Germany from the core countries of the former Soviet Union, i.e., Ukraine, Belarus and the Russian Federation, and from those countries that emerged from the former Yugoslavia, i.e., Slovenia, Bosnia, Croatia, Serbia/Montenegro and Macedonia, where 54 life story interviews were conducted. The research was part of the International Forced Laborers Documentation Project, carried out by the Institute for History and Biography at Hagen University, on behalf of the Foundation "Remembrance, Responsibility and Future" in 2005-2006. This chapter focuses on phenomena related to the mass repression against former forced laborers of Nazi Germany after their return from the Reich, or its formerly occupied territories, to the countries of the former Soviet Union and Yugoslavia, in or shortly after 1945.

Many of these returnees assumed that the worst was over, and were certain that their compatriots would treat them better than the Germans and their allies had. This study asks questions about how former forced laborers were made objects and victims again, this time by their home countries and societies of origin, and looks at how the returnees tried to cope with this renewed repression. These questions will be approached from the different perspectives of states, societies and repatriates respectively, though the former forced laborers' individual views will predominate. This approach will be facilitated by differentiating various manifestations of oppressive actions, and ascertaining whether they were designed to be outright means of destruction, or instead as everyday acts of politically-motivated punishment, or moral or economic degradation. In addition, the individual perception and interpretation of those who were repressed will be analyzed, because acts of repression not only have immediately palpable short-term effects, but may also have deep psychological impact and long-term consequences. These consequences are best uncovered in personal accounts, since they hardly ever become the subject matter of official files.

One of the characteristics of using oral history is the intermingling of various layers of time within personal experiences. While this may be problematic in terms of factual reconstruction, it does open up interpretive potential. This is illustrated by an excerpt from Belarusian former forced laborer Raisa B.'s recollection of her interrogation by the Soviet secret service in the summer of 1945, shortly after her return from three years of forced labor in Germany:

> When I came to the KGB, I was afraid. Even more, as I did not come from the GDR. Not from the direction of Berlin, which later belonged to the GDR; when Germany was divided into four zones, there was the GDR. Is that correct? And there, there was all our military. And I had been in the FRG. At that time, only the word "FRG" was horrible, because it was said that the FRG, the Federal Parliament, the Federal Armed Forces were our primary enemies. One was not even allowed to say these words. And I was so frightened—what should I say and how should I say it—that I had been in the FRG, in West Germany. West Germany—that was terrible. And I lied and mentioned a city, I do not know which one, mentioned a Polish city. I have got an excerpt from KGB Donetsk, there this town is mentioned. I lied, just to avoid saying that I had been in the FRG. I would not have been released. I would have been deported right away.[1]

Although in the beginning this narrative concerns the first confrontation with the Soviet secret service upon return in the autumn of 1945, the perceived danger of this confrontation is put into terms relevant only in the early 1950s and onwards. This gives us an idea not only of the long-term nature of the perceived threat, but also of the confusion of the concrete circumstances of this threat through the years and decades.

Especially in Slovenia, the long-term effects of World War II on the whole seem to have been distinctly complex due to the demographic and political interferences from 1940 to 1945. There was not only an ethnic confrontation within Yugoslavia but also between various factions of Slovenians, e.g., partisans, collaborators, and Home Guard members.

Even to this day, some former forced laborers from Slovenia, particularly those who were forcibly resettled by the Axis powers, have felt like second-class victims in comparison to the partisans, who triumphantly emerged from the civil-war-like situation in Yugoslavia after 1945.[2] They have continuously struggled to find their place in society, both socially and politically, as recent research has shown.[3] In some neighborhoods, relationships are still being defined along the social and political lines that were set up during World War II.[4] Joze J., who was interned in Dachau after trying to escape from forced labor in 1943, remembers his liberation in April 1945 and subsequent return that summer:

> ... I was afraid because I had been [working] in the disinfection [area] and everybody knew about it. Because we then talked about it with Pogorelec, he is the one who accompanied Mušič, he said, "So you were not arrested?" I said that I had been terribly lucky that I had been in Zagreb. It is interesting that there were no retributions against each other in Zagreb, you know. In Ljubljana people still know [people] who had been a member of the White Guards and so on. In Zagreb, there was none of this.[5]

Joze J. still has not come to terms with his role during internment in the German camps. He tried his luck; he was convinced that the shelter of big cities—in contrast to the general circumstances in small villages—mitigated the danger of being held responsible for actual or alleged conduct during World War II because one could remain more anonymous. Still, most returnees went back to their native villages.

Repressive Actions of the Receiving States and Societies

Although there has been increased research on the repression of returning former forced laborers of Nazi Germany, their personal narratives reveal, more compellingly than the socio-historical studies, the extent of the arbitrariness with which repatriates were often confronted. Repatriates were accused on the basis of unfounded denunciations, put on trial without adherence to any constitutional standards, and sentenced to excessive terms in camps or prisons. Although they were among a host of other groups to be confronted with the Gulag system, former forced laborers still showed specific individual perspectives towards the experience.

Igor G., a former Soviet POW who did four years of forced labor in various German labor and concentration camps, was accused of high treason and collaboration upon his return. He remembers how he was sentenced to 15 years of internment in a penal camp by a Soviet military tribunal:

Two men ... hmm ... who had been arrested together with me ... were forced to sign these denunciations. They were told, "Either you sign or we lock you up." They signed, but to me they said, "We will revoke the charges immediately."

Interviewer: "And when did you manage to confront them about this?"

Hmm ... well ... We had been together in a cast, that was all before ... before the arrest. Yes. Well, to cut it short, the jury reads out the indictment. I listened, listened, listened, listened. Nothing complied with reality. Everything was provocation. I was granted the final word. I stand up and start saying that all this does not comply with reality, that everything had been so and so and so. I look at them, they sit there, smoke, talk to each other, nobody listens. I fell silent and sat down. I sat silently for ten minutes and they were talking to each other. The president of the tribunal stands up and asks me: "Was that all?"[6]

This illustrates how effective denunciations, formal justice and repressive policies intertwined and left hardly any way out. In this case, the arrestee had to serve a term of ten years in a labor camp, which he could leave only after Stalin's death.

In the countries of the former Yugoslavia, one can spot a more complex approach towards former forced laborers compared to what happened in the Soviet Union. To begin with, they potentially had to face the threat of political screening by the UDBA police force. As its outcome was generally unclear, fear of repression was widespread and the danger was perceived as inherent, as is shown by this account of Andria M., a Serbian repatriate who was deported to do forced labor as a child with his family in 1941. This is his impression of their homecoming in the summer of 1945:

They [Yugoslav nationalists] tried to convince us that we should not go back to Yugoslavia, that it is hell there, that a certain Tito has come to power there, and that those who return from Germany will be killed. However, my father was not taken in by this.[7]

Regardless of the actual existence of looming repression back home, there were many rumors and contradictory political strategies and interests in the camps of the Allies, where most of the former forced laborers had to decide on their next step, or rather, which official offer to accept—if there was any alternative at all. Of course, this atmosphere of anxiety and uncertainty was mixed with the real danger of reprisals on return; however, there was still more individual scope for the affected Yugoslavs than for Soviet repatriates. The screening and investigations in Yugoslavia were less widespread and comprehensive.

Nevertheless, with the victorious partisans still struggling to establish their grip on power, repatriates could be confronted with straightforward denunciation,[8] as is revealed in Angela D.'s narration. She had been deported for political reasons in late 1942 and describes her return in July 1945 after two and a half years of forced labor in Germany:

> I have already said this before, that we were astonished when we faced our liberators. They were the kind of people who even begrudged us water; with this machine gun he [a Yugoslav guard] patrolled in the train back and forth. On the other side there were the English with their caps, but they were only subordinate soldiers. They told us that they would bring our people water. So, I do not know, we were looked at with such hatred. I do not know what they imagined who or what we were.[9]

This account, first and foremost, demonstrates the inimical and fearful atmosphere upon the arrival of the repatriates. Although the liberators were on one side and the liberated on the other, most of the actors involved seemed to be filled with mistrust towards their counterparts. As the liberated were perceived as possible traitors or collaborators, the liberators approached them with suspicion and, therefore, rather appeared to be new oppressors.

During the subsequent civil war, much revenge killing and other forms of retaliation took place. This was partly fuelled by or turned into an ethnic confrontation between Serbs and Slovenians, respectively, and Croats afterwards,[10] which becomes clear in this account from Milan D., a Serbian former forced laborer who joined the partisans after he escaped from the Reich in 1944:

> So I became a soldier, a partisan. And we went for some ... some actions at night to various villages. I was mostly impressed when we were at Hrtkovci. That is a mixed Croatian, Hungarian, Serbian, a mixed village, and there were many traitors there: Serbs as well as Croats and ... and that was a bl - ... a black spot in the Srem [a region in the northern part of Serbia]. And there we received the order ... we did not kill anybody there, we did not drive anybody away, but we loaded approximately ten cars with ham, bacon, lard, everything [speaking louder] gathered together, loaded in our cars and brought them into the forest.[11]

Very soon, the allegiances and front lines were drawn according to ethnic affiliations, thereby in a way continuing structural patterns that had also been brutally established during the Axis reign, only now they were roughly turned upside down. In the same way that Serbs, who on the whole had been bad off during occupation, and Croats had to suffer for their collaboration with Germany, Communist guerrilla fighters now became the hunters instead of the hunted.

Still, there was no regular system of sanctions against repatriates, but rather erratic sentences meted out which were mostly restricted to the final year of the war and to the period immediately following the homecoming of former deportees,[12] as emphasized by the aforementioned Angela D.:

> My husband always said to me, "You were lucky to have returned home, that they did not kill you like the others."
>
> Interviewer: "That was a little later, right? Because, at that time they no longer did this…"
>
> Yes, a little later; no, they did not do this any more.
>
> Interviewer: "Actually it did not really matter then, in July [1945] it was still a little early, there was no amnesty yet, a lot could still happen."[13]

Here, the account of the survivor does not correspond with the knowledge of the interviewer. Unfortunately, the interviewer intervened, stopping the narration of the interviewee, which likely would have taken a different course. The interviewee suddenly felt urged to justify herself as she allegedly had luckily escaped possible execution, against the odds, as her husband termed it. Whether the danger was real or not, at this point finding out about the family discussion and subsequent evaluation would have been far more relevant in the interview than reaching consensus between interviewer and interviewee on alleged historical facts.

On a judicial level, the new wielders of power in Slovenia prosecuted some former slave laborers from Dachau, who were accused of collaborating with the enemy under camp conditions. This was, more than anything else, a demonstration of mistrust towards all forced deportees who did not fight as partisans, but had to endure the German camp system. The vast majority were victims who then had enormous difficulties in justifying their conduct to their compatriots back home. Joze J., a Dachau survivor, relates his evaluation of the trial:

> With us, one thing happened at this Dachau trial. There were a lot of functionaries of the Communist Party and those who had come home, for whom there were no jobs. Either you had to replace someone who had returned or to track down someone for them. And one solution was the Dachau trial.[14]

Popular perception still went along rather practical lines. In this case, the political complexity behind the trial seems either to have been lost on the respondent or, again, could possibly have interfered with his own strategy which he developed and performed throughout the course of the interview to justify his role in the camp. On the other hand, his memory seemed to work in an obviously and consciously selective way. That does not make it any easier to estimate the reliability of this account. However, in general it can be said that after enduring the immediate post-war situation, quiet acceptance of the new political and social hierarchy guaranteed most of the Slovenian former forced laborers an unmolested life.

Coming Home After Forced Labor

The notorious filtration process of former forced laborers on their return from Germany to the Soviet Union[15] had a deep impact on many of them. Although findings have shown that female forced laborers returning to rural communities were far less strictly screened in the filtration camps, even among this group we can find descriptions of persistent fear of repression that undermined the respondents' life with insecurity and mistrust, as the aforementioned Raisa B. tells us:

> My life after returning from Germany to the Soviet Union did not become any easier. I have experienced so much, my entire life I have shivered. I have never written in the records of the cadre department that I had been in Germany. I always wrote that I had lived under the occupational regime. And when there was an assembly held and somebody was summoned, I always thought: "Oh, maybe they have come because of me." I was afraid that they would send me to prison. This way my life went by. Only my husband knew that I had been to Germany.[16]

Fear and mistrust not only became rooted in the everyday lives of former forced laborers, it also dominated the way they formed and perceived social relationships. In these cases, only the immediate family members or perhaps only their partners were privy to their past. While others hardly mention the filtration in interviews because it appeared to them to be a regular, unspectacular element of their homecoming, the substantial influence on the lives of many of the repatriates again reveals that there is, indeed, a traumatic long-term dimension of forced labor which goes far beyond the actual assignment in Germany.

For women, one strategy to conceal one's forced labor past was to change one's name through marriage, as for example the same Belarusian respondent was advised to do:

> Then I was invited by the leader of the pedagogic cabinet and she was talking like this, openly. And her husband was a navy colonel. And she herself came from somewhere near Magnitogorsk. And she said: "Raisa Yakovlevna, I also came from a family of persecuted people. However, when I married this navy officer and went away from there, I changed my name and they stopped keeping me under surveillance. You have to change your name." I say, "But how can I change it?" "Well, somehow you have to marry." And who could you marry there, if one was constantly living in fear. I was afraid to open my mouth. There was only military anyway. This meant that I had to fool somebody. "Now, well, I send you to Oblono." And the husband of this cousin said, "I have got this military attorney there, a very good friend."[17]

It becomes clear that there were obvious advantages to this strategy, but at the same time it required enormous personal engagement and even involved other people. Nevertheless, the restricted situation of former forced laborers could become so precarious that they even considered this far-reaching option.

Forged biographies were another remarkable feature of the repatriates' ways of dealing with their experience of obvious disadvantage in their home countries, especially in the former Soviet Union.[18] For repatriates in general, and those who returned via Soviet camps in particular—but also for many other former forced laborers—the predicament of not being masters of their own lives was prolonged for years after 1945. Thus, at various stages they tried to influence the courses of their lives, for example, by forging documents. This already started with attempts to escape deportation by claiming that they were younger than they actually were. The forging of facts also happened during their time as forced laborers when they tried to maneuver through the racial hierarchy of the Third Reich, e.g., by concealing that they were Jewish. It became a strategy of sorts in the displaced person (DP) camps in Germany as an attempt to avoid forced repatriation.[19] In the filtration camps throughout the Soviet post-war dominion, it was used to circumvent mentioning potentially or actually compromising details of one's stay in Germany. Finally, this was developed into an everyday practice whenever former forced laborers had to deal with authorities and with colleagues and superiors at their workplaces back home, providing at least a small means of mitigating the considerable obstacles most of them had to face. Sometimes, recruitment to the Red Army after repatriation even served to cover the traces of forced labor for the enemy, because then the returnee came home as a respectable soldier in 1947 or 1948 instead of returning as a suspicious deportee in the summer of 1945.[20]

Renewed or newly founded social networks, again most prominently in the former Soviet Union, opened up another possibility to escape the otherwise virtually omnipresent process of sanctioning,[21] to which, in any case, the male city dwellers among the repatriates were exposed.[22] The reestablishment of relationships beyond friends and family or the building up of new social connections, primarily at the workplace, often helped former forced laborers to overcome the many difficulties that were involuntarily placed in their way, among them often being exclusion from further education and from professional advancement.

Galina A. tells how she managed to find a job in Moscow upon her return to the Soviet Union in 1945 after three years of forced labor in Germany:

It was said that there should be written "temporarily." That ... they said...

Interviewer: "What ... how one had to write it."

One had to formulate it this way. He said: "I conferred. In the personnel department nobody knew anything."

Interviewer: "And how did you formulate your application?"

I wrote, "I request you to employ me temporarily ... without right of lodging and right of residence." How did this work? In a free bed, where nobody was sleeping. And sometimes in one bed with Verochka Skvorchkova.

Interviewer: "In the hall of residence?"

And when the police came for a control, I hid in the cupboard.[23]

Her account shows the readiness of former forced laborers to improvise and to accept temporary solutions in order to somehow get settled under the unfavorable circumstances of life back home. It also illustrates how dependent they were on friends' and colleagues' readiness to create some semi-legal spaces where they could (re-)construct their existence, as they were constantly in danger of being discovered by mistrustful officials.

While building up social networks went quite well in the countryside, it remained an exception in bigger cities. An important turning point in the lives of many of the deportees was Stalin's death and the subsequent political upheaval it caused throughout the Soviet realm in the mid-1950s. This stirred hope in many former forced laborers like Russian Marya V., who was sentenced to ten years of camp internment for treason upon her return from two years of forced labor for the Germans in 1945. She remembers her own and her families' and friends' efforts to obtain her rehabilitation:

> Yes, and later, that they would clear it up after the war—well, I thought, maybe they are actually going to clear it up; there will come, (maybe) there will come a time. Well yes, that is, I have, indeed, told you that my sister, my mother wrote, I wrote, and there actually was a letter from Nikitov—from the lieutenant colonel. I do not know, what would have been otherwise, everyday I pray for him to the Lord. They came here to the site of the crime, interrogated all witnesses ... and, based on the follow-up investigation, they rehabilitated me in 1956.[24]

There are two dimensions to consider here: one is the year-long hope of those affected that a different time might come, wherein they would finally obtain legal (and potentially economic, political and professional) rehabilitation. This hope was realized for some of them, but remained a treacherous prospect for many. The other is the societal dimension that

even those who achieved formal governmental or legal acknowledgement could not be sure that this also meant the end of all types of social
marginalization that they had experienced in the meantime.

Dealing with the Experience of Forced Labor

The importance of silence in the interview situation and its impact on
interpretation has been regularly emphasized by numerous oral historians.[25] Two kinds of silence seem to prevail among survivors of forced
labor, particularly the survivors of racially motivated Nazi persecution.
The first one is basically the absence of recordable speech, which is
often revealed by the shortness of interview transcripts despite the
considerable length of the interview on the whole. Of course, age and
health play a role in this; however, only if one takes the implications
of unspeakable experiences into account will we be able to get a complete picture of the difficulties of narrating traumatic experiences.[26]
The second kind is characterized by a lack of emotional involvement,
although the factual events can well be related.[27] This can either be the
prolonged effect of forced labor or, indeed, a coping strategy. On the
other hand, the great distance from the events combined with the very
advanced stage of the individual lives of former forced laborers, and
their perspectives on their lives as a whole, might enable the witnesses
to place their suffering into the context of their previous and later biographies. If they managed to overcome the immediate traumatic impact,
they could speak about their suffering as one element within the course
of their lives, rather than as something that has continuously uprooted
them.

At the same time, the interview situation has also produced shame
between the interviewees and their often much younger counterparts. For
example, women from Eastern Europe, who were otherwise quite willing
to talk about their memories, refused to speak about certain elements of
deportation, e.g., details of the transport in cattle cars to Germany, the
medical inspections in the transit camps, and their confrontation with
the allegedly liberating Red Army soldiers towards the end of the war
and in the filtration camps on the way back.[28] For them, liberation only
ended the racial or political persecution by the Nazis; in addition to the
political screening of the NKVD (the forerunner of the KGB), they were
still part of sometimes violent relations between the sexes.

The end of the war did not mean the end of all threats for many of
them,[29] like the aforementioned Marya V. She recalls the repeated interrogations by the NKVD that took place in early 1945:

I go there, it is the same again, he has laid the table. "And, did you think about it?" I say, "Yes, I have thought about everything, yes, I have pondered it all. I want to go home; I have not seen my mother for so long." Now well, thus far. And he, he butters me up pretty much, like "queen" and "fur coats" and all such things. I say to him, "I do not wear any German rags, you see. And I have not got anything else on me, I have," I say, "I did not sell myself, I am not involved in anything." Anyway, I knew, that for connections to the Germans—that this was the end, if I return and everything is from Germany, who would believe me. Yes, and he just said, "Nevertheless, think about it again." On the third—and in the following night I am summoned again to him. However, this time the guard had already locked the door. Now well, I immediately understood what was going on, he was already heavily drunk. And he starts right away, he is not only talking to me, he also starts to come closer violently. He already wanted to push me on the bed, then, of course, I strongly, hmm, really kicked him, he fell against the oven and that was that.[30]

This encounter shows various elements which were all part of the danger for women of being raped: bribery with food and clothes, promises of future welfare or outright blackmailing under the threat of using alleged or actual wrongdoings of the affected woman during World War II to legitimize whatever reprisal and, on top of that, the sheer physical force of mostly more than one man. If women decide to talk about this at all in an interview situation, they generally preferred to talk about it as if it were only hearsay or as something that happened to a relative or acquaintance.[31]

Another aspect of silence during interviews is that interviewees may simply lack the words to express their processed memories in a way that seems appropriate to them, as one female Ukrainian interviewee, former agricultural forced laborer Nadya S. who lives in Germany today, epitomized: "You can experience a lot, but you cannot tell everything."[32]

This may have some connection to a lack of individual eloquence and education, but also to the very impact of traumatizing events. Furthermore, these days many interviewees find themselves confronted with a vast literature, with documentaries and feature films that seem to already occupy the means of expression. This is a very complex interplay[33] and, of course, also depends on access to and consumption of various kinds of media. However, these factors are increasingly implicit in the way in which interviewees try to create images of their memories.

Related to this issue are the written sources that some of our interviewees have produced about their past. Sometimes they prefer to point to them as authorized sources for the description of their experiences, thereby delegating possibly hurtful confrontation to the printed paper. This can mean consciously holding back information which seems unsuitable or too private or hurtful for the interview situation, as it might either be beyond the interviewee's grasp, or, by way of psychological transference, thought to be beyond the interviewer's understanding, especially when he or she is not a contemporary of World War II and is considerably younger than the eyewitness. Still, through the dynamics of the interview or the presence of insufficiently suppressed memories, traumatic experiences may sometimes be revealed, leading to tears and/or silence, which often result in breaks or turns of the narration. Although generally not considered part of a "successful" narration, these ruptures in a biographical account can be very telling. While the concealed meaning is a problematic issue, this occurrence can be fruitfully integrated into the interview situation. These situations can potentially unearth deeper layers of memory, but mostly the concomitant uneasiness is so unbearable that both participants prefer to try to overcome them as soon as possible.

However, the spontaneous reaction of an interviewer is mostly directed towards comforting the interviewee, thereby helping to overcome the uneasiness of the situation. At the same time, it could potentially hinder the further disclosure of the apparently unspeakable content that had just been unearthed. After some moments of consolation and support, experienced interviewers try to take up exactly where the narration was cut off; however, a good deal of meaningful content probably remains beyond speech.

Specifics of Racial Persecution and Its Aftermath

In the recently war-torn countries of former Yugoslavia, interviews reveal how past and present experiences of persecution overlap. This is found mostly among respondents from Bosnia, who had to escape from their country during the civil wars of the 1990s. Osman H., a Roma who had been deported to forced labor in a Croatian concentration camp as a child with his entire family in 1941, fled to Germany from recent acts of war in his home country in 1992. His recollection begins in the distant past and gradually moves towards the present:[34]

When I was ten years old, I managed to escape from the concentration camp after endless maltreatment and insane torture. When my father was released from the concentration camp, he stayed alive only for two more years. He experienced many terrible things. He was also maltreated and tortured. Both of my parents died during the great famine after the war, to be precise. When they were released from the concentration camp, the fight against hunger started. There was almost nothing to eat. First my mother died, then my father, too. What shall I do now? Shall I kill myself? If I am deported from Germany and I am not allowed to stay here, then I will commit suicide. I have got nobody; who would accommodate me? Even my medical care would not be guaranteed any more. Should I be deported, I would commit suicide. I am very ill and do not want to be a burden for anybody. My leg hurts, my back, as well, and therefore I have difficulties breathing and cannot breathe properly any more. These are the consequences of the Yugoslav civil war, when we were hiding in the water night after night because of fear of the soldiers. My wife and I were hiding in the water most of the time. The doctors diagnosed chronic inflammation of the joints. When an operation had to be performed on my eye, I stayed in hospital for four days. I can only mention again and again that I have nobody to turn to.[35]

Relating the consequences of events in the Nazi and Ustasha concentration camps triggers a balancing of the present misery of the interviewee. As the present situation threatens to result in deportation to Bosnia, the haunting memories of World War II and civil war are unearthed again and, mediated through the topic of hospital stays, intermingle with present day exigencies. Apart from specific cultural or ethnic concepts of time that become visible here, one encounters desperate attempts to integrate various but sometimes similar traumatic experiences into one person's biography in the first place. It is part of this mixing up of the chronological order that Germany as the country of past persecution and forced labor suddenly and confusingly becomes a safe haven from present atrocities, albeit an ambiguous one. Restricted rights of residence, refused work permits and regularly renewed short-term exceptional leaves force survivors to lead a precarious existence. Still, there is a positive impact on their view of Germany and the Germans, even in historical perspective.

Summary

For forced laborers, homecoming was a fragile process with many events occurring within a constantly changing, dominantly unfavorable political landscape. They faced hunger, destruction of property and at times violent social relations, especially those between men and women. Female former forced laborers were likely accustomed to this attitude from the Germans; however, they were still dismayed by the Red Army soldiers' contempt and general assumption that they had allegedly "sold" themselves to the Germans. The former involuntary foreign workers of Germany, male and female alike, had to find a place for themselves quietly, unassumingly, and under the suspicious attention of the social milieu that transcended family and friends. In the countryside they could hope for support from their social environment, where everybody knew each other. However, that was still a double-edged sword, as this closeness could result in solidarity as well as strict exclusion. In the end, former forced laborers could still find themselves being forced to move to another place, often actively driven away by zealous secret service officials. In the big cities they were better off if they kept information about their past to themselves. There, chances were considerably greater if no one took an interest, but suspicion was pervasive. On the other hand, social and economic aspirations—mostly realized in cities—could spark trouble for repatriates. An unskilled female worker on a *kolkhoz* would in most cases be left alone by the secret service, while officials would surely have developed an interest if someone sought university entry.

It seems that in the Soviet Union, the repressive potential former forced laborers had to endure rested to a large extent with state, party and economic functionaries, administration officials and, of course, the secret service. It was spread, generally speaking, from a center. Whereas in Yugoslavia, the actual sources of repression were not so clearly distinguishable and rather reflected various lines of confrontation of the war and even pre-war eras. Here, neighborhoods, villages and workplaces seemed to be more intertwined with governmental power structures. Nevertheless, the deep mistrust and potential hostility is a striking commonality between the two countries' official conduct towards former forced laborers.

The frequent time leaps that occur in our interviewees' narrations show how experience usually dominates chronology as their means of orientation. Underprivileged national groups like Ukrainians in the Soviet Union or Slovenians in Yugoslavia or ethnic minorities such as Roma integrated repression into a life course structured by adversities, tending not to assign too much specificity to single incidents. At the same time, it must have been deeply disturbing for people who thought they would belong to the majority or exert some kind of supremacy in their respective countries—such as Russians or Serbs—and still found themselves "frozen out" from the social hierarchy because they had been captured and forced to work for the enemy during World War II. Our interlocutors seemed to deal with things that happened to them rather "thematically," permanently drawing comparisons between different incidents of persecution, forced labor, physical harm, and everyday adversities. Hence, it is hardly possible to get direct access to memories of World War II forced labor and its consequences, but a complex view of individual attempts to come to terms with traumatic experiences can be carved out. It shows how our interviewees have constantly tried to develop strategies to integrate these experiences into their biographies.

Post-war repression made the stay in Germany an officially acknowledged stigma in the biographies of the former forced laborers. Thus, the experience of forced labor has become a long-term point of reference for many of them. Of course, its importance varies with the length of the period of captivity in Germany and with the concrete circumstances of the internment. Still, the interpretation of their course of life seems to hinge largely on this past, as later success is often claimed to have been achieved despite deportation to the Reich, while lost chances and prospects are often described as after-effects of forced labor for Nazi Germany.

Notes

1. Translation of International Forced Labourers Documentation Project (IFLDP) interview with Raisa B. (History Workshop Minsk, Belarus, 17.8.2005), 33.
2. See documentation of IFLDP interview with Elka G. (Slovenia, 20.7.2005).
3. Silvija Kavcic, *Kollektive und private Erinnerungen slowenischer Überlebender des Frauen-Konzentrationslagers Ravensbrück [Collective and Private Memories of Slovenian Survivors of the Women's Concentration Camp Ravensbrück]*, Paper at the conference "Oral History in (post) socialist societies" in Freiburg, 3-5 November 2005.
4. See documentation of IFLDP interview with Anton K. (Slovenia, 9.8.2005).
5. Translation of IFLDP interview with Jože J. (Slovenia, 27.2.2006), 58.
6. Translation of IFLDP interview with Isaak (Igor) G. (Memorial Moscow, Russia, 27.7.2005), 7.
7. Translation of IFLDP interview with Andria M. (Serbia& Montenegro, 29.7.2005), 8.
8. See documentation of IFLDP interview with Janez B. (Slovenia, 8.8.2005); documentation of IFLDP interview with Andria M. (Serbia& Montenegro, 29.7.2005).
9. Translation of IFLDP interview with Angela D. (Slovenia, 18.3.2006), 36.
10. See documentation of IFLDP interview with Joze B. (Slovenia, 15.9.2005); documentation of IFLDP interview with Milan D. (Serbia& Montenegro, 28.7.2005).
11. Translation of IFLDP interview with Milan D. (Serbia& Montenegro, 28.7.2005), 21.
12. See documentation of IFLDP interview with Anton K. (Slovenia, 9.8.2005).
13. Translation of IFLDP interview with Angela D. (Slovenia, 18.3.2006), 36.
14. Translation of IFLDP interview with Jože J. (Slovenia, 27.2.2006), 58.
15. See, also on the following, e.g., Pavel Polian, *Deportiert nach Hause. Sowjetische Kriegsgefangene im "Dritten Reich" und ihre Repatriierung* (München/Wien: Oldenbourg, 2001); Ulrike Goeken, *Repatriierung in den Terror? Die Rückkehr der sowjetischen Zwangsarbeiter und Kriegsgefangenen in ihre Heimat 1944-1956*, Dachauer Hefte, 16 (2000): 190-209.
16. Translation of IFLDP interview with Raisa B. (History Workshop Minsk, Belarus, 17.8.2005), 40f.
17. Ibid., 35.
18. See documentation of IFLDP interview with Viktor Z. (Memorial, Russia, 20.7.2005); documentation of IFLDP interview with Ruzica N. (Serbia & Montenegro, 24.3.2005).
19. See documentation of IFLDP interview with Vasyl B. (England, 13.3.2006).
20. See documentation of IFLDP interview with Vadim N. (Memorial Moscow, Russia, 17.7.2005).

21. See ibid. and documentation of IFLDP interview with Mikhail B. (Memorial Moscow, Russia, 29.7.2005); documentation of IFLDP interview with Galina A. (ditto, 19.6.2005).

22. See Polian, Deportiert, 182.

23. Translation of IFLDP interview with Galina A. (Memorial Moscow, Russia, 19.6.2005), 37.

24. Translation of IFLDP interview with Marya V. (Memorial St. Petersburg, Russia, 25.6.2005), 40.

25. See e.g., Shoshana Felman and Dori Laub, *Testimony: Crises of Witnessing in Literature, Psychoanalysis, and History* (New York and London: Routledge, 1992).

26. This refers mainly to slave laborers, but under a number of conditions it also applies to civilian laborers, e.g., if they lost a relative or close friend during forced labor, were sent into humiliating circumstances or suffered from extraordinarily violent treatment, e.g., extra punishments, penal camps, prisons, etc.

27. See documentation of IFLDP interview with Iosif G. (History Workshop Minsk, Belarus, 2.8.2005).

28. See documentation of IFLDP interview with Nadya S. (Germany, 2.11.2005).

29. See documentation of IFLDP interview with Liudmila T. (Russian Academy of Sciences, Russia, 11.10.2005).

30. Translation of IFLDP interview with Marya V. (Memorial St. Petersburg, 25.6.2005), 34f.

31. It also makes a difference whether they are talking to a male or female interviewer, whether their counterpart is the same age or considerably younger. Moreover, the impact of the generational gap between interview participants is an issue in itself. The members of our project included a core of elderly, established interviewers, but also a considerable number of younger colleagues. While interviewees tended to seek reassurance and recognition from the older interviewers, they easily slipped into a teacher-like position when confronted with people who could have been their grandchildren. However, these general remarks become refined through further targeted research.

32. Transcription of IFLDP interview with Nadya S. (Germany, 2.11.2005), 14.

33. See Kobi Kabalek, Spuren vergangener Geschichte/n: Die NS-Zeit in Interviews mit jungen Deutschen aus der ehemaligen DDR [Traces of bygone (hi)stories: The NS-era in interviews with young Germans from the former GDR], Paper from the conference "Oral History in (post) socialist societies" in Freiburg, November 3-5, 2005.

34. See documentation of IFLDP interview with Omer A. (Bosnia, 16.5.2005); documentation of IFLDP interview with Osman H. (Bosnia, 23.7.2005).

35. Translation of IFLDP interview with Osman H. (Bosnia, 23.7.2005), 7.

5

Resisting Oppression: Stories of the 1980s' Mass Insurrection by Political Activists in the Eastern Cape Province, South Africa

Jan K. Coetzee and Geoffrey T. Wood

Introduction

Economic pressures were the predominant motivation that prompted the 1990 decision by South Africa's former apartheid government to commence serious negotiations with the principal opposition movements. This move ultimately resulted in democratization. Unlike many Western states, apartheid South Africa never really recovered from the global economic shocks of the early 1970s, which prompted a series of halfhearted, and later full-scale, reforms. In turn, the crisis of racial fordism—a production paradigm centering on traditional mass production methods coupled with the racial division of labor and the wider subordination of South Africa's black majority—was worsened by waves of mass resistance, encompassing the mass strikes of 1973 (Durban) and 1974 (East London), the 1976 Soweto uprising, and, finally and most importantly, the mass insurrection of the 1980s. Yet, while there is an extensive literature on the fall of apartheid, much of the latter has concerned itself with broad political and economic processes, and key leaders, while the role of individual grassroots actors has often been neglected. The mass movements that were instrumental in forcing an end to apartheid were structured in such a manner as to be resilient in the face of state repression. The latter encompassed high levels of internal democracy, with a strong emphasis on grassroots participation and mobilization. The most successful of these movements were the labor unions, and the United Democratic Front—a loose coalition of community organizations.

This study focuses on the experiences of political activists in Grahamstown, a secondary urban center in the Eastern Cape Province of South Africa, drawing primarily on the life histories of nine individuals.[1] It is hoped that through a detailed study of this nature, additional light may be shed on the exact nature of the resistance, and its effects on the lives of individuals at its epicenter. The project relies on individual memories. The life histories on which it is based allow us to learn about the way in which these young activists experienced the mass uprising against apartheid. As one of them recalled:

> [W]hen I went to the University of Zululand. That was in 1982: there was a consolidation point. We were able to link the struggles that we were involved with in the schools, with the broader issues around the community.... So yes, I would say people became much more mobilized.[2]

Another activist became involved in the struggle against apartheid in his mid-teens. He recounted:

> I was doing my standard six then and became politically aware. I was involved in some school boycotts then. Even the security forces called our school a notorious school... We didn't have a well thought out strategy as to how we [were] going to embark on our programs and how we [were] going to take up political campaigns. We just acted spontaneously.[3]

A third activist describes his early political involvement as follows:

> I first left school completing my standard eight in 1977. I joined a Rhodes [University] student group, which started a newspaper. I became involved as their reporter. My job was to gather any news from the township. They used the projects such as the "Release Mandela Campaign," the strikes and the boycotts. In 1979 I got involved in a group called SPP (Surplus People Project), working on forced removals. I would say that was the one thing that gave me insight because it meant going to such areas threatened with removal.[4]

The circumstances that led to the individuals becoming politically involved are complex and differ from case to case, reflecting not only actual experiences, but also subjective interpretations thereof. All of the activists came from backgrounds of poverty, but it was at a time when it seemed possible to bring about improvement in this situation.[5] Many had their education disrupted as a result of the school boycotts of the late 1970s and early 1980s. However, these experiences were common to millions of South Africans, and only a few assumed leadership positions in those organizations that emerged to oppose the status quo. The reasons underlying activists' decisions to become involved in the struggle are complex, and would *inter alia* include the fact that the halfhearted "reforms" of the then P.W. Botha government created the impression that the system was no longer immobile; the black-dominated trade unions were becoming ever more assertive in challenging workplace injustices; the heavy-handed reactions of the authorities to any form of protest; and the role of a range of community organizations (in some cases influenced by activists who had links to the African National Congress (ANC) underground) that were instrumental in raising political awareness. Each of the activists told a unique story, and although their collective accounts cannot be seen as a representative sample of popular sentiments and experience, they do provide an enlightening perspective of events that changed South Africa irrevocably.

Origins of the Resistance

Between 1983 and 1987, South Africa was rocked by internal turmoil of a type unprecedented in the country's history. While the origins lie in many years of social, economic and political injustices, the turmoil was sparked by two ill-advised "reforms" that were intended to make the core aspects of apartheid work better. Firstly, while recognizing the permanent presence of at least some urban blacks, the Black Local Authorities systems denied African town dwellers any real political rights, at the same time aiming to co-opt local leaders. In practice, those willing to assume office in local councils lacked popular backing; chronic underfunding and the essential powerlessness of this extra layer of government ensured that the system never succeeded in gaining any vestige of wider legitimacy. Secondly, a new "Tri-Cameral" constitution introduced two junior, but visibly subordinate, houses of parliament for South Africa's "Colored" and Indian minorities. This reform proved equally unpopular in African, Colored, and Indian areas, as it was clearly designed to deny all but whites real political rights. The subsequent wave of resistance was only broken by two successive States of Emergency proclaimed on July 20, 1985, and June 12, 1986 respectively, thousands of detentions (apartheid-speak for imprisonment without trial), and the militarization of white South African society. These basic facts mask the full complexity of the nature of the resistance, of regional dynamics, and of the myriad of organizations that arose to represent the interests of black South Africans. The revolt was initially confined to the Vaal Triangle townships. However, it spread countrywide through a combination of activism, the increasing influence of bodies such as civic associations that had sprung up in most South African centers, and the alienating nature of the state's initial attempts to curb the resistance.

It should be noted that while the mass insurrection of the 1980s only began in the Vaal Triangle in 1983, in the Cape the battle lines had already been drawn by the 1980 school boycotts, and the attendant violent resistance shared many of the characteristics of the later revolt. During 1979, the Grahamstown police assisted in the establishment of a vigilante grouping, the Peacemakers.[6] This grouping became intimately involved in the 1980 school boycott in Grahamstown. In July 1980, over thirty school pupils were arrested, following a wave of arson and stonings directed against school property and the businesses and homes of members of the Peacemakers.[7] This violence continued into October, when pupils attacked members of the vigilante grouping en route to a meeting with parents and teachers to discuss mechanisms for ending the boycott. At the time there seems to have been considerable tension between parents and students as to the usefulness of the boycott.[8]

The 1980 school boycotts share a number of characteristics with the mass insurrection of the mid-1980s. Firstly, originally peaceful protests soon escalated into violence.[9] Secondly, the protests represented not only conflict between the community and outside authority, but also revealed deep-seated divisions within the community, between older conservative elements and the youth. Thirdly, the protests were partially crushed by means of mass detentions, a similar mechanism to what was employed in the mid-1980s. Finally, the boycott energized the student leadership and it represented the logical extension of the activism of 1976.[10] Many of the activists who told their life stories revealed that their first involvement was in the school boycotts. The effects of these boycotts were not only greater political awareness, but also in terms of the disruptive effects to secondary education—many of the activists finished their schooling relatively late as a result, several were forced to continue their studies in different urban centers.

In the 1982-1983 period, the government made a number of proposals to change the influx control system and set in motion the process towards implementing the tri-cameral system.[11] The "Koornhof Bills" proposed to increase the controls placed on black migrants, while the Black Local Authorities Act greatly increased the powers of the generally unpopular and corrupt black Community Councils into town or village councils, ostensibly similar to those operating in white areas.[12] The black Community Councils had been established in 1977, with intention of " co-opting a section of the urban population as agents for the state at local level."[13] The Councils were forced to increase service charges due to the collapse of the monopoly on beer sales, an incapacity of the

Bantu Administration Boards to "match income with expenditure in the 1980s," and the losses incurred in the provision of housing and services. These developments provided the impetus for the launch of the UDF in August 1983, an umbrella organization of civic groupings, trade unions and student organizations.

The first signs of the 1980s insurrection reached Grahamstown in September 1984. This first major incident of "unrest" concerned neither the Tri-Cameral Constitution nor the Black Local Authorities, although these issues contributed to the reality of the everyday life of the activists who told their stories. Scholars boycotted school in memory of the death in detention of black consciousness leader Steve Biko in 1977. Five hundred scholars marched from Joza to Fingo Village.[14] At the corner of Victoria and Albert Roads, they were dispersed by police using shotguns and *sjamboks*.[15] When the pupils regrouped, teargas was used. Several activists who told their stories were present at the march, and provided detailed accounts of the police action against the demonstrators. This march was to represent a formative political experience for many of the activists who told their stories.

Although the mass insurrection was caused by far broader political and economic conditions, there is little doubt that heavy-handed police action alienated many, and reinforced opposition to the status quo. The police had a strongly militaristic organizational culture, in addition to the role played by the army itself. The latter's presence in the townships greatly politicized its role and challenged the conventional mold of civil-military relations. By 1985, up to 35,000 SADF troops were deployed internally to counter the disturbances.[16] Meanwhile, up to three quarters of policemen were also committed to these tasks.[17]

The role of the South African Police (SAP) was even more contentious than that of the army in the 1980s. The "fundamental policy" of the police was that the "political system must be defended and protected with all powers at its disposal."[18] SAP riot control techniques tended to be very heavy-handed and seem to have learned little from the tactics employed by European police forces.[19] These riot control techniques remained framed by perceptions of unfavorable terrain, climatic conditions and the size and aggression of opposing mobs.[20] Officially, crowd control was seen as a military operation, for which the police had to be "combat ready."[21] Shotguns, *sjamboks* and teargas, versus specialized riot protection gear and other equipment in the case of European police forces, ensured a higher degree of casualties on both sides. In addition, young and inexperienced policemen were often placed in situations where demands were placed on them beyond their emotional capabilities and training. This led to increasingly severe responses by the police when faced with hostile mobs.[22] In the case of Grahamstown, this resulted in the increased use of firearms by the police and, consequently, higher casualties. In addition, these responses deepened the cleavages between the established authority and its opponents.

It is significant that several of the activists interviewed revealed that it was the actions of the police that contributed to their assuming a more active political role. For example, one activist had been following a crowd of *toyi-toyiing*[23] youths at a funeral at a distance when he was arrested. In that period, he recounted, "one could easily be detained and beaten up and not even taken to a police station." He was taken to a house in white Grahamstown, where he was repeatedly assaulted and then released. He related: "As long as there was trouble in the location, ... getting picked up was a high possibility. And the person picked up would pay the price for what they term trouble in the location."[24]

Bearing the marks of a severe beating, this activist was asked to address a political rally, and tell the audience what had happened. He was, in his words, "still a bit young," and thought that "addressing a big crowd was scary." He described "shivering before [he] got on the platform," and explained that, while he believed "it was unsafe to be involved, ... it was not worth retreating."[25]

Communities Divided

As violent resistance increased, it became evident that much of the popular anger was directed against representatives of the authorities within the townships, most notably black town councilors.[26] This was in line with the ANC's stated position of targeting black town councilors, police force members, and others who had collaborated with the apartheid government.[27] These actions reflected deep-seated divisions within communities, between a small, generally older and conservative minority, many who were materially benefiting from the state's then policy of co-optation of selected figures, and a far greater number of generally much younger discontents. Again, some of the violence paralleled the earlier conflict between the older "Peacemaker" vigilantes, and the school boycotters. The attacks on town councilors led to many resigning their positions, and thus succeeded in bringing the local authorities system to its knees, although it never totally collapsed. Some black councilors did however fight back. In 1984 the government began issuing them firearms. By 1985, 20 percent of the councilors were armed,[28] which seems to have achieved little more than contributing to the spiraling violent resistance and reprisals.

In addition to the town councilors and black policemen who were actively involved in opposing the mass resistance, many of the older generation within the community, often the parents of activists, had mixed feelings about the struggle of the young. For example, after a visit by the security police and some intensive interrogation at his home, one activist's parents blamed him for what had happened. He explained,

> It was somewhat disturbing because it was the first time that police had ever entered our home and my parents were somewhat shaken. They blamed me for this kind of treatment, saying that the police were there because of my involvement. They insinuated that I was bringing some kind of curse to the family through my activities.[29]

Similarly, another noted that:

> Even me, I was discouraged at some point by my parents to be part of the struggle. At that time people were hopeless. Honestly speaking, each and every parent was concerned about his or her son or daughter, so therefore we were persuaded to distance ourselves from these things. As you know, the youth has got its own historical role or mission to accomplish. Some of our mates had serious conflicts with their parents. They were given strict instructions by their parents that if they were not going to tow or follow the line they must take a decision either to leave or find another home. Really, parents were scared, very, very scared through their ignorance.[30]

Although less spectacular than the violent clashes between representatives of the local authorities and the activists, this less visible division between generations was probably of greater significance. Yet, some of these divisions were overcome by the fact of the unprecedented repression of the late 1980s.

A division that was not so easily overcome was the racial one, between black and white Grahamstonians. One of the most visible manifestations of the discontent was in the endemic stonings of vehicles (mostly those driven by whites), on Raglan Road (leading through both the white and African/black parts of Grahamstown), which then formed part of the N2 highway between Cape Town and Durban.[31] As one activist remarked: "Whites were also seen as responsible for the oppression and the people targeted them."[32]

The highly conspicuous attacks on white motorists deflected attention from the more intense, hidden struggles in the township between those who were co-opted into existing structures of authority and those seeking their demise. However, these incidents also reflected the faceless side of the rebellion and the bitter harvest of entrenched racial segregation. In return, they often triggered disproportionate responses by the white government and government officials.[33]

Finally, there were attacks against the symbols of the existing order. As one interviewee explained:

> Beer halls were also attacked because the system encouraged the community to indulge in liquor so that they could not realize that they were oppressed. If beer halls were destroyed then people would stop spending the whole day drinking there. We also showed our anger by attacking other symbols of oppression.[34]

The state-owned beer halls were an obvious target in that the revenue collected from them was directly used for the implementation of apartheid. Seemingly irrational destruction of property was often used by state propagandists to portray the violent resistance as aimless. Yet, activities of this sort, as well as other indirect forms of collective action, while rarely considered in the literature on resistance in the developing world, "form an everyday part of the consciousness and action by the African proletariat."[35]

The Organizations of Resistance

The street committee system lay at the center of popular resistance. The street committees first originated in the Cradock township (the brainchild of Cradock schoolteacher, Mathew Goniwe, later assassinated by an official death squad), and the system gradually spread countrywide. These committees, themselves reporting to area committees, were based on the principle of retaining the anonymity of street-level leaders. Detained activists were rapidly replaced, and records were kept of detainees and of those who had vanished.[36]

The civic associations provided more formal organization. They were affiliated with the United Democratic Front (UDF), a broad umbrella organization, that brought together not only civic groupings countrywide, but also trade unions, women's associations, youth groupings, and a range of other community organizations. The UDF had been formed in the early 1980s, in direct response to both the Black Local Authorities Act, and the introduction of the Tri-Cameral System.

In Grahamstown, the Grahamstown Civic Association (GRACA) had originally been formed to encourage people not to vote in town council elections, but by the mid-1980s it had become involved in political education. The life stories revealed some tensions between this organization and the street committee activists. Despite widespread opposition to apartheid rule, the civic movement in Grahamstown had bitter internal conflicts, with two rival leaders both "feeling they owned individual groups of people."[37]

When confronted with a divided civic movement seemingly imposed from above, a group of activists decided to organize the street and area committees independently. Each street had a committee of ten, electing an executive for every five streets. Communication between committees was by word of mouth, considerably hampered by the complexity of structures, and the fact that two entire street committees, of "Y" and "N" Streets were arrested.

Although both the Grahamstown Civic Association (GRACA) and Grahamstown Youth Congress (GRAYCO) made repeated attempts to bring the street committees under their control, the street committee activists refused, preferring to retain some form of autonomy. Indeed in defiance of the civics, the Grahamstown street committees organized a consumer boycott, which, again, brought the younger activists into conflict with many of the older generation. However, despite these organizational divisions, contact was retained with activists from other centers involved in the organization of street committees, such as Malgas and Goniwe (prior to his assassination).

Underground Resistance

By the middle of the 1980s, following on successive waves of state repression, much of the resistance was driven underground. Immediately after the declaration of the first State of Emergency in July 1985, a large number of the leadership of black Grahamstown was arrested, forcing the remaining activists to enter a secret world of operating underground. One of the most important challenges to the authorities in this period was the organization of the 1986 consumer boycott. Other measures included rent boycotts and renewed efforts to force black town councilors (constituting the unacceptable local government structures) to step down.

Amidst ever-tightening control measures and efforts by the security police to combat these programs of defiance, one of the activists believes that the strong system of street committees had been very successful. He asserted:

During that time we were able to make sure that we set up street committees at grassroots level, and in that sense we were able to involve a lot of elderly people who were not involved before.

I was involved in making sure that they were set up in all the streets. So I went from street to street, setting them up. Chairing those meetings, making sure that people elect their leaders at the street level, providing guidelines as to what the functions of the street committees would be, determining the frequency of meetings, etc.

The street committees did not only confine themselves to political issues; the issues that were put forward were quite interesting because they included issues that would have a direct effect on their lives. Issues like death in the neighborhood, water that has been thrown out and smelling—those kinds of issues were very important to people. They could not speak freely at the meeting and this was a first taste of democracy for most of the people. For the first time they also got to know the word accountability.[38]

Nonetheless, the position of the activists soon proved untenable, as evidenced by the following remarks:

They were right on our heels. So we had to hide during the same time. Sleep here today, sleep there tomorrow—you never slept in one place. Always during the day you were looking over your shoulder if no one is following you. So it was quite a sort of life that was not right—we were quite aware of the security risk. So it was this kind of bioscope-like situation. You were always on the run, like a hare, scared. Living in fear of the unknown.[39]

Similarly, another noted:

We were all on the run. For instance, during that time we were not sleeping at our places. At some point you don't tell your friends where you sleep. It was quite a nasty period. If one asked you a question you asked yourself: why was he asking that question? You became suspicious when you saw a strange face. Even at our meetings, we sometimes became suspicious when one was asking specific questions. You questioned almost everything, and you had a negative attitude at the same time.[40]

Despite considerable optimism that the street committee system would weather the repression, the state actually succeeded in breaking much of the system of resistance that had been so carefully constructed. Yet, a victory for the state proved largely illusory. The spirit of the resistance had not been broken, and other organizations, most notably the trade union movement and the churches, assumed a leading role in opposing the government in the late 1980s. In the interim, however, many activists found themselves incarcerated. While a limited number of life stories cannot provide a comprehensive vision of detention without trial, it is possible to identify certain general patterns and trends.

Detention without Trial

In terms of the provisions of the two States of Emergency proclaimed during the 1980s, people could be held in prison or in police cells for lengthy periods. On July 21, 1985, the first State of Emergency was declared, confined only to certain regions, including Albany (the region within which Grahamstown falls). In the first five days after the declaration, at least thirteen Grahamstown residents were detained[41] with over 441 detained countrywide.[42] Detention without trial could also include periods of solitary confinement. Access to a lawyer and relatives was severely restricted and political prisoners were initially not allowed reading material, additional toiletries or food from outside. After challenges by relatives, lawyers for human rights, church bodies, and other human rights organizations, these provisions were later revised and relaxed.

During March 1986, the first State of Emergency was lifted.[43] Resistance nevertheless continued in Grahamstown throughout that year, notwithstanding the declaration of a nationwide second State of Emergency on June 12, 1986,[44] evidence to the outside world was the stoning of vehicles, petrol-bombing of houses and necklacings (placing a used car tire around someone's neck and setting it alight).[45] Behind the scenes, the street committees began to rebuild their structures. However, the second State of Emergency was to be applied with "unprecedented harshness," ultimately aimed at breaking the backbone of the resistance.[46] By November 1987, the UDF's organizations were collapsing.[47]

All the activists whose life stories were collected were detained during the second State of Emergency, a reflection of the mass arrests that took place during this period. Although each individual's experience was in some manner unique, it is apparent from their stories that the detention process had a number of distinct hallmarks. These included not only isolation from their communities, but also attempts to divide them, and the periodic use of torture. Torture was used as an *ad hoc* means of "punishment," in an effort to force activists to recant earlier beliefs (to "turn" them), as well as to gain information from them.

Most of the activists were picked up by the security police at odd times of the day, confirming that very specific searches for them had taken place. One of the activists relates the events around his arrest in the following way:

> Yes, I remember very vividly my arrest on the 9th of December 1986. On the day before, some of my comrades were arrested and we knew that the police were actually stepping up pressure. I used a particular place as a hiding spot. I didn't even tell my comrades where I was hiding. I didn't trust anybody. On the evening of the 8th, when I went down to the place at 10 o'clock, I got scared and my body just told me that something wrong was going to happen. I just got that kind of instinct.
>
> I woke up at about 5 a.m. When I woke up I just heard footsteps and somebody knocking on the door. Then when I look[ed] outside, I saw that the whole house was surrounded by police, security, SADF and the peace was just invaded. Then I knew that they have come for me.[48]

Interrogations were a central aspect of life in detention for almost all detainees. These normally involved the same security police members in each individual case. Topics covered in interrogations ranged from banal details of the detainee's personal life, to the detainee's actual role in political organizations, to imagined major conspiracies. Not only was there constant fear of torture, which seemed particularly prevalent in the Eastern Cape, but in addition it was often those conducting the interrogations who determined how long the individual would stay in detention. Interrogations were held at all hours, with no advance warning. As one activist described:

> I think it was more a feeling of fear rather than anger. When we were in the cells the police would come and interrogate us. So we lived in the constant fear of—we didn't know when they were going to come. And you knew that some of the people who were detained before you were also assaulted in trying to extract information.
>
> Sometimes they would leave you there for the whole week and they would not come. And then they would come and give you a piece of paper and say that you must write everything that you have done. Then they would come back again and if they see that you are not happy with what you have written, they would say: "Nonsense." They would intimidate us and say: "We know all the activities you are involved in, so don't try and be clever. Write everything you have done." So it was that kind of constant harassment, psychological torture in a sense.[49]

It was African detainees who experienced the worst living conditions in detention. Many did not even have beds, but were given mats to sleep on the floor. They were issued blankets (often unwashed) but rarely sheets. Similarly, the prison diet was often rather sparse, consisting largely of porridge, bread, black coffee, and *samp*.[50]

Despite the deprivations of life in detention, for many the time in prison was also a time of learning. Informal classes, mostly dealing with contemporary political issues and radical political thinking, were conducted by fellow detainees. The very nature of incarceration of groups of dissidents by a minority regime maintained by a limited number of officials, allows for exchange of ideas, mutual encouragement and the furthering of the ideas of resistance. During the heyday of South Africa's repressive siege maintained by the two successive States of Emergency, it was not possible to detain the majority of the political activists in single cells. They were often locked up together with fellow activists. The majority of detainees report being politically enriched by the discussions/seminars/lectures that took place during their incarceration. These classes were never as structured or coherent as those organized by the long-term political prisoners on Robben Island[51] but, at the same time, they offered much to those who had only had limited exposure to broader political debates. Generally, these classes were organized by older political prisoners, many of whom had spent time on Robben Island or elsewhere as political prisoners prior to the mid-1980s. One former detainee characterized them as follows:

They ... then became teachers to us who had not had that opportunity to be on Robben Island. So they led the discussions. They gave us the lectures. They taught us, and then there were open sessions for us to debate issues, and to challenge some issues with the little we had from outside, what we learnt in the township. So I would say, they were the people that one could say were the political gurus in the prison.[52]

At the stage of this activist's detention, the situation in the prisons had improved quite substantially as a result of constant streams of complaints to the prison authorities, and his reports of life in detention are somewhat less grim than those activists who had been incarcerated a few months earlier. The ability of detainees to make complaints was later greatly circumscribed by modifications to the regulations governing detention, which imposed heavy penalties for malicious objections.

Ironically, the system of detention without trial failed in its objectives of isolating activists. Rather, it brought together two generations of discontents: the new radicals, a product of the schools boycotts of the 1980s and the street committees, and an older generation of activists, who had a far broader experience of the limits and possibilities of various political organizations. It also provided the basis for future organizational unity. The younger activists were representatives of the street committees and of the community and national political movements that had largely emerged from within South Africa. The older activists were in many cases representatives of the then-exiled ANC. The period in detention brought the former into direct contact with a core of ANC members, while for the latter it was a chance to disseminate the ideals of both the ANC and the South African Communist Party. The political discussions relieved some of the monotony and frustrations of detention, and highlighted the need for perseverance, as one activist recalled:

I cannot run away from the fact that sometimes there was anger. But the fact that we could use political discussion played a very important role to politicize us further. In particular the youth was very angry, sometimes uncontrollable, and very militant. The one aspect that kept us going was that we were of the opinion that our political objectives were not to fight individuals but to destroy the system. That kept us going.[53]

In addition to the isolation and the unpredictable nature of the verbal interrogations, there was always the possibility of physical torture, some details of which have been provided by the story of one of the activists. A scrutiny of court records will reveal that his experiences were by no means unique. In 1985 he experienced his first of several bouts of detention, because he was the object of an investigation into arson at two schools in the township. During this first stint behind bars he described experiencing the following:

For the first two weeks I could not make out what exactly was taking place because I was being assaulted. The police wanted more information from me. They wanted me to incriminate certain people in the township. So for the first two weeks I was under stress but for the rest of the time [± 20 months] I could feel that I was going to get a mental breakdown because I was alone in the cell, outside on the outskirts, on a farm police station. Nothing to do, no music, no written material, not even a Bible, having a bucket system in the cell which I was made to change once a week. The conditions were very, very bad and that was a very, very difficult time for me.

For the first two weeks I was tortured. The interrogation started from the day I was detained until two days before I was released. The form of torture used to be: a rubber thing that they put around my head; they used to tie my hands to the back; they put leg irons on my feet; I had to lie on my stomach on the cement floor. So they used to do quite a lot of funny things. At times they took a needle, trying to push it into my flesh. At one stage they took me to a dam at Indwe where they pushed me into a sack and they let me float on the water for about five minutes. It was very, very cold and I was feeling very, very dizzy at that time.

All the time I was in that detention I was never ever able to see my family. My family last saw me when I was picked up by the police and they only saw me when I came back. They didn't even know where I was kept. As for the lawyers, there was no chance of seeing any attorney.[54]

There were many deaths in detention in the 1980s and several instances where detainees simply disappeared after they had officially been "released." Those who were subject to physical torture faced the danger that they, too, might become one of the many who met with lethal "accidents." As one remarked:

Yes, that feeling was always there. Because of the treatment that I got there, I didn't even know what would happen the following day. You see, I also had that fear. Because of the brutality of the police one would suspect that one day one might die. I mean even our experience, the experience I got and of some people that died in police cells, people like Steve Biko and the others. So I always thought maybe I would be one of those people who would die one day.[55]

Despite the availability of support structures, some of the activists found it difficult to adapt after their release. According to one of them, he was disturbed emotionally and physically and could not cope with the conditions or with the situation that he found himself in after his release. He revealed:

The scars I carried after my prison experience took time before I could get rid of them. We had sessions and these sessions involved what we called "stock taking" whereby people would reflect on their involvement during detention and even before detention. We would then also relate what we were involved in.[56]

As a result of his relatively favorable financial position—during his time in prison his employer paid his salary—this subject faced accusations that he was an informer. His situation was not helped by a personality clash with an older detainee, who had spent time on Robben Island and therefore provided some inspiration to the other detainees. When he lent some money to another detainee, this subject found himself in an even worse position. He explained:

> He had some monetary problems, and I gave him some money, telling him that I was not lending him the money but that I was actually giving it to him. This money I was giving him led to more allegations that the reason I had money to give to fellow comrades was because the security police had deposited such money into my account for me to use for such purposes. This other man also alleged that I had organized a youth group called Amabotho, in order for them to assassinate him.[57]

The persistent accusations that he had been an informer ultimately proved too much for him, and led to his emotional collapse. He described his predicament thus:

> I think I would have coped with the situation had it only been the onslaught of the oppression from the police, but once it involved my surname [family honor] it then began for me to have wider implications. I also had the sort of feeling that even my cell mates when they were visited by other parents or relatives would share this information with them. In turn their family or relatives or friends would go back to the community and share the information with the rest of the community. This made me feel isolated in a way and I felt as if I was losing my identity. This even made me fear the day I was to be released. In a way I was not looking forward to my release because I feared the attitude that would be waiting for me when I went back into the community. For me that was the toughest part of my detention. That incident happened only two months before my release.[58]

This subject continued by commenting:

> That was a period in which I almost lost my life. For a long time after that I could not even go to sleep. The emotional scars were quite deep and I would hear footsteps in the middle of the night. I can see people standing in the street, perhaps in a group, but I couldn't bear seeing people being in a group next to my home. Every time I saw people standing next to my home, I had this feeling or I thought that these people had come to kill me because they had heard this information from prison and they had now come to act upon it. That was a very difficult period for me.[59]

The heavy psychological price paid by some of the activists bears some testimony to the strains of life in detention. Although the detainees often provided emotional support to each other, at times divisions reappeared, often encouraged by the authorities. While for many, detention provided an opportunity for broadening their political education, it was also a time of fear and uncertainty. Despite the experiences of detention, none of the activists who told their stories expressed any regret at their decision to become politically involved.

Retrospective: After the Insurrection

While several activists reported that they had been severely trauma-tized by their periods in detention, most felt that they had personally benefited from their role in the insurrection, along the lines expressed below by one of them:

> I think in a sense it made me stronger—being there. Because when I was there I had a lot of time to myself to reflect on my life, and how I have been doing things. I think it made me a much more disciplined person than before, because I was able now to be more patient, more determined to do and to succeed.
>
> The detention strengthened me in my political views. When I was arrested the security police who arrested me, threatened me by saying that they would make sure that when I came out I will no longer be active again. They would be making me suffer, so that I could regret being involved. But I think on the contrary, when I came out I was stronger than before. What kept us together was that kind of common cause. All of us belonged to the same ideology which is the ANC ideology. So we had a lot of political classes and discussions even in detention and that strengthened us.[60]

When asked whether he thought that what he had endured could be regarded as worthwhile, another activist responded:

> It was worth the while, because my political involvement also sharpened my think-ing and helped me to listen very carefully when one is expressing himself. Secondly, my political experience really changed my life in terms of being tolerant to other views. In jail, that was one of the points that was stressed by some of the comrades: what we must really understand is that there are other schools of thought. Thirdly, our contribution is to deliver something good in life. The ultimate objective which is nothing else but the freedom of the people of South Africa as a whole, irrespective of their political convictions or affiliations. Those years (although very tough) brought about that we were able to see the fruits of such suffering for the development of the society as a whole.[61]

Although South Africa's political transformation in the 1990s was the product of a complex range of factors, all of the activists expressed pride in the role they had played in bringing about democracy. One activist summed up the process of change as follows:

> Those things made him [P.W. Botha] find that the country is getting out of hand and he was forced to declare a State of Emergency. After that the [struggle] continued, with people making a lot of sacrifices, to such an extent that he was to suffer a stroke and give up completely. The new person [de Klerk] realized he could not take the same trend.... [62]

Conclusion

The narratives presented here originate from a life history research project on the memories of former political activists. The activists re-flect on and articulate their involvement in the struggle leading to South

Africa's political transformation. Memory is commonly agreed to be a person's capacity to recall or summon information stored in her/his mind. So, remembering is often depicted as a mental act of "thinking of things in their absence."[63] But memory also has a deeper dimension because our memories are bodily experienced and expressed. The narratives in this chapter illustrate both of these dimensions. On the first level, these narratives relate in an almost matter-of-fact manner the programs of defiance, the education that resulted from political discussions while in detention, the anger directed at an unjust system, the financial worries during incarceration, etc. On the second level the stories deal with the blame expressed by parents for drawing the family into trouble, the disruption to private life because of living in hiding, the fear of being on the run, the terror of being interrogated, the anguish of pending mental breakdowns after assaults and torture, the deep emotional scars, the distrust of people perceived to have come for you, etc.

Many accounts of the demise of apartheid are stories of organizations and forces, or of a few leaders and intellectuals, but they often neglect the experiences of individual actors at the grassroots level. This necessarily brief summary of the stories of a handful of individuals provides an alternative perspective on the waning years of apartheid. A number of themes and issues emerge from these accounts.

Firstly, while activists may have shared tactics, and indeed, been indirectly guided on questions of broad strategy by the exiled liberation movements, many of their activities were based on their own choices, often despite weak organizational backing or, indeed, chronic organizational infighting.

Secondly, while South Africa is now a dominant party system under the ruling ANC, with a weak and fragmented opposition, the legacy of semi-autonomous community activism has, particularly in regions such as the Eastern Cape, ensured the persistence of a civil society, with local groupings of activists remaining willing to challenge—albeit now predominantly by peaceful means—unpopular decisions and policies of national government. At this point, thirteen years after the first democratically elected government came to power, there are indications that the uncritical mass support for the ANC as liberation movement-turned-government is gradually being replaced by factions within the movement and by a proliferation of political viewpoints.

Thirdly, unlike many countries in Central and Eastern Europe, one of the compromises of South Africa's transition was that there was never a full exposure of the identities and roles of police informers. Moreover, the memories of times in prison include accounts of individuals shifting allegiances, some of whom now hold government positions. This represents some rather unfinished business, particularly as many who remained loyal to the ideals of the struggle were later marginalized after the transition. However, all of these issues represent only aspects of the real face of South Africa's transformation. Through their actions, these individuals contributed to a major reconfiguration of South Africa's political institutions.

Notes

1.   All the interviews took place during the first six months of 1994. The authors are grateful to Canon Ezra Tisani, Makhosandile Tisani, Mzwakhe Ndlela, and the activists who told us their stories, for their contribution in making this project possible.
2.   Activist A.
3.   Activist B.
4.   Activist G.
5.   J.C. Davies, "Why Do Revolutions Occur?," in *The Practice of Comparative Politics*, ed. P.G. Lewis et al. (London: Longman, 1978).
6.   *The Argus* (Cape Town), 27 October 1980.
7.   *The Argus* (Cape Town), 11 July 1980.
8.   Frank Molteno, *Students' Struggle For Their Schools.* (Cape Town: University of Cape Town, Centre for African Studies, 1980), 2-15.
9.   *The Argus* (Cape Town), 16 May 1981.
10. Molteno.
11. William Cobbett et al., "A Critical Analysis of the South African State's Reform Strategies in the 1980s," in *State, Resistance and Change in South Africa*, ed. Peter Frankel et al. (Johannesburg: Southern Book Publishers, 1988), 20.
12. Tom Lodge and William Nasson, *All Here and Now: Black Politics in South Africa in the 1980s* (Claremont: David Philip, 1991), 34.
13. J. Grest, "The Crisis of Local Government in South Africa," in *State, Resistance and Change in South Africa*, ed. Peter Frankel et al. (Johannesburg: Southern Book Publishers, 1988), 94-95.
14. *The Cape Times* (Cape Town), 13 September 1984.
15. Sjamboks: long, stiff whips, originally made of thick hide.
16. Simon Baynham and Geoffrey Wood, "Securing Protection and Defense," in *Policy Options for a New South Africa*, eds. Fanie Cloete et al. (Pretoria: Human Sciences Research Council, 1991), 226.
17. Ibid., 230.
18. Republic of South Africa, *White Paper on the Organisations and Functions of the South African Police* (Pretoria: Government Printer, 1988).
19. Baynham and Wood, "Securing Protection and Defense," 233.
20. Ibid, 230.
21. Republic of South Africa, *White Paper on the Organisations and Functions of the South African Police.*
22. *Business Day* (Johannesburg), 12 December 1985.
23. Toyi-toyiing: dancing characterized by high-stepping movements typically performed at protest gatherings or marches.

24. Activist I.

25. Activist I.

26. *The Cape Times* (Cape Town), 12 June 1986, 21 July 1986, 22 September 1986. See also Commissioner of Police, *Annual Report of the Commissioner of South African Police: July 1984 – June 1985* and *July 1985 - June 1986*. (Pretoria: Government Printer, 1985 and 1986).

27. *The Daily Telegraph* (London), 3 October 1985.

28. Capital Radio (Cape Town), 9 April 1985.

29. Activist B.

30. Activist D.

31. *The Cape Times* (Cape Town), 5 September 1985 and 17 April 1986.

32. Activist A.

33. *The Cape Times* (Cape Town), 12 May 1986.

34. Activist B.

35. Robert Cohen, "Resistance and Hidden Forms of Consciousness Among African Workers," in *Work and Industrialization in South Africa*, ed. Eddie Webster et al. (Johannesburg: Ravan), 135.

36. *The Sunday Times* (Johannesburg), 2 March 1986.

37. Activist A.

38. Activist F.

39. Activist B.

40. Activist G.

41. *The Cape Times* (Cape Town), 21 July 1985; 24 July 1985.

42. *The Cape Times* (Cape Town), 27 July 1985.

43. *The Cape Times* (Cape Town), 8 March 1986.

44. Commissioner of Police, "Annual Report, July 1985 – June 1986," 23.

45. *The Cape Times* (Cape Town), 12 June 1986; 21 July 1986; 22 September 1986.

46. Lodge and Nasson, "All Here and Now," 87

47. Ibid., 99.

48. Activist A.

49. Activist H.

50. Samp: coarsely ground maize, or porridge made from this.

51. Jan K. Coetzee, *Plain Tales From Robben Island* (Pretoria: Van Schaik Publishers, 2000), 27-31.

52. Activist D.

53. Activist H.

54. Activist C.

55. Activist I.

56. Activist D.

57. Activist D.

58 . Activist D.

59. Activist D.

60. Activist C.

61. Activist E.

62. Activist H.

63. Barbara Misztal, *Theories of Social Remembering* (Maidenhead: Open University Press, 2003), 9.

6

Struggling with a Horrendous Past: Rwandans Talk about the Aftermath of the Genocide

Hessel Nieuwelink

It is important that they confess and tell that they did so. These people give testimony, it hurts and [...] I feel very bad. Then I want to do something very bad to him or her. [...] I want revenge. The same thing needs to be done to them!
— *Ancilla, a survivor*

To reconcile with someone who killed people was very difficult. But we cannot rebuild our country if there is no reconciliation. I started to reconcile with people in order to prepare the country for the children.
— *Innocent, a survivor*

Introduction

During the genocide in Rwanda in 1994, more than 800,000 people were killed, mostly Tutsi. Others were tortured, raped, or enslaved. Approximately 200,000 Hutu participated in the killings, and many more participated in other ways in this organized campaign of mass murder. The genocide was coordinated at the national level, but in this densely populated country, villagers performed an important role during the killing campaign.[1] Now, almost fifteen years later, survivors, perpetrators and bystanders alike live in the same village and are confronted with one another every day.[2]

In order to find out how Rwandans deal with the legacy of the genocide, I interviewed fourteen "ordinary" Rwandans.[3] I asked them about their experiences during the genocide, how they dealt with this horrible past and their opinions on the mechanisms concerning the transition of the country. Truth, justice and reconciliation were therefore recurring themes in the interviews and in their narratives. All interviewees were more or less capable of expressing their ideas about these notions. Many interviewees considered these concepts relevant, important and necessary. Nevertheless, some of them relativized the possibility of justice because they felt that in the context of genocide, justice is never really possible. In addition, a few interviewees stated that reconciliation was not an option for them; they were striving for revenge and retaliation.

A certain level of trust between the interviewer and interviewee is of utmost importance when interviewing survivors, bystanders, and perpetrators of a genocide. It was not possible for me to build such relationships, because I was in Rwanda for only two months and wanted to interview people of diverse backgrounds. I was, however, introduced to every interviewee by an acquaintance, frequently someone working for a local nongovernmental organization – and that facilitated trust. As some interviewees confirmed, this go-between increased their readiness to be interviewed and to talk about their past. Their willingness to speak can also be explained by the fact that they are used to talking about the horrific events of the genocide, since they spoke about their experiences during *gacaca* proceedings, gatherings of survivors, and with relatives and friends.[4]

Although all interviewees spoke about their experiences of the genocide, at least some of them were still silent about certain events. The way in which Donatila, a survivor from the northern province of Gysenyi, spoke about the first days of the genocide is telling. She recounted: "I [fled] with my sister, the one who was raped in 1991. And then she was once more raped. Others were killed, horribly, with clubs, with stones. But I and my sister were only raped. [...] From that day, I don't realize what happened."[5] In the first instance, she mentioned that her sister was raped. A few moments later, Donatila said that she was raped as well. After that, she did not mention the sexual violence again. Although Donatila was not completely silent about this experience, she did not want to discuss it any further. Many interviewees were willing to talk to me about their experiences, but Donatila's silence illustrates how not everything was extensively discussed, and certainly not comfortably. The interviewees did not talk about particular topics for various reasons, which included: shame, the fact that they think they feared endangering themselves by voicing their opinions about their community and governmental policies, the lack of a trustful relationship between the interviewee and interviewer, and, in the case of women interviewees, the fact that I was male. Nevertheless, the interviewees did describe many experiences. Although Donatila mentioned the rape only once, she was willing to disclose that she had experienced sexual violence.

Even though these Rwandans were willing to talk to me about their pasts, nearly all of them strongly emphasized their desire to remain anonymous. Consequently, all of the names in this chapter are pseudonyms. One interviewee explained their common motivation for requesting anonymity: "You don't know what kind of regime there will be in ten years, so it is better to be anonymous."[6] To some extent, most interviewees were still uncertain about their own safety and were afraid that their opinions could harm them in the short or long run. Additionally, their feelings of insecurity can be explained by the fact that several Rwandans have been killed because of their testimony at gacaca.[7]

In order to have a broad view of existing opinions in Rwanda on transitional mechanisms, I opted to interview people with different backgrounds for this research. To that end, I interviewed eleven survivors, two bystanders, and one perpetrator, who was incarcerated for more than ten years. Three interviewees live in Kigali, five in a village in the province Kigali-Rural (where the mayor was prosecuted by the International Criminal Tribunal for Rwanda), three in the northern province Byumba, and two in the northern province Gisenyi. Because most interviewees only speak the local language, the majority of the interviews were carried out with the help of a translator, who translated from Kinyarwanda to English.[8]

This chapter deals with the ideas of ordinary Rwandans with regard to the transition in their country. The focus will be on their opinions on the notions of truth, justice and reconciliation, but reflection on the interviewees' interpretation of the past will precede these discussions.

Rwandans Interpreting the Past

The interviewees for this project experienced horrors unimaginable for an outsider. They witnessed family members being killed. Several women were raped. Many hid on roofs and in latrines for weeks on end and were in constant fear that they might not live another day. Most respondents began talking about their personal experiences during the genocide without being directly asked about the genocide. When Gentille, a survivor who lived in Kigali, was asked whether she was married, she answered: "My first husband was killed in 1958. With my first husband, I had three children. One of them died in the war of 1958, the other two were killed in the genocide. With my other husband I had eleven children, they died in 1994."[9] She and other interviewees directly related general questions about their lives to the events of the genocide. For them the genocide was still all around them; everything was connected to this horrible episode.

The interviewees had different opinions on the question of when the genocide started. Emerthe and Janvier, two survivors, asserted that the genocide began in 1959 when, on the eve of independence, Hutus seized power and killed thousands of Tutsis. Janvier explained: "It started back in 1959. [...] They started calling us snakes. The snake had to be killed. [...] They started killing people from that time. Then the sixties, then the seventies. The final was this genocide of 1994. But it started in '59."[10] Ever since the late fifties, Tutsis have been killed and the genocide was, in this line of thought, only an intensification of the killing. Other interviewees, however, said that Rwanda was quite peaceful until the civil war started in 1990. Innocent, a survivor, said: "The tensions started in 1959 when the Tutsis started to be killed. [But during] the Habyarimana regime, those things were quiet. [...] We started to fear in 1990, when the RPF[11] started the war."[12] Innocent and other interviewees lived peacefully during a period considered by Janvier as part of the genocide or at least as a prelude to it. These variations in experience can be explained by pointing to the degree of peacefulness in different regions, as well as to their personal perceptions of the period before the genocide took place.

Several interviewees explained why they thought the genocide had taken place and how so many people came to participate in it. One of the reasons they mentioned was the existence of hatred among Rwandans. Emerthe, a Tutsi from the province Byumba, commented: "The cause was hatred between Hutu and Tutsi. [...] The Hutu hated the Tutsi. The Hutu didn't want to hear any word of a so-called Tutsi."[13] Therefore, Hutus killed Tutsis. The hatred was an important part of the genocidal ideology.[14] Félicien, a Hutu who admitted to having killed several Tutsis and was imprisoned for more than ten years, gave another reason for participation in the genocide. He believed that the Rwandans are by political culture obedient, and when asked why Rwandans participated in the genocide, he said: "If the current leaders don't want to see this banana plantation, the population will start to remove the plantation without being asked 'Why are we removing the banana plantation?' We do it just because the leaders have said so."[15]

When talking about the causes of the genocide, most respondents did not offer explanations on why the mass killings themselves took place. They mostly explained why people participated in the campaign.[16] This discrepancy can be clarified by the fact that most of the interviewees had attended school for only a few years and were unaccustomed to analyzing societal developments. Consequently, they searched for the causes of the genocide in their direct environment, and not on a national level. Joseph, a Tutsi who finished the Rwandan military academy in the 1980s, was the only interviewee who gave an explanation for the planning of the genocide: "If [the government] made a peace-agreement with the RPF, they had to share places in the government, in parliament, in the army. So the government forces tried to reduce the electoral and military potential of RPF in killing Tutsis and opposition."[17] According to Joseph, the governmental elite planned the genocide for strategic reasons, because they were afraid of losing power.[18]

How Rwandans interpret and talk about the past will affect the functioning and effectiveness of transitional mechanisms. Some Rwandans prefer to discuss the period since independence while others only focus on the more recent past. The fact that most interviewees did not mention the root causes of the genocide and the strategic reasons of the elite to plan the mass killings may affect the readiness of these people to allow the government to perform an important role during the transition of the country. However, their very willingness to talk to me about these horrific experiences was a good sign, even though the issues discussed below show that there is still a long and bumpy road that has to be traveled before a stable society can be reached.

The Empowerment and Impediment of the Truth

A key question in dealing with the past is whether the subject wanted to remember or forget what happened. Most interviewees said that they wanted to know what happened to their relatives and which persons were responsible for these murders. Odette, a Tutsi from the province of Gisenyi, explained what exactly she would like to know: "Up to now I don't know what happened to my husband. [...] I would like to know where the bones of my husband are. That is the truth I am looking for."[19] Many interviewees still lived with these kinds of questions. For them, knowing what happened meant that they wished to be informed about their individual situation. When speaking about this subject, most did not say they wanted to know who planned the genocide and for what reason. The interviewees only mentioned this national truth-finding process when they expressed their disdain for those who were being prosecuted by the International Criminal Tribunal for Rwanda (ICTR) and still denied that the genocide occurred. Perhaps the interviewees felt they already know why the genocide took place and who was responsible for the planning. However, it is also possible that the interviewees were still mainly concerned with the consequences of the genocide on a more personal level.

Several interviewees stressed the importance of truth finding. They said that they were not able to rebuild their lives as long as they remained uninformed of the events that led to the death of their relatives. Bernadette, a Tutsi who lost her husband, explained: "There are killers who tell the truth but also those [who] don't tell the truth. [...] I want those people to tell the truth and then I can put it away."[20] More than ten years after the genocide took place, these individuals were still looking for information about the remains of their loved ones. For Bernadette, until she found out where the remains of her husband were, she was not able to start looking into the future. One important function of the truth in this context is that it can enable survivors to carry on with their lives.

However, being confronted with the horrors of the past can also be very disturbing. Immaculée, who lost several children during the genocide, said: "It is good to know what happened, but then I experience those moments again and I don't want that."[21] On the one hand, Immaculée expressed a strong desire for information about the crimes committed against her loved ones. On the other, she did not want to relive the events of 1994, because that made her feel depressed. Knowing what happened can be indispensable, but it can also be disruptive.

Another survivor, Emerthe, who lived in a small village in the province Byumba, also talked about the consequences of facing the horrors of the genocide. She explained:

It is difficult to hear the truth. [...] When I am [at gacaca], normally I feel I want to cry. The local authority has two books about the people who have died. Two [of my] children are inside this book. When they start [reading] the names of those who have been killed, they call the names of my children and I feel very bad. [Then] I go back home, things start to roll in my mind and I feel bad. I start feeling so sad, recalling what happened. [Therefore] I want to forget what happened.[22]

For Emerthe, being confronted with crimes of the past was more of a stumbling block than a prerequisite for rebuilding her life. Emerthe's case therefore questions the assumption that knowing the truth will enable survivors to leave the past behind. The Israeli philosopher Avishai Margalit argues that for most survivors, being confronted with crimes is not the best way to overcome the past. "[T]he idea of reliving the past takes its toll when the past was deeply humiliating. You cannot relive humiliation without being humiliated anew."[23] Although Margalit's proposition makes sense, many interviewees stated that they wanted to know what happened. It seems that some survivors are willing to be humiliated again in exchange for recovery in the long run.

For most interviewees, knowing the truth is important but insufficient. They would like the community, and especially the perpetrators and their families, to acknowledge the offenses. Immaculée, a survivor, needed for the perpetrators to admit their crimes. She reasoned, "[If] he tells the truth, I feel very happy [...] because then the truth is established."[24] For her, as well as for others, acknowledgement of the crimes was essential to rebuilding their lives. They did not say that it was also important that the impact of the crimes be recognized—that might have been too much to hope for—but it was implicit.

Several interviewees emphasized that there were still perpetrators who denied their role in the genocide, or contested the fact that the genocide took place at all. Emerthe, for example, who lost several children and her husband, talked about the repudiation by perpetrators: "Among the ones who killed, there are some who [acknowledge] that they did so. And others, they don't want to [acknowledge] that they did so, although I know they did."[25] For Emerthe it was very difficult to hear that some people refused to acknowledge their guilt. This viewpoint is supported by the policy of the Rwandan government to encourage perpetrators to acknowledge the crimes they have committed. However, during gacaca, many perpetrators similarly acknowledge their guilt without showing any emotion. Therefore, this sort of acknowledgement diminishes the value of these confessions and questions the desirability of official incentives for perpetrators to acknowledge their guilt.[26]

According to Augustin, however, it was not only the perpetrators that refused to tell and accept the truth. He was a Hutu who was imprisoned for two years because several survivors claimed that he had killed three Tutsis. He was released after being exonerated by other survivors. Augustin commented that, "Sometimes when a survivor sees a Hutu, but he is not a killer, they say: 'He is a killer. Put him in prison.' What they have to do, [is] to tell the truth. Don't say: 'That Hutu is a killer' if he is not."[27] Augustin believed that in order to rebuild the country, Tutsis needed to accept that not all Hutus participated in the genocide.

In sum, the majority of the interviewees said that they did want to know what happened, because it was essential in enabling them to move on. The confessions of perpetrators are of great value as well. Confrontation with the past, however, can also be disruptive. Consequently, some of the survivors preferred to forget what happened.

Reckoning with the Past

The meaning of justice varies among survivors of mass atrocities. Whether the focus should be more on retribution or restoration is a fundamental dispute.[28] The opinions of the persons interviewed for this research differed on this subject. Nevertheless, they all agreed that a reckoning with the past through the organization of criminal trials, is indispensable in order to achieve justice. Ignace, a survivor who is also a judge at gacaca, argued: "To me justice means that if someone is a killer he must be punished. If someone is in a prison but he did not do anything during the genocide, he must be let free. That is justice."[29] The research conducted by Timothy Longman, Phuong Pham, and Harvey Weinstein in Rwanda in 2002 had a similar outcome. More than nine out of ten respondents agreed that criminal prosecution is a necessary element of justice.[30]

For seven of the interviewees, criminal trials and punishment were the sole elements of justice. According to them, justice is established only when trials have taken place and perpetrators have been punished. For them, justice was therefore largely a retributive phenomenon. However, other interviewees argued that trials were not the only component of justice. They described several elements that are a constitutive part of justice as well. One of these elements is financial compensation. Emerthe, a survivor from the province of Byumba, concluded: "Those who killed, let them be punished. Those who have lost relatives and loved ones, they should be compensated in monetary terms."[31] For survivors to recover, it is crucial, according to Emerthe, that they do not live in poverty. Financial compensation can aid in their recuperation not only because they have more money to spend. The fact that victims received a sum of money also signifies that their grief was related to the conduct of these criminals. For survivors, payment from the perpetrators can be a form of acknowledgement that enables the rebuilding of their lives. Félicien, who participated in the genocide, agreed with Emerthe. He emphasized the importance of psychological as well as financial recovery: "[Survivors need to regain] the respect they had before. The value they had needs to be compensated. Not only in monetary terms, but also respect. If [a perpetrator] says: 'I want to ask for forgiveness,' the person feels very prestigious."[32] For these interviewees—who emphasized that compensation and rehabilitation are also constitutive elements—justice was not only a retributive phenomenon. To establish justice, restorative measures were necessary as well.

Punishment is part and parcel of retributive justice. Most interviewees agreed that punishment was necessary, especially for those who planned and instigated the genocide. One interviewee, Emerthe, remarked that she considered trials to be important, but not punishment. She explained: "I don't give punishment a lot of attention. I want to teach my grandchildren that it is bad to kill, bad to hate. It is good to love your country; this means loving your people. [...] God will punish for me, it is in my mind."[33] Since she was strongly religious, she was content to defer punishment from worldly authorities to God. Another survivor, Bernadette, also addressed this issue, pointing out that punishment was insufficient. She said: "That [perpetrators] are in prison is important, but it is not enough. It is not equal to what they did! There is nothing equal to someone who killed many people. [...] There is no punishment for them which is hard enough."[34] Although people have to be punished, it will never be satisfying.

Many interviewees favored a different kind of punishment for those who planned the genocide than for those who followed orders. Augustin, a bystander, said: "The punishment depends on what they did. Authorities who told people to kill others, they must be punished extremely. More than those who executed." [35] Although the second group was directly responsible for the death of their loved ones, these interviewees said that the organizers were more responsible and therefore deserved a harsher punishment. Joseph, a survivor and a former RPF soldier said that if he had to choose, he wanted the planners to be punished: "If we compare the two situations and if you demand me to [choose], I will prefer to punish Bagosora and to let free the others who killed my family."[36]

Most interviewees maintained that the planners of the genocide had to be punished severely. They differed, however, as to the exact meaning of this punishment. To some, the death penalty was the only just punishment. Ancilla, a survivor, said: "Perpetrators give testimony, it hurts and [...] I feel very bad. Then I want to do something very bad to him or her. [...] I want revenge. The same thing needs to be done to them!"[37] She was clearly hoping for a form of vengeful justice. When speaking about the prosecution of planners at the ICTR, Immaculée, a survivor from Kigali, declared that she also wanted some sort of revenge. She said: "Why should [Bagosora] fear to say the truth here? It is better that he come here and tell the truth. So people can beat him."[38] Immaculée's wish to harm Bagosora is an important reason why these trials did not take place in Rwanda.[39] Odette, also a survivor, remarked that she no longer knows what kind of punishment has to be given to this group:

"Some years ago, I wanted one punishment: to kill them. But now I have no definition of punishment. I want justice and let the judges give the punishment."[40] Odette's stance raises the issue of the way in which some survivors' thinking about justice can change over time.

Another group of interviewees considered imprisonment to be a just punishment for the planners of the genocide. Augustin, a bystander, maintained: "The punishment [for] them is to put them in prison for their whole life. That is their punishment."[41] Joseph, a survivor, agreed. For him, it was important that the planners be removed from society. Consequently, he applauded the fact that the trials against the planners at the International Criminal Tribunal for Rwanda did not take place in Rwanda but in Arusha, Tanzania. He reasoned: "To have them in Arusha is okay. To send them [to] Rwanda is not good because of political problems. So to send them to Arusha or judge them in another country is okay."[42] Joseph was the only interviewee who was satisfied with the International Tribunal's location outside of Rwanda. For the other interviewees, the tribunal's location, or rather its remoteness, was their main problem. This group wanted to participate during the trials and/or see the perpetrators being prosecuted.

The interviewees suggested a different kind of punishment for those who carried out the genocidal plans. In principle, they felt that imprisonment was not the proper punishment for these perpetrators. Janvier, a survivor from Kigali, said: "[J]ailing people is not a solution. […] [The planners] are very hard to tame, so they have to be jailed. Others [can] be tamed, be educated. To show what is bad, what is good for society."[43] This stance allows the perpetrators' return to society on the condition that they are 'taught' how to behave. Augustin, a bystander, offered a different reason for not imprisoning them. "I was in prison, and to be in prison is very bad. So it will be better to give them the punishment of labor."[44] The situation in Rwandan prisons is miserable. Due to the high number of perpetrators, the prisons suffer overcrowding, and every year over a thousand deaths result from the prison conditions.[45] Therefore, Augustin considered imprisonment to be too tough a measure for those who carried out the genocide.

According to several interviewees, depending on their conduct during the genocide, some persons from this group of perpetrators deserved a prison sentence. Innocent, a survivor, stated: "Someone who was very strong and when he killed people said, 'I am very okay, I wanna kill ten people per day.' Those people have to be imprisoned."[46] Furthermore, some maintained that a prison sentence for low-level perpetrators could also be dependent on their behavior during gacaca. Emmanuel, a by-stander from the province Kigali-Rural, was unequivocal in his opinion: "Those who tell the truth, they can give them the punishment of labor. But those who don't tell the truth, those have to be sent to prison."[47] Those perpetrators who were clearly motivated to participate in the genocide as well as those who did not show remorse are entitled to a sentence similar to the one planners deserve.

The idea that those who committed genocidal crimes deserved punishment was widely accepted among the interviewees. They maintained that without the punishment, there would be no justice. On the other hand, the claim that RPF soldiers should be prosecuted for crimes against humanity was controversial. Some interviewees denied that the RPF committed any crimes. Innocent, who was saved by the Front, said: "The RPF must not be put to trial. Although some people say that the RPF killed people, that is not true. It was in the war. The RPF was there to fight against someone who had a gun. If you let him, he is going to kill you."[48] Others (a former RPF soldier and two Hutus) however, pointed out that some RPF soldiers did commit crimes. Félicien, a perpetrator, said: "If RPF did so, it was only individuals. They have to be punished on an individual basis."[49] Research by Longman, Pham and Weinstein reported a similar outcome. A large majority of the Hutus and only one out of three Tutsis found that the Front needed to be prosecuted.[50] The disagreement between Rwandans over the question of whether the RPF should be prosecuted makes clear that achieving justice is not only a question of organizing trials. Determining which crimes and individuals should be prosecuted is a fundamental issue.[51]

Criminal trials constitute an important element of justice for the interviewees. Most believe that those who planned the genocide deserve harsh punishments. Nevertheless, half of the interviewees considered justice to constitute more than the prosecution of perpetrators. For them, justice should also have a restorative element. The vision of justice described by these interviewees is quite similar to the governmental policy on transition, so the mechanisms implemented have the general approval of most of these interviewees. However, their opinions are also largely influenced by the local situation.

Between Retaliation and Reconciliation

In the aftermath of genocide, survivors have to find ways to pick up the pieces of their lives. Although this process is always very complicated, it was particularly difficult in Rwanda, since perpetrators, bystanders and survivors lived on the same hillside (again). Therefore, the question of whether survivors were prepared to live next to perpetrators and are perhaps even willing to reconcile with them loomed large. In their research, Timothy Longman and Théonèste Rutagengwa found that a majority of the Rwandan survivors felt that reconciliation was important.[52] My research points to a similar outcome. Almost all interviewees claimed that they were willing to reconcile with their former tormentors, although the wish for retaliation was not absent. Ignace, a survivor, said for example: "Reconciliation is very important but it needs many efforts; it is very difficult."[53] He and other interviewees were in principle willing to reconcile but they recognized that it would be a difficult and long-term process.

The interviewees were, however, not willing to reconcile with all perpetrators. Janvier, a very religious man, explained why he was not willing to reconcile with the planners of genocide. "They are devils. [...] They have done the worst!"[54] If people are seen as devils, it is clear that is impossible for reconciliation to take place, especially for the religious survivors.

Emerthe, an elderly survivor, explained that she had a problem with reconciliation. "Those who want reconciliation, let them have it. The government wants those who killed to be forgiven. [...] But I cannot forgive and forget. I [live next to] the perpetrators because the government wants it, not because I [do]."[55] Her comment not only demonstrates that some Rwandans had doubts about the possibilities of reconciliation, it also shows that on a superficial level the government's policy was effective. Emerthe lived alongside perpetrators because the government strove for "unity," but she was actually not content with doing so. Her situation raises the question as to the depth of her fellow citizens' preparedness to reconcile. Their stated readiness may be no more than an expression of compliance with state policy. A change in that policy could have a potentially significant impact on the country's reconciliation process.

When the interviewees talked about reconciliation, they only referred to their local community. Perhaps they considered that there were no longer tensions at the national level because they assumed that most planners were either prosecuted or had fled. Another explanation is that interviewees did not receive information about the functioning of political institutions and therefore were not aware of the possible necessity of reconciliation at the national level.

The interviewees similarly described the meaning of reconciliation. According to them, reconciliation meant that people were prepared to live together. Janvier, a survivor from Kigali, said, for example: "Reconciliation means putting us together. To be families. Not killing one another. [...] These victims have lost their family, okay, but it is not reversible. We have to live together."[56] However, the interviewees have different opinions about the meaning of living together. On the one hand, Ancilla and Immaculée, both survivors, felt that living together meant being tolerated in their village. Immaculée explained: "The importance is that [Hutus] allow me to fetch water in their compound. That kind of interaction was not here before."[57] It seems that for them living together meant no more than the absence of violence. Contact between neighbors was not necessary.

On the other hand, for some interviewees, living together needed to be more than just being tolerated. Innocent, a survivor, explained:

> When there is a wedding in this house, [Hutus] have to be here and bring something to drink. And if someone is sick [...] they come and we bring that person who is sick to the hospital. [...] People have to meet, people have to share everything. Like how the life was before the genocide.[58]

One explanation for the different interpretations of living together derives from the circumstances under which they lived. Innocent and some other interviewees said that they had contact with Hutus and felt secure. Ancilla and Immaculée said that they did not have much contact with Hutus and did not always feel secure. For these women, it seems that being tolerated is already a great accomplishment while the others are used to more than just living next to one other. Both descriptions show that the interviewees felt that they had no choice but to live together. These interviewees go along with government policies for pragmatic reasons. For their own well-being, they were prepared to forgive those persons who killed their loved ones.

The interviewees stressed several reasons for reconciliation. Innocent, a survivor, explained that it could prevent future conflicts. "To be reconciled with someone who killed people was very difficult. But we cannot rebuild our country if there is no reconciliation. I started to reconcile with people in order to prepare the country for the children."[59] Innocent argued that the problems he had concerning reconciliation were of less importance than the necessity for his children to live in a peaceful country. Joseph, who lost several family members, provided a different explanation: "[Survivors] need reconciliation. [...] It is a psychological problem to have an enemy every day. [...] To make you one again, reconciliation is a principal need."[60] According to him, survivors need to reconcile with the perpetrators in order to function in society, so it is in their own interest.

This point of view is quite similar to the ideas of the former president of the South African Truth and Reconciliation Commission, Desmond Tutu. He argued that everyone's humanity is related to that of others. Feelings of anger and revenge destroy the humanity of both persons. Thus, forgiveness and reconciliation are in the interest of survivors.[61]

There is consensus that several conditions have to be met in order to achieve reconciliation. According to interviewees, knowing what happened to relatives who were killed was an important condition. Odette, who lost her husband, stated: "Reconciliation is not possible without the truth. And without that for me there is no pardoning. I can only pardon if I know where my husband's bones are."[62] Knowing the truth would have made it easier for Odette to reconcile. But as we have seen above, being confronted with horrible deeds perpetrated against one's family could also lead to a desire for revenge. Therefore, knowledge of what happened can be a necessary condition for reconciliation but can also hinder the process.[63]

Another condition for reconciliation for some was that perpetrators ask for forgiveness. Janvier, a survivor from Kigali, said: "You come to me to ask for forgiveness. [...] Then I will think about forgiving you."[64] When perpetrators ask to be forgiven, the balance of power may shift and consequently the survivor is, at least temporarily, more powerful than the perpetrator. A third condition is the prosecution of perpetrators. Some interviewees emphasized the necessity that perpetrators be punished before they are able to reconcile with them. Augustin, a bystander, said: "If someone is a killer, and he is punished, after his punishment he is out. He says: 'It is true, I was punished for what I did.' Then after the punishment reconciliation is also possible."[65] Their reasoning is that those who are punished can be forgiven because they have paid for their crimes.

The reasons these interviewees gave in order to explain why reconciliation was important are persuasive. However, there are survivors from other mass atrocities who are unwilling to reconcile with their former tormentors.[66] The willingness of these interviewees to reconcile has therefore to be explained, partly at least, by the specific characteristics of Rwanda. One explanation is that because of the age-old gacaca, Rwandans are used to a model of conflict resolution that is focused on the restoration of mutual relationships. Another explanation is the central role of the Christian church in Rwanda that stresses the importance of forgiveness and restoration of disrupted relationships. The politics of the government can also be viewed as one explanation since it has emphasized the necessity of unity and reconciliation through several policies. Finally, the fact that Rwandans have no other option than to live together can also explain their willingness to reconcile. Survivors of other mass atrocities are most often not forced to live side by side with the perpetrators. Perhaps these explanations clarify the fact that these Rwandans are more inclined toward reconciliation than survivors of other mass atrocities, in which these factors are more or less absent. Emerthe's remark that she was only prepared to live with perpetrators because the government wanted her to, shows us that while Rwandans comply with this policy, they may well have different feelings about it and questions about the durability of the process. Their acquiescence to the state's will rather than their own may ultimately hamper reconciliation.

Conclusion

More than ten years after the genocide took place, many interviewees were prepared to reconcile with those who carried out the "crime of crimes." At the same time, punishment of these persons was of great importance. In particular, according to the interviewees, the planners of the genocide deserved severe punishment, while low-level perpetrators should accept their guilt and ask for forgiveness so that they can return to society. The goal of reconciliation for these Rwandans was to live in a peaceful society. Because many survivors are forced, due to the lack of space, to live next to the perpetrators and their families, they argued that they have no other option than to try to rebuild their country together. Therefore, the outcomes of this research support the policies of the Rwandan government. The gacaca system enjoyed particular support among the interviewees and can be seen as an essential mechanism to the transition.

For the interviewees, the transition process was local. They were hardly informed about national issues, let alone the activities of the International Tribunal for Rwanda, which is located in Tanzania. In a rural country like Rwanda it is thus of great importance that a reckoning with the past takes place in every village. Without that local element, a transition can most certainly not be effective or just. On the other hand, during local truth-finding processes, the role of national political leaders will be left out of the picture. Mechanisms with a focus on the role of the national elite are therefore of great importance as well.

Among scholars who study the transition of post-conflict societies, there is debate about which mechanisms are most effective.[67] Some argue that tribunals are essential; others claim that truth commissions are better equipped to help rebuild the country. Based on this research, it can be argued that both mechanisms have important benefits for Rwandans. The truth commission's restorative focus largely corresponds with the ways most interviewees wish to deal with low-level perpetrators. Furthermore, it also focuses on truth-finding and can consequently help the reconciliation process that many interviewees have described as important. Nevertheless, punishment of those who planned the genocide through criminal trials was considered very important for the interviewees in order to reckon with the past. The international emphasis on criminal trials as the most important transitional mechanism is therefore partly justified. However, criminal trials do not focus on the restoration of disrupted relationships, truth finding, or other interests of survivors. Moreover, according to many interviewees, justice is more than the organization of criminal trials. Therefore, both mechanisms have important advantages but lack certain qualities that are necessary for a just transition. On the basis of this study, and the larger-scale investigations noted above, it is clear that a combination of mechanisms will need to be implemented in order to establish an effective form of transitional justice in Rwanda.

Notes

1.   Scott Straus, "How many perpetrators were there in the Rwandan genocide? An estimate," *Journal of Genocide Research,* 6 (2004): 85-98 and Scott Straus, *The Order of Genocide: Race, Power, and War in Rwanda* (Ithaca and London: Cornell University Press, 2006).

2.   African Rights, *Death, Despair and Defiance* (London: African Rights, 1995) and Jean Hatzfeld, *Into the Quick of Life. The Rwandan Genocide: The Survivors Speak* (London: Serpent's Tail, 2005).

3.   By "ordinary" Rwandans, I mean people who do not belong to the cultural, political or economic elite. In addition, I also interviewed government officials, journalists and several professionals working for nongovernmental organizations.

4.   Gacaca is a traditional local court system where many low-level perpetrators are tried. Interestingly, all persons who were asked to be interviewed were willing to cooperate. Jean Hatzfeld encountered the same attitude among survivors; see *Into the Quick of Life*, viii.

5.   Donatila, interview in Kigali, December 14, 2005.

6.   Interview with a pastor, Kigali, December 13, 2005.

7.   Human Rights Watch, *Killing in Eastern Rwanda* (Human Rights Watch: New York, 2007).

8.   Two interviewees, Joseph and Janvier, spoke English and those interviews were carried out without a translator.

9.   Gentille, interview in Kigali, November 30, 2005.

10.   Janvier, interview in Kigali, November 28, 2005.

11.   The Rwandan Patriotic Front (RPF) invaded Rwanda in 1990 from Uganda. In 1994, the Front was responsible for the overthrow of the genocidal government and has ruled the country since.

12.   Innocent, interview in the province of Kigali-Rural, December 12, 2005. Habyarimana ruled the country from 1973 until he was killed on April 6, 1994. His death was the starting sign of the genocide. Gérard Prunier, *The Rwanda Crisis: History of a Genocide* (London: C. Hurst & Co, 1997).

13. Emerthe, interview in the province of Byumba, December 11, 2005.

14. Human Rights Watch, *The Rwandan Genocide: How It Was Prepared* (New York: Human Rights Watch, 2006).

15. Félicien, interview in the province of Byumba, December 11, 2005. Straus' research shows that obedience was one of the most important reasons to participate; see *The Order of Genocide*, 133-140. According to several researchers, the political culture in Rwanda can be characterized as highly obedient. Prunier, *The Rwanda Crisis*, 57. Although Félicien said this was the reason he participated, it must be considered that for a perpetrator it is better to say that he was told to participate by the authorities than to say that he killed out of belief.

16. The existence of hatred between groups and a culture of obedience are important explanations for the genocide, but are not sufficient. It does not, for example, explain why the genocide took place in 1994.

17. Joseph, interview in Kigali, November 25, 2005.

18. According to several scholars, this is an important cause of the genocide. African Rights, *Death, despair and defiance*, xvii and Benjamin Valentino, *Final solutions: Mass Killings and Genocide in the Twentieth Century* (Ithaca and London: Cornell University Press, 2004).

19. Odette, interview in Kigali, December 14, 2005.

20. Bernadette, interview in the province of Kigali-Rural, December 9, 2005.

21. Immaculée, interview in Kigali, December 10, 2005.

22. Gentille, interview in Kigali, November 30, 2005.

23. Avishai Margalit, "Is truth the road to reconciliation?" in *Experiments With Truth: Transitional Justice and the Processes of Truth and Reconciliation,* ed. Okwui Enwezor (Kassel: Hatje Cantz, 2002), 61-64.

24. Immaculée, interview in Kigali, December 10, 2005.

25. Gentille, interview in Kigali, November 30, 2005.

26. Urusaro Alice Karekezi, Alphonse Nshimiyimana and Beth Mutamba, "Localizing justice: gacaca courts in post-genocide Rwanda," in *My Neighbor, My Enemy: Justice and Community in the Aftermath of Mass Atrocity,* ed. Eric Stover and Harvey M. Weinstein (Cambridge: Cambridge University Press, 2004), 69-85, 79.

27. Augustin, interview in the province of Kigali-Rural, December 9, 2005.

28. David Bloomfield, Teresa Barnes and Luc Huyse, ed., *Reconciliation After Violent Conflict* (Stockholm: International Institute for Democracy and Electoral Assistance, 2003); Rama Mani, *Beyond Retribution. Seeking Justice in the Shadows of War* (Cambridge: Polity Press, 2002), Martha Minow, *Between Vengeance and Forgiveness: Facing History after Genocide and Mass Violence* (Boston: Beacon Press, 1998) and Andrew Rigby, *Justice and Reconciliation: After the Violence* (London: Lynne Rienner Publishers, 2001).

29. Ignace, interview in the province of Kigali-Rural, December 11, 2005.

30. For their research, they surveyed 2,091 Rwandans in 2002. Timothy Longman, Phuong N. Pham and Harvey M. Weinstein, "Connecting justice to human experience," in *My Neighbor,* ed. Stover and Weinstein, 206-225, 213.

31. Emerthe, interview in the province of Byumba, December 11, 2005.

32. Félicien, interview in the province of Byumba, December 11, 2005.

33. Gentille, interview in Kigali, November 30, 2005.

34. Bernadette, interview in the province of Kigali-Rural, December 9, 2005.

35. Augustin, interview in the province of Kigali-Rural, December 9, 2005.

36. Joseph, interview in Kigali, November 25, 2005. Bagosora is said to be one of the masterminds of the genocide. Linda Melvern, *Conspiracy to Murder: The Rwandan Genocide* (London and New York: Verso, 2004).

37. Ancilla, interview in the province of Byumba, December 11, 2005.
38. Immaculée, interview in Kigali, December 10, 2005.
39. Payam Akhavan, "The International Criminal Tribunal for Rwanda: The Politics and Pragmatics of Punishment," *American Journal of International Law*, 90 (1996): 501-510.
40. Odette, interview in Kigali, December 14, 2005.
41. Augustin, interview in the province of Kigali-Rural, December 9, 2005.
42. Joseph, interview in Kigali, November 25, 2005.
43. Janvier, interview in Kigali, November 28, 2005.
44. Augustin, interview in the province of Kigali-Rural, December 9, 2005.
45. Human Rights Watch, *Struggling to Survive: Barriers to Justice for Rape Victims in Rwanda* (New York: Human Rights Watch, 2004), 16-18.
46. Innocent, interview in Kigali, December 11, 2005.
47. Emmanuel, interview in the province of Kigali-Rural, December 9, 2005.
48. Innocent, interview in the province of Byumba, November 12, 2005.
49. Félicien, interview in the province of Kigali-Rural, December 9, 2005.
50. Longman et al., "Connecting justice," 214.
51. For a description of crimes against humanity committed by the RPF, see Filip Reyntjes, "Rwanda, Ten Years On: From Genocide to Dictatorship," *African Affairs*, 103 (2004): 177-210.
52. For their research they interviewed up to two hundred Rwandans. Timothy Longman and Claude Rutagengwa, "Memory, identity, and community in Rwanda," in *My Neighbor*, ed. Stover and Weinstein, 162-182.
53. Ignace, interview in the province of Kigali-Rural, December 11, 2005.
54. Janvier, interview in Kigali, November 28, 2005.
55. Emerthe, interview in the province of Byumba, November 12, 2005.
56. Janvier, interview in Kigali, November 28, 2005.
57. Immaculée, interview in Kigali, December 10, 2005.
58. Innocent, interview in the province of Kigali-Rural, December 12, 2005.
59. Ibid.
60. Joseph, interview in Kigali, November 25, 2005.
61. Desmond Tutu, *No Future Without Forgiveness* (New York: Doubleday, 1999), 37-38.
62. Odette, interview in Kigali, December 14, 2005.
63. Ervin Staub argues that under the right circumstances the confrontation with the past will help reconciliation, "Preventing violence and generating humane values: Healing and reconciliation in Rwanda," *International Review of the Red Cross*, 85 (2003): 791-806. In a different article he shows that trauma counseling can lead to more openness towards reconciliation, Ervin Staub, Laurie Anne Pearlman, Alexandra Gubin and Athanasa Hagengimana, "Healing, Reconciliation, Forgiving and the Prevention of Violence after Genocide or Mass Killing: An Intervention and its Experimental Evaluation in Rwanda," *Journal of Social and Clinical Psychology*, 24 (2005): 297-334.
64. Janvier, Interview in Kigali, November 28, 2005.
65. Augustin, interview in the province of Kigali-Rural, December 9, 2005.
66. See for example Miklos Biro, "Attitudes toward justice and social reconstruction in Bosnia and Herzegovina and Croatia," in *My Neighbor*, ed. Stover and Weinstein, 183-205.
67. Payam Akhavan, "Justice and Reconciliation in the Great Lakes Region of Africa: The Contribution of the International Criminal Tribunal for Rwanda," *Duke Journal of Comparative & International Law*, 7 (1997): 325-348. Bloomfield, Barnes and Huyse, ed. *Reconciliation After Violent Conflict*, Mani, *Beyond Retribution*, and Minow, *Between Vengeance and Forgiveness*.

7

Leaving Silence Behind?
Algerians and the Memories of Repression by
French Security Forces in Paris in 1961

Jim House

Introduction

Between 1958 and 1962, Algerians in the Paris region were subjected to a policy of state terror by the French security forces under Paris police chief Maurice Papon in the context of the French state's war with the pro-independence Algerian National Liberation Front (FLN). In theory, the aim was to crush the FLN's organizational structure, responsible for raising the money within the emigrant community that provided most of the funding for the nationalists' armed struggle in Algeria. In reality, this repression affected all sections of the Algerian population, and aimed to force Algerians into political submission by threats, intimidation and violence.[1] Violence peaked in September and October 1961, as Algerians were brutalized, kidnapped, tortured, and assassinated during routine policing operations and acts of "reprisal" by police officers for FLN assassinations of security force personnel.

It was in protest against both the police violence and the nighttime curfew that Papon had placed on Algerians, that the FLN organized the demonstrations of October 17, 1961. At least 30,000 Algerian migrants from the Paris region peacefully attempted to converge on central Paris in a move also designed to appeal to French and international public opinion at this crucial time in the negotiations taking place with the French state at the end of the war.

These demonstrations gave the Paris police the opportunity to vent its hatred of Algerians. During the night of October 17-18, many dozens of

Algerians were clubbed to death, shot at, drowned in the Seine, and over 11,000 were detained in appalling conditions in requisitioned stadiums. At least 500 Algerians were seriously injured. While the French media were far from silent in the weeks immediately following the massacre, a successful official cover-up soon ensued. The mainstream French left, split on the question of Algerian independence and the Cold War, was both unable and unwilling to mount mass, unitary protests after October 17, 1961.[2] In addition, high levels of police violence against metropolitan French demonstrators, such as the police killing of nine anti-fascist protestors in Paris on February 8, 1962 at the Charonne metro station, provoked a mass response from the left that further hid the October 1961 events.[3] At the end of the Algerian War of Independence (1962), the French state introduced amnesty measures covering all aspects of military and policing operations during the conflict.[4]

However, on the Algerian side, events moved just as swiftly to foreclose public visibility and ultimately memory. The Provisional Government of the Algerian Republic did not want the October 1961 violence to complicate its negotiations with the Gaullist government. Crucially, in the struggles for power witnessed during the transition to independence in July-August 1962, the French FLN Federation lost out to the factions behind Ahmed Ben Bella.[5] President Ben Bella thus had little desire to cultivate the memory of the French FLN Federation's role during the war.

All of these developments therefore left Algerian migrants in France in a sort of memorial "wasteland" after 1962, with little, if any, "space," or forum and memory vectors for the voicing and/or transmission of the memories of October 1961. In the face of these highly constricting conditions of political and social "illegitimacy" for the memories of October 1961, many Algerians in France adopted a strategic silence. The reasons for this silence, and the forms it took, represent one key memorial dimension that this chapter examines, before moving on to analyze the chronologically differentiated pattern of leaving silence behind that some Algerians followed in relation to their experiences of repression. Finally, the chapter studies the transformations in these memorial dynamics due to the greater public visibility and social credence that October 1961 has enjoyed since the late 1990s, even if the vast majority of Algerians have remained silent about their difficult wartime pasts.

The approach adopted in this chapter follows Luisa Passerini's suggestion that "it is constitutive of the definition of a silence to find out its limits, its context, and its reference: in respect to whom and what is it a silence?"[6] This study focuses on Algerians who had publicly spoken of their experiences in October 1961 during the 1990s. The interviews I conducted examined the events themselves but also included the reasons for interviewees having kept silent during several decades, and their subsequent motivations for having left that silence behind. This approach allowed interviewees to objectify their own memorial strategies. In addition, I interviewed memory activists who have campaigned for the official French recognition of October 17, 1961, many of whom are themselves of Algerian heritage and whose parents were in France during the Algerian war. This research also included material from numerous interviews with French anti-colonial and humanitarian activists from the war period, and an analysis of documentary film, Internet, and newspaper sources.

My analysis of this material aims to probe the articulation between individual and social memory,[7] the processes of private and public silence and/ or forgetting of "contested pasts,"[8] the relationship between experiential and non-experiential memories,[9] the context for the solicitation of testimony, and the various uses to which testimony can be put. My questions also examined political and social events in France, in Algeria, and what Paul A. Silverstein calls the "transpolitical space" within and across these two countries, as exemplified by the political activism of sections of the Algerian diaspora in France and their descendants.[10]

1960s-1970s: Silence but Not Forgetting

Just as public silence can be multi-layered, so, too, can private silence, or the confining of one's experiences to the familial sphere. This was the strategy adopted during the 1960s and 1970s by the vast majority of the former demonstrators as well as the 130,000 or so Algerians living in the Paris region at the time.[11]

Of course, the memories Algerians have of the October 1961 events are themselves diverse, and for some traumatic. Twelve years old at the time, Khaled was one of the demonstrators from the suburban Nanterre shantytowns fired at by police on October 17 as they attempted to march across the Pont de Neuilly bridge towards central Paris. Khaled was not injured, but he did get buried under a pile of protestors. In interview, Khaled, today a teacher in the Paris suburbs, discussed the variation in experiences that Algerians endured on and after October 17:

> For those that went to the protest and who managed to escape from the repression, it was a demonstration, they thought "we've taken part in something." For those who participated but who suffered physically, with clubbings and the like, I think a deep

suffering has remained within them. Unfortunately, there are those that disappeared forever and whose families don't even know what became of their bodies. In that case it's impossible to move beyond grieving.[12]

As more Algerians came forward from the 1980s to give testimony, few doing so had actually lost a close family member in October 1961, suggesting that the greater the emotional pain endured, the less likely one was to speak out.

Unless they had witnessed violence themselves, it was not always easy for Algerians in Paris during the late war period to ascertain whether the killing of a loved one, colleague, or friend resulted from a police or an FLN punitive action. This fostered the idea of a "mysterious war," as one former shantytown resident put it.[13] The Algerian war was not just a civil war in terms of Algerians fighting the French, it was a multiple civil war, with Algerian nationalists fighting each other, and punitive executions within each camp: evoking this intra-Algerian violence remains largely taboo within the Algerian migrant communities. Additionally, some Algerians (termed *harkis*) fought alongside the French security forces, further compromising the possibility of any shared memories of the war in Algeria or France.[14] Some Algerians may therefore not have wanted to remember painful wartime experiences, and thus they deliberately avoided speaking of the past. As Madame Arouali, a resident of a shantytown in suburban Nanterre in 1961, points out in Ali Akika's documentary film *Les Enfants d'octobre* (October's Children): "What a lot we had to endure at that time!"[15]

There are also important generational aspects to consider. For those Algerians who went to the October 17, 1961 demonstrations as children, the full significance of the event might only have been realized later, either via evocation within the family—which was quite rare—or from contact with memory carriers. Events then became reinterpreted in the light of a new context. Farid Aïchoune was taken as a ten-year-old by his mother to the Algerian women's demonstration of October 20, 1961 in protest against the repression of the October 17 demonstrations. Since his parents had not spoken about their wartime experiences, during the 1960s he had forgotten the general context in which the October demonstrations had occurred. He recalled, "as an adolescent, I had taken on the collective memory of the French, *i.e.,* Charonne, that's to say I had obscured my own history."[16]

As this remark suggests, many Algerians were not transmitting their memories of the war—and of October 1961—to their children. There were arguably a number of reasons for this linked to the situation of emigration. Many Algerian male migrants entertained the "myth of return," but constantly put off their departure back to Algeria. This resulted in a long-lasting provisional status and disposition, and their stays in France became ever longer. How could such Algerians, who had supported Algerian independence, verbalize a decision to stay in the country of the former colonizer, where racism and structural socio-economic inequality remained real issues? What did their wartime experiences in France signify if these migrants did not then go back to Algeria? How could Algerians admit to their children that the independent Algeria for which they had struggled did not correspond to their hopes, as the one-party FLN failed to introduce real democracy? Furthermore, for the Algerian state, Algerians in France were in some respects "illegitimate" nationals (emigrants), just as, for the French state, Algerians' wartime experiences were also considered "illegitimate."

The status of the migrant was characterized by a certain number of silences regarding the hardships endured in exile (*al-ghorba*). As the sociologist Abdelmalek Sayad has shown, Algerian migrants had to give their families in Algeria the impression that their stay in France had been a success, so that their families would not "lose face" in relation to other families and/or the village group. Consequently, Algerian migrants returning home tended to downplay the loneliness, and even in some cases the physical violence they had experienced in France. This often resulted in a "collective illusion" for potential Algerian emigrants regarding the true nature of emigration.[17]

Furthermore, throughout the Algerian war, many police or army tactics inflicted upon Algerians brought forms of public humiliation that the authorities knew would prove difficult to recount at the time and, presumably, after the event. These tactics included: enforced nudity, beatings, injuries to sexual organs, and sexual abuse.[18] The very decision to speak out and denounce abuses brought Algerians face to face with the French judicial apparatus that was an essential element of the colonial system. Likewise, colonial power relations undermined the ways in which Algerians were treated by and thus viewed the French medical system that was responsible for validating their claims of physical abuse.[19] Additionally, if all the community had suffered during the war, was it not selfish to draw attention to one's own sufferings or those of one's family? The popular Kabyle saying that "the past is dead" (*li fat met*) exemplifies how Algerians might have been encouraged to look to the future rather than to the past.[20] This may have encouraged Algerians to "move on" after the war with the reasoning that since colonialism was over, they would be better off not dwelling on this painful past, but concentrating on improving social conditions.[21]

Some Algerian parents deliberately did not transmit their painful wartime experiences so as not to compromise the attitude their children had towards France. As sociologist Saïd Bouamama put it: "it wasn't to obscure the past but to go beyond it ... that parents kept quiet" in relation to painful wartime experiences, which October 1961 constituted.[22] The researcher Jean-Luc Einaudi, speaking of his interview work on October 1961 in the 1980s, described how, when Algerians did agree to recount their experiences in front of their children, these children were often hearing their parents' stories for the first time.[23]

Furthermore, even if Algerians had wanted to speak out publicly in France in relation to their wartime past, many were afraid to do so. We know that the effects of state terror often induce silence for many years afterwards by instilling fear.[24] Such silence, when induced, is not necessarily forgetting: some carry a "bodily memory" of the violence (the physical and psychological pain of injuries received) that still affects them every day.[25] In addition, the post-1962 period saw remarkable continuity regarding the French state's attempts to socially and politically control the Algerian communities in France.[26] Accordingly, many Algerians in France tried not to draw the attention of the police onto themselves.

The case of one former demonstrator, Belkacem, illustrates many of these points. He had avoided the violence on the demonstration of October 17 by pretending to be Italian, and not Algerian, when stopped by police, and he had managed to escape the police cordon near the Champs-Elysées in which he found himself. However, Belkacem was arrested in late October 1961, suffered violence in a detention center outside of Paris, and was then flown to Algeria where he spent the rest of the war in detention, eventually returning to Paris in 1963, where he remained. Summarizing the period between 1961and 1995, during which he did not talk about his experiences, Belkacem explained: "[I]t's as if there was some sort of blockage there.... I said to myself that I simply couldn't talk about it [the events of October 17] for reasons of personal safety, and in order to live a problem-free life, to bring up my children, and keep out of trouble. So I never spoke about it." In 1963, he went on, "on my return to France [...] it wasn't that I had forgotten about 17 October, but that I had completely turned over a new page in my life, had decided to prioritize other things, like my personal life, my career. I never talked about 17 October." He asserted that this attitude was typical of other Algerians he knew.[27]

Some Algerians had been solicited for testimony by opposition groups and journalists immediately after the October 17, 1961 violence. However, after November 1961 this oppositional context had mostly disappeared, and had resulted in no shift in the official version that, beyond the political left, retained considerable credence. There was, officially, no massacre on October 17, 1961, nor had there been any state terror. As Khaled put it, this violence was "something that no one knew about and that everyone denied."[28] This silence within French society re-enforced the marginalization of Algerians' wartime experiences. As Annette Wieviorka has shown, the context in which testimonies can be "heard" and listened to is crucial.[29] When no groups are willing to take on board certain experiences, individuals often retreat into silence.

All of these factors meant that publicly, but also in many cases privately, there was not a "context for the transmission of memory."[30] Former demonstrator Khaled explained that two conditions had to exist for him to speak openly about his wartime experiences. "On the one hand," he noted, "society ha[d] to accept the situation and on the other, those that have experienced these difficulties themselves need to be ready and backed by associations." He did not speak publicly of his experiences before the 1980s. His "double trauma" of having witnessed violence as a child in Algeria and then again as a twelve-year-old at the October 17 demonstrations meant that, for him, the episode "needed to be shut out, and not spoken about again, because it was too painful."[31] As Michael Pollak concluded in one of his studies of Holocaust memory: "remaining silent about the past stems less perhaps from forgetting than from a way of dealing with memory according to the conditions for communicating it at a given moment of one's life."[32] Just as a congruence of factors had combined to ensure the rapid loss of public visibility of the October 1961 violence soon after the events, so a variety of reasons therefore explained the persistence of this public silence in France.

Furthermore, we also need to understand the attitude of the Algiers regime which declared 17 October "National Emigration Day" in 1968, thereby moving from official silence about the repression to highly visible, instrumentalized commemorations that sought to emphasize the links between Algerian emigration and the Algiers regime. Many Algerians could not identify with this message, as a gulf had developed between the Algerian state and many of its citizens, in particular those in France. However, the lengthy annual dossiers devoted to the October 1961 violence in the publications of the Algerian state-run association in

France for its migrant workers—the *Amicale*—often contained interview testimony from Algerians who had been in Paris in 1961.[33]

Where memorial voices can be traced for this period, they often belong to various counter-memorial strategies. The French far left and the Algerian and wider "Arab" far left challenged the respective silence of the French state and the French Communist Party and the official Algerian instrumentalization of October 1961, as a new radical political "space" emerged in France in the wake of the student and worker protests of May 1968. For example, the Paris branch of the Arab Worker's Movement (*Mouvement des travailleurs arabes*, MTA, 1972-1977), close to the Maoists, and hostile to the Algerian *Amicale*, brought the French and "Arab" far left together over the evocation of October 1961.[34] The MTA, and the radical left-wing politics of the time, provided a key meeting ground and forum in which some former FLN militants from the war and French former anti-colonial activists as well, transmitted their memories of the war to a receptive audience. The MTA was comprised of student radicals from Tunisia or Morocco, and young people whose Algerian parents had been in France during the war, but who, for the reasons previously outlined, had often not heard of October 1961 from their parents. This radical political activism therefore provided a forum for revisiting war and migrant memories—and those of October 1961 in particular—in a sort of "semi-public" sphere,[35] since most of the former wartime activists involved in these campaigns were not discussing these issues in a family context.

Shifting Memorial Voices: 1980-1998

After the Gaullists, in power since 1958, lost both the presidency and legislative elections to the left in 1981, there was no change in the policy of official silence on the October 1961 events, despite the new political, social and cultural framework. The Socialist left had little political capital to gain from evoking a war that had been as divisive on the left as it was nationally.

A key carrier of the memorial activism at this point was the counter-cultural movement Without Borders (*Sans-Frontière*, 1979-1985), set up by some former members of the MTA who realized in the late 1970s and early 1980s that there had been a lack of memory transmission from many Algerian parents to their children.[36] These activists sought to appropriate memories of October 1961 in order to counteract the social silence and forgetting with regard to colonial violence and immigration. For the *Sans Frontière* activists, the "Beur" generation of the 1980s—the sons and daughters of North African migrants who emerged as political actors challenging racism in the early and mid-1980s—needed to incorporate these transmitted memories of the war.[37] For the younger generations, the October 17, 1961 demonstrations could symbolize colonial and post-colonial racial violence and its impunity,[38] and also provide a "narrative of resistance" to racism.[39]

From this point onwards a rich intergenerational memorial dynamic began to emerge within the Algerian migrant communities and their descendants in France, one whereby the mantle of memory activism was taken on by the next generation. Over the next twenty years, as memory activist Mehdi Lallaoui puts it, the descendants of Algerians in 1961 "picked up the thread again of this painful, violent memory" from their parents to ensure that these events did not disappear forever.[40]

However, memory activism was not limited to the descendants of Algerian migrants. Algerian immigrant Kamal was active in organizing meetings on October 1961 in the Paris suburb of Saint-Denis, away from any national media publicity. Kamal had been in France since 1948, and had attempted to demonstrate on October 17. Like Belkacem, he had pretended to be Italian to avoid arrest. A few days later, the police raided his hotel and machine-gunned one of the residents in front of him, resulting in that man's death. Like Belkacem, Kamal was taken to the identification centre at Vincennes outside of Paris, where he too was subjected to physical assault by the police. Kamal, who had been active in the FLN during the war, was conscious of the problems of memory transmission of the Algerian war within the Algerian migrant communities, hence his decision to promote this memory.[41]

Within the Algerian communities in France there was a Franco-Algerian dynamic at work in the memorial activism surrounding the October 1961 events that was capable of bringing together those with an experiential memory of the repression and their descendants. Protests against the violent repression in Algeria during October 1988 of demonstrations against poor socio-economic conditions, corruption, and lack of democracy—leading to at least 500 deaths—illustrate this process.[42] Such protests drew more parallels to October 17 than to many other instances of violent repression of Algerian nationalist street protests in Algeria during the war. This revealed the particular historical consciousness forged in France that had developed by 1988 in relation to the October 1961 repression within sections of the Algerian migrant communities. The link between October 17, 1961 and October 1988 was used by Algerians and their descendants in France to critique what they saw as the betrayal of the hopes of the Algerian people by the one-party FLN that had been in power since 1962, and to link demands for social justice in Algeria with the struggle against racism in France.[43]

In France in the 1980s, the memory activism regarding the October 1961 violence in France had only started to find a real "space" in which Algerians' wartime experiences could be heard. However, from 1990 onwards, a new campaigning association called In Memory's Name (*Au nom de la mémoire*, hereafter ANM), supported by established antiracist organizations, provided a more consensual forum for the public expression of Algerians' memories. ANM also shifted some of the focus of memory activism, formulating specific demands to the French government for symbolic reparations in the form of truth, recognition and justice that continue to frame the debates on October 1961. This activism corresponded to what Mark Osiel calls the "social movement for factual recovery"[44] that would seek to transmit Algerians' memories and solicit their testimonies on a more systematic basis with the main initial aim of proving that a massacre had indeed occurred on and around October 17, 1961.

The two documentary films on October 1961 that came out in the early 1990s—*Le Silence du fleuve* ("The River's Silence," 1991), co-produced by Mehdi Lallaoui (one of the founders of the association ANM), and *Drowning by Bullets* (1992) by Alan Hayling—are emblematic of the process of greater public disclosure of wartime memories, and the mixture of memory work and historical work undertaken by activists during this period. Both films used oral testimony as part of a multi-vocal counter-narrative, involving victims of violence in addition to deliberate or accidental witnesses. In these works, testimony as counter-knowledge challenges the state version of events and the sense of justice and legitimacy with which state actors attempt to surround themselves.[45] However, both of these carefully constructed films feature far more French than Algerian interviewees, and these Algerian interviewees are often the former French Federation FLN leaders, or at least high-ranking officials. It is apparent that many ordinary Algerians experienced problems in speaking publicly.

Leaving Silence Behind?: 1998

In France, the national-level politics of memory regarding the October 1961 events came to occupy an increasingly central place in the media and political debate after 1997. These developments impacted upon the memorial dynamics within the Algerian migrant communities themselves, on the less publicly visible memorial initiatives at the grassroots level, and on the memorial dynamics within the family, as Algerians were solicited to speak of their experiences in October 1961 by journalists, researchers, and younger family members.

Several examples illustrate this process. The key event grounding the October 1961 repression within public consciousness in France was the evocation of this repression during the highly publicized trial (October 1997-March 1998) of former police chief Maurice Papon for crimes against humanity during Vichy.[46] The trial itself, however, did not examine Papon's alleged individual responsibility in the October 1961 killings. In response to this, Jean-Luc Einaudi wrote in the newspaper *Le Monde* that the "massacre" of October 17, 1961 had occurred "under Maurice Papon's orders." Papon duly sued him for libel.[47]

Einaudi's defense team coordinated a wide range of written and oral testimony for the trial. Khaled, for example, provided written testimony of his experiences as a demonstrator on October 17. Khaled had known Einaudi since 1995. In January 1999, just before the Einaudi libel trial, Khaled had agreed to be interviewed for the second major book on October 17 that Einaudi was preparing.[48] Khaled described giving written testimony to the trial as "leaving anonymity behind out of refusal" at what was occurring, given the situation whereby Einaudi, and not Papon, was sitting in the dock at the libel trial.[49] Khaled knew that Papon had been responsible for violent repression in Algeria in the Constantine region during 1956-58 at the very height of the Algerian war.[50] Significantly, it was in Algeria, rather than France, that Khaled had suffered his worst wartime experiences as a young boy. Therefore, he told himself: "This man [Papon] should not be allowed to get away with it." While Khaled had become active in relation to October 17 within an associative context after the October 1988 repression in Algeria, he had not spoken about the October 1961 events to his children. His attitude had been to keep these events at a distance, like "an historical event, that's to say [...] not an event that I experienced. [*I spoke about it*] as if it was an historical event like the 1914-1918 war."[51] The Papon case drew him out of this position. Khaled's testimony, as a strategic, albeit solicited form of leaving silence behind, helped Einaudi win his case, which gave greater juridical certainty to the idea that wide-scale illegal killings by police of Algerians had taken place in October 1961, despite the lack of official French recognition.

A second instance further demonstrates the variety of strategies adopted by Algerians regarding speaking about their experiences of

October 1961. In October 1995, Belkacem attended the annual October 17 commemoration in central Paris and was stopped by a journalist seeking to contact those who demonstrated in October 1961. This led to an interview the same day with the French national television channel TF1, and Belkacem agreed for his name to be used. From this point onwards, the Algerian political party with which Belkacem was associated—the secularist, left-leaning Union for Culture and Democracy (*Rassemblement pour la culture et la démocratie*)—began to organize official commemorations of October 17, 1961 in France. Thereafter Belkacem, like Khaled and Kamal, seems to have developed a very conscious strategy of going public. For Belkacem, speaking out constituted a political intervention in both French and Algerian spheres to pressure the French state to recognize the massacre, and force the Algerian state to fully accept the important role played by Algerian migrants during the war of independence.[52]

The interviews with Belkacem also gave an interesting insight into the link between social remembering and memorial dynamics at the individual and family level. The wide publicity given to October 17, 1961 stimulated the interest of his grandchildren, and his children, who wanted him to talk to them about the event. Belkacem pointed out:

> With my children now older, and newspapers and television speaking more of October 17, my children, who are now fathers, have begun to ask me questions along the lines of "now you need to give us some details," now, you see, and it took place in 1961, we are in 2005, and I am only starting to explain to my children what happened.[53]

This interest and memorial stimulus from the descendants of Algerians, creating a virtual memorial circle, has been observed by analysts of Algerian migration.[54]

Belkacem then campaigned successfully for a memorial plaque to the October 1961 repression, to be raised in his suburban town outside Paris. Belkacem asserted that he felt more protected now that historians work on October 17. Yet, Belkacem, like Khaled, was very aware of how unrepresentative he was in having spoken at such national, local, or even family levels. Belkacem co-founded the Association for the Memory of October 17, 1961 (*Association pour la mémoire du 17 octobre 1961*). Whilst handing out flyers to advertise this association locally, Belkacem met an Algerian who told him: "I've been living here since 1961 but have never spoken to anyone about it, you are the first person that I have spoken to about October 17." Belkacem noted that former demonstrators were only gradually coming forward to his association.[55]

Much work remains to be done to create a more comfortable atmosphere in which Algerians will speak of their experiences, and French rather than Algerian voices still predominate the books and documentaries produced on October 1961. One interesting exception to this remaining unequal process of public disclosure, can be found in the documentary film by Ali Akika, *Les Enfants d'octobre* ('October's children'), which examines the experiences of the Arouali family from Sidi Okba in Algeria, who were living in the Nanterre shantytown of Rue des Paquerettes in October 1961.[56] The film's director, Ali Akika, was a friend of one of the daughters, Alima. Here another type of semi-public disclosure is at work: the documentary film with restricted circulation, shot by someone whom the family trusted.

The Arouali family, active within the FLN, demonstrated on October 17, 1961. The whole family found itself on the Pont de Neuilly, when one of the daughters, Aïcha, who was twelve at the time, was shot at by police. The bullets passed between her legs, and she escaped injury. The family setting is interesting, since all of the daughters went to the demonstration. Immediately after the repression, Aïcha Arouali described her experiences in the underground film by Jacques Panijel, *Octobre à Paris* ('October in Paris'), which was shot with the help of the FLN in the Paris suburbs between November 1961 and February 1962. This film aimed to give voice to Algerians.[57] In Ali Akika's documentary, when Aïcha revisits her testimony in Panijel's film, her mood changes from one of nervous laughter in recounting what happened to tears, as Aïcha expressed "It's moving [...] these are quite difficult memories."

This film presents a more complex approach to the question of memory and testimony. It is part of a wider development of the period since the Papon-Einaudi trial of 1999, as greater societal credence relating to the violence in Paris in October 1961 meant that the emphasis on the need for campaigners to mobilize "proof" diminished, although such campaigns have not entirely disappeared. This process illustrates Paul Ricœur's observations on the multiple uses which testimony can serve.[58] Memory campaigners had successfully created a "space" within which Algerians' memories of October 17 could be heard in their divergence and sometimes contradictions, and were therefore not explicitly linked to their status as counter-narratives.[59] This development partially re-centered the debates away from a focus on Papon and the police and more on the Algerian demonstrators, their memories, migratory trajectories and the considerable complexity of Algerians' wartime experiences.

These developments since the late 1990s may well also have been linked to the greater time lapse—both from the event and the subsequent waves of memorial testimonies of that event—that brings with it, "more reflection, analysis, surfacing of connections," as victim groups become aware of the testimonies of others and situate themselves within a wider framework.[60] There is therefore both a quantitative and a qualitative transformation underway regarding these memorial dynamics. This ongoing process is all the more complex given that many descendants of Algerian migrants, from adolescents to those in their forties, are currently engaged in memorial projects or historical studies relating to the October 1961 repression. Such people provide a further context for Algerians to share the experiences, and their work provides a "layering" of memorial voices.[61]

Conclusion

Alongside the regained visibility in French public consciousness of the October 1961 repression, and the greater possibilities for "hearing" what Algerians have to say about their experiences, is a less reassuring issue. Post-colonial power relations continue to weigh upon many Algerians' willingness to come forward to speak in the French national media or political arena, or even within a family context, just as the post-colonial situation influences the conditions of reception of such memories by their descendants.[62] Feelings of marginality and vulnerability persist within the Algerian wartime generation. As we have seen, silence in relation to police violence can be left behind at different levels (family, semi-public contexts, local, national), at different moments, and for different reasons. The types of disclosures have varied. The social and political contexts in and between France and Algeria influence these developments, which are closely associated with the wider memorial landscape of the Algerian war and its many competing memories. In many respects, the history of the memories of October 1961 represents in microcosmic form the tensions and dynamics of the post-colonial condition of Algerian migration, a condition in which the figure of the Algerian war continues to play a significant if only partially understood role.

Notes

1.   See Jim House and Neil MacMaster, *Paris 1961: Algerians, State Terror, and Memory* (Oxford: Oxford University Press, 2006); Linda Amiri, *La Bataille de France : la guerre d'Algérie en métropole* (Paris: Robert Laffont, 2004).
2.   See House and MacMaster, *Paris 1961*, chapters 4-8. The term "October 1961" will be used as shorthand in this chapter to refer to the peak of this violence dur-

ing September-October 1961. However, given the memorial and historiographical focus on the 17 October 1961 demonstrations themselves and their repression, most of the discussion focuses on the demonstrations of 17 October 1961, and this specific date is indicated wherever possible.

3.   See Alain Dewerpe, *Charonne 8 février 1962. Anthropologie historique d'un massacre d'Etat* (Paris: Gallimard, 2006).

4.   See Stéphane Gacon, *L'Amnistie: de la Commune à la guerre d'Algérie* (Paris: Seuil, 2002), 255-296.

5.   Gilbert Meynier, *Histoire intérieure du FLN, 1954-1962* (Paris: Fayard, 2002), 659-676.

6.   Luisa Passerini, "Memories between Silence and Oblivion," in *Contested Pasts: The Politics of Memory,* ed. Katharine Hodgkin and Susannah Radstone (London: Routledge, 2003), 238-254, 249.

7.   See James Fentress and Chris Wickham, *Social Memory,* (Oxford: Blackwell, 1992); Paul Ricœur, *La Mémoire, l'histoire, l'oubli* (Paris: Seuil, 2000).

8.   Hodgkin and Radstone, ed., *Contested Pasts.*

9.   Maurice Halbwachs, *Les Cadres sociaux de la mémoire* (Paris: Albin Michel, 1925/1994); *La Mémoire collective* (Paris: Albin Michel, 1950/1997).

10.   See Paul A. Silverstein, *Algeria in France : Transpolitics, Race and Nation* (Bloomington and Indianapolis: Indiana University Press, 2004).

11.   On Algerian migration in France at this time, see Neil MacMaster, *Colonial Migrants and Racism: Algerians in France, 1900-62* (Basingstoke: Macmillan, 1997), chapter 11.

12.   Interview, Aubervilliers, 15 October 2002. To protect anonymity, the first names only of some interviewees are given. All interviews were conducted by the author (in French).

13.   Interview with Muhammed, a Moroccan living in one of the suburban Nanterre shantytowns in 1961 (Paris, 19 February 2002).

14.   Gilles Manceron and Hassan Remaoun, *D'une rive à l'autre : la guerre d'Algérie de la mémoire à l'histoire,* (Paris: Syros, 1993); Benjamin Stora, *La Gangrène et l'oubli* (Paris: La Découverte), 200-202, 206-208, 261-265.

15.   La Lanterne / Images Plus, 2000 (Forum des images, Paris, VDP20998). On the Nanterre shantytowns during the late-war period, see Monique Hervo, *Chroniques du bidonville : Nanterre en guerre d'Algérie, 1959-1962* (Paris: Seuil, 2001).

16.   Interview with Farid Aïchoune, Paris, 7 June 2002.

17.   Abdelmalek Sayad, *La Double absence : des illusions de l'émigré aux souffrances de l'immigré* (Paris: Seuil, 1999). For a striking literary evocation of this theme, see Rachid Boudjedra's novel *Topographie idéale pour une agression caractérisée* (Paris: Denoël, 1975).

18.   Raphaëlle Branche, *La Torture et l'armée pendant la guerre d'Algérie 1954-1962* (Paris: Seuil, 2001), 331-334.

19.   Sayad, *La Double absence,* 257-303, "La maladie, la souffrance et le corps" (first published 1981).

20.   Interview with Farid Aïchoune, Paris, 7 June 2002. The cultural transformations undergone by migrants over the years may well have eroded the possible effects of this invocation, by encouraging Algerians to make symbolic demands relating to past violence as part of a general trend within French and other societies.

21.   Interview with Saad Abssi, Gennevilliers, 18 April 2003. Saad Abssi was a senior FLN cadre in Paris and Lyon during the war.

22.   Interview, Lille, 6 April 2001.

23.   Interview, Paris, 22 October 2002.

24. See Marguerite Feitlowitz, *A Lexicon of Terror: Argentina and the Legacies of Torture* (New York and Oxford: Oxford University Press, 1998).

25. Interview with Muhammed, who still suffers back pains from brutalization during security force raids in the suburban Paris shantytown where he was living·in 1961 (Paris, 19 February 2002). The term "bodily memory" comes from Kristin Ross, *May '68 and its Afterlives* (Chicago and London: Chicago University Press, 2002), 34.

26. Jim House, "Contrôle, encadrement, surveillance et répression des migrations coloniales: une décolonisation difficile (1956-1970)," *Bulletin de l'Institut d'histoire du temps présent*, 83 (premier semestre) :144-56.

27. Interview, Sarcelles, 6 December 2005.

28. Interview, Aubervilliers, 15 October 2002.

29. Annette Wieviorka, *L'Ere du témoin* (Paris: Hachette, 2002).

30. Fentress & Wickham, *Social Memory*, 122.

31. Interview, Aubervilliers, 15 October 2002.

32. Michael Pollak, "La Gestion de l'indicible," *Actes de la recherche en sciences sociales*, 62 (3): 30-53, 51.

33. See the dossiers in *L'Algérien en Europe*, 111 (13-29 October 1970): 5-15; 134 (11-26 October 1971): 4-17; 156 (1-15 October 1972): 5-10.

34. On the MTA, see Rabah Aissaoui, "Le Mouvement des travailleurs arabes: Ethnicity, Antiracism and Political Mobilization amongst Maghrebi Immigrants during the 1970s in France," in *Shifting Frontiers of France and Francophonie*, ed. Yvette Rocheron and Christopher Rolfe (Oxford: Peter Lang, 2004), 115-133.

35. I am grateful to Raphaëlle Branche for discussions on this term.

36. Mimoun Hallous, "Les grandes heures du Mouvement des travailleurs arabes," in *Douce France : la saga du mouvement beur 1983-1993*, ed. Ahmed Boubeker and Mogniss H. Abdallah (Paris: Im'Média, 1993) 80-82.

37. On these antiracist movements of the early-mid 1980s, see Saïd Bouamama, *Dix ans de marche des beurs : chronique d'un mouvement avorté* (Paris: Desclée de Brouwer, 1994). ·

38. Jim House, "Antiracist Memories: the case of 17 October 1961 in historical perspective," *Modern and Contemporary France*, 9, 3 (August 2001): 355-68. See also House & MacMaster, *Paris 1961*, chapters 10 and 11.

39. Fentress & Wickham, 117.

40. Interview, Marseille, 27 February 2002.

41. Interview, Paris, 14 October 2002.

42. On this repression, see Abdel Aïssou, ed., *Octobre à Alger* (Paris: Seuil, 1988).

43. Interview with Khaled, Aubervilliers, 9 December 2005.

44. *Mass Atrocity : Collective Memory and the Law* (New Brunswick, N.J. and London: Transaction Publishers, 2000), 270.

45. Karen Slawner, "Interpreting Victim Testimony: Survivor Discourse and the Narration of History," 2004, article available at http://yendor.com/vanished/karenhead. html (accessed 26 March 2007).

46. See Richard J. Golsan, ed. *The Papon Affair: Memory and Justice on Trial* (London: Routledge, 2000).

47. Octobre 1961 : pour la vérité, enfin," *Le Monde*, 20 May 1998.

48. See Jean-Luc Einaudi, *Octobre1961 : un massacre à Paris* (Paris: Fayard, 2001),177-178. Einaudi's first book on October 1961 was *La Bataille de Paris, 17 octobre 1961* (Paris: Seuil, 1991).

49. Interview, Aubervilliers, 15 October 2002.

50. See House & MacMaster, *Paris 1961*, 48-60.

51.   Interview, Aubervilliers, 9 December 2005.
52.   Interview, Sarcelles, 6 December 2005.
53.   Interview, Sarcelles, 6 December 2005.
54.   Silverstein, *Algeria in France*, 154: David Lepoutre and Isabelle Cannoodt, *Souvenirs de familles immigrées* (Paris: Odile Jacob, 2005), 13-14, 295.
55.   Interview, Sarcelles, 6 December 2005.
56.   See footnote 15.
57.   Interview with Jacques Panijel, Paris, 21 February 2002.
58.   Ricœur, *La Mémoire, l'histoire, l'oubli.* , 201-8.
59.   See the Internet site of the campaigning association "17 October 1961 against forgetting" (*Le 17 octobre 1961 contre l'oubli*): http://17octobre1961.free.fr/pages/Temoin-Docu.htm (accessed 27 March 2007). See also Olivier Le Cour Grandmaison, ed., *Le 17 octobre 1961 : un crime d'Etat à Paris* (Paris: La Dispute, 2001).
60.   Feitlowitz, 78.
61.   See Elizabeth Jelin and Susana G. Kaufman, "Layers of Memories: Twenty Years After in Argentina," in Timothy G. Ashplant, Graham Dawson, and Michael Rooper, ed. *The Politics of War Memory and Commemoration* (London: Routledge, 2000), 89-110.
62.   Abdellali Hajjat, *Immigration postcoloniale et mémoire* (Paris: L'Harmattan, 2005).

Part III

The Transmission and Distortion of Memory

8

"Privatized Memory?" The Story of Erecting the First Holocaust Memorial in Budapest

Andrea Pető

The political transition of 1989 in Hungary brought up competing versions or interpretations of the very same event: for instance, people asked whether the country had been liberated from Nazi Germany or occupied by the Red Army in 1945. In this chapter I analyze a case that illustrates this point: the lack of a reconciliation strategy and the controversial operation of the people's courts or tribunals in the aftermath of the war, which contributed to a divided collective memory about the Holocaust in Hungary. As Larry May has argued, "if reconciliation cannot be achieved (…) the very possibility of a stable court system, the hallmark of the rule of law, is jeopardized."[1] (That is one of the reasons why the post-1989 conservative turn in historiography was questioned by survivors, perpetrators, and bystanders who questioned the legitimacy of post-1945 lustration as a transition to the rule of law.)

The other reasons why the memory of the Holocaust is divided in Hungary and why the responsibility of "ordinary" Hungarians has never been assumed and talked about widely, are related to the manner in which post-war lustration was carried out. The legal framework, strictly regulated by the act of law relating to the people's tribunals as well as the penal code, made it possible for perpetrators (those who were identified by the jurisdictional mechanisms) to get away with their crimes with impunity—either by legal means (with the assistance of lawyers) or by other means (such as threats and blackmailing).[2]

For post-Holocaust Hungary, May's argument is also valid: "Trials are not the only possible remedies for group-based harm. Other reconciliatory strategies will provide what victims are owed, and also sometimes better exemplify the principle of equity that is crucial, especially for crimes that involve large segments of the population as both victims and perpetrators."[3] In this chapter I use the case of the war crimes committed at Csengery Street No. 64 in the Sixth District of Budapest to trace how the possible interpretations of post-Holocaust transitional justice were formed. An important point is that this case led to the erection of the first privately funded Holocaust memorial in Budapest. Therefore we need to explain why "private" memories failed to intersect with collective memory of the Holocaust.

The Case

In mid-October 1944, it was exceptionally warm in Budapest. "It was nice, jacket weather" as one of the eyewitnesses told me in an interview.[4] Since March 19, 1944, Hungary had been under German occupation as a "reluctant ally." The quickest and the most effective deportation in the history of the Holocaust was already underway: 500,000 Jews were deported just in a few months.[5] The Horthy regime was already concerned about the rapid advance of the Soviet troops and Romania's successful armistice with the Allied Forces. Thus, in a radio broadcast, Horthy announced an armistice on October 15, 1944. By that time, Budapest's Jewish citizens had been "gathered together" into houses marked by the Star of David or into the ghetto ready for deportation.[6]

On October 15, 1944, at Csengery 64, in the center of Budapest, in one of the houses marked by the Star of David, the Jewish residents were listening, in the courtyard, to the radio of the non-Jewish concierge. The concierge had graciously put the radio into his open window, because Jews were not allowed to own a radio. This house was very close to the headquarters of the Arrow Cross party, the Hungarian Nazi party, on Andrássy Avenue. When the declaration of armistice by Horthy was broadcast, the inhabitants of Csengery 64 reacted positively. For the first time in many long months, the Jewish tenants hoped that their sufferings might be over and that their male relatives, who were on forced labor service, might soon return home. People in the neighboring houses had started to remove the yellow stars from their buildings. The Jewish male tenants who had gathered in the courtyard (who were either very young or too old or unfit for forced labor service) decided that they should keep guard at the gate during the coming night. They suspected that the Hungarian Nazis, the Arrow Cross, would prevent Hungary from making peace with the communist Soviet Union and would do their utmost to seize power.[7] Subsequent events proved their suspicions to be well founded. Later that same day the occupying German troops forced Horthy to appoint Szalasi, the head of the Arrow Cross party, as prime minister. He then ordered Hungarian soldiers to continue the obviously hopeless fight against the Red Army.

There are four reasons why the events at Csengery 64 on October 15, 1944, are important to our analysis of how the different actors and institutions shaped the memory of this traumatic event of the Holocaust in subsequent decades. First, during the night of October 15, the apartment building was looted by the Arrow Cross and SS troops; 18 tenants were massacred in their own apartments. Even the survivors explained how there had been a shot before the looters got into the house, thereby constructing an alibi: there was a shot, so they needed to get in to restore order. Even in the midst of illegal conditions there was a half-hearted attempt to act "legally."[8] Although it was wartime, this massacre was regarded as an extraordinary event. Hungarian police willingly assisted the Germans in transporting Hungarian Jews outside the country, but murdering Jews, mostly elderly men and women, in their own apartments in the center of Budapest was not acceptable. Consequently, a Hungarian police investigation team was sent to Csengery 64 with the task of assuring the inhabitants that this massacre was a single and unauthorized private "action."[9]

Second, the armed group which committed the massacre was allegedly led by a woman, Piroska Dely, who after a high-profile people's court case was sentenced to death in the late spring of 1945. Very few women were sentenced to death as war criminals in Hungary, and Dely's case at the people's court was one of the first. We know very little about the gender dimension of World War II history in countries collaborating with Nazi Germany, so an analysis of this case will contribute to a gendering of historical memory of the events. Third, the survivors of this massacre erected the first "private" Holocaust monument, a marble plaque in Budapest, marking the location of the massacre.

Fourth, I was able to conduct interviews with the survivors about their present struggle to keep this plaque at its original site. Together with the people's court transcripts and the press coverage, this offers unique source material with which to analyze memory and trauma.

The People's Court and the Memory of Survivors

In the post-Holocaust period, the definition of democratic values and the task of determining such values were to be undertaken by the people's tribunals, or courts (among other bodies). Ernst Cassirer, writing about post-war reconstruction, says that only constitutions "written into citizens' minds" can work.[10] In Europe and later in Japan, it was the task of the tribunals examining war crimes to define these crimes with the available legal instruments, to punish those who were guilty, and to show norms and values in the post-Holocaust world through education and information. In Hungary the basis of post-Holocaust jurisdiction, the 1945 act on people's tribunals, was thrown together in a hurried manner. For this reason, it was a controversial act—and it was also criticized on legal and political grounds.[11] Historians evaluating transitional justice in Hungary have made two critical legal and political arguments concerning the activity of the people's courts.

The legal argument states that it is illegal to apply retroactive justice in a legal system, but underlines the international pressure—coming from outside the Hungarian legal tradition—to introduce retroactive justice: the Soviet Army was stationed in Hungary at the time. Another legal argument points out that the non-professional court (with one professional judge and five civil appointees from five political parties) was alien to the Hungarian legal tradition. The critical political arguments consider that the tribunals were instrumentalized by the Communist party in their struggle for power (1945-1947) and offered ways out for "minor members of the Arrow Cross." The consensual narrative (right and left) evaluating the activity of the people's tribunals agrees that they served as a weapon in the class struggle and that they existed outside the Hungarian legal framework because they were introduced under retroactive legislation.

The people's tribunals were greatly influenced by the Hungarian Communist party, which was in charge of the Ministry of Interior during the coalition government. A vital interest was to undermine publicly the previous Horthy regime and to place responsibility for the defeat in war onto the Arrow Cross party.[12] Hungary's social and political climate in 1945 was very different from that of subsequent years. The 1945 act on people's tribunals was a rough sketch; the newly appointed judges, who lacked experience, had to interpret it. Court cases were undertaken quickly and sometimes without thorough investigation—which was impossible in the immediate aftermath of the war. The main aim was to prevent people from taking the law into their own hands. Moreover, the semblance of legality was needed after the cataclysm of the war. Somewhat later, new laws were passed to regulate the function of people's tribunals more strictly as the postwar situation was consolidated and the political climate hardened due to the Cold War: Act VII of 1946 was followed by Act XXXIV of 1947, which regulated the proceedings.[13]

The process of regulative justice was overshadowed by the Soviet occupation of Hungary; indeed, it served as a starting point for the Sovietization of the country's judicial system. The critics of postwar lustration placed the people's tribunals outside the legal framework, labeling the whole process as "Stalinist justizmord" while ignoring the crimes that needed to be punished. The individualized focus of the procedure offers different modes and frames of explanation: the myriads of details emerging during a trial offer several points for questioning the "justice of the justice system" to paraphrase Michael Walzer's term of the "justice of war." The lustration system was instrumentalized, which left all actors feeling wounded and convinced that their case had been handled unjustly.

The court, all of whose members were men, judged women for their alleged war crimes. In this way, the people's tribunal also served as a corrective force capable of restructuring the gender hierarchy, the "matriarchy born in need" after World War II.[14] As far as female perpetrators were concerned, the gender politics of the court was to punish those women who were active members of the Arrow Cross party: even if they did not commit murder, their political consciousness needed to be broken. Female defendants receiving milder sentence were those who argued that they had been powerless victims acting under the orders of men.

The trial of Piroska Dely was one of the first people's court trials in Budapest; it began on March 13, 1945. The first case had been launched on February 4; it ended with the public execution of two male war criminals for mass murder.[15] Until September 16, 1945, the activity of the people's court was regulated by decrees. The trial of Piroska Dely, who was accused of participating in the massacre at Csengery 64, began as a "normal" criminal case. One of the surviving victims of another looting that took place on the same night in the adjacent Hársfa Street, recognized Ms. Dely on the street, followed her to her home, and then reported her in a neatly handwritten letter to the police—which has been preserved in the Historical Archive of the Municipality of Budapest. The battles between the Germans and the Red Army raged on in the western part of Hungary until early April, but Piroska Dely was convicted of burglary in March 1945.

The civil courage and initiative of the surviving victim, however, changed the course of the events. Piroska Dely became a widely known symbol of female war crime perpetrators in Hungary. Perpetrators, when planning their acts, always assume that no witnesses will remain alive. But Andor L., who lived at Csengery 64, returned from deportation.[16] During the looting and massacre at Csengery 64 on October 15, 1944, the clear intention of the perpetrators was to eliminate all witnesses: some tenants were killed on the spot, while others were gathered in the courtyard and forced to march to the nearby police station for interrogation and possible deportation to the death camps. The perpetrators of the massacre returned the same day, arresting those who had managed to conceal themselves. But some of those taken to the police station returned home safely, and even some of those deported to the death camps managed to survive. The survivors never forgot their losses, and they wanted the tragedy to be remembered.

This was the story of Andor L. On October 15 when the massacre took place, Andor L. was in forced labor service; as a result of the massacre, he lost his wife, father and son. He himself did not witness the event. He was in his late forties, an educated and successful businessman with international experience. When Andor L. returned home, he wanted to ensure that those responsible for the crimes should be punished; he did his utmost to find the perpetrators.[17] He regularly visited public sessions of the people's court, and so it happened that he went to the first court hearing of Piroska Dely. During the trial he recognized the pattern of the looting on October 15, 1944. Some of the survivors of the massacre and the subsequent deportation had told him the story, and so he submitted a report to the police, declaring that he himself was able to identify the perpetrator of another burglary as the same person who took part in the massacre at Csengery 64.[18] In the first police hearing of March 5, 1945, Andor L. gave his testimony in first person, as if he himself had been present on October 15 and as if he himself had witnessed the events. He testified that he saw Dely in an Arrow Cross uniform.[19]

This marked the beginning of the notorious Piroska Dely case; the active role of Andor L. mobilized the survivors of Csengery 64. Testimonies of the survivors recorded at the police station and later heard during the court hearing, were contradictory in several respects concerning events at Csengery 64 on October 15, 1944. There are factual differences between the testimonies recorded at the police station in March 1945 and those subsequently heard during the trial on April 25, 1945. Csengery 64 is a three-story apartment building; it lay two hundred meters from the Arrow Cross Headquarters and was marked with the Star of David. In each apartment, several families were cramped together. Thus, each of the witnesses had literally different "spatial" perspectives of what they could see and what they testified at the court.

The initial testimonies given to police did not even agree on the number and identity of the people entering the apartment building on that warm October night. Some witnesses remembered men in Arrow Cross uniform or with armbands as well as German soldiers and SS personnel (of Hungarian German extraction). The precise relationship between these armed men and Piroska Dely was also unclear. Some witnesses could not even recall the presence of a woman among the looters:

> Then I saw myself that a truck stopped, and Arrow Cross men and SS soldiers were jumping out of it together. I did not see a woman with them, which does not prove anything because perhaps she was the last to jump out. I looked at them for a second. One woman was among them. Our parents told us this.[20]

An issue raised in the testimonies was whether Dely had been wearing an Arrow Cross armband or even a uniform. The testimonies are contradictory:

> A. P: Did the Arrow Cross men wear uniform?
>
> B: Yes.
>
> A. P. And the Germans, were they also in uniform?
>
> B. I do not know.
>
> C. I have seen an armband. That is for sure.
>
> B. Yes, there was an armband. I believe they were wearing armbands. I do not think they were wearing the Arrow Cross uniform you can see in documentary movies.
>
> C. No, but they were wearing leather riding boots, with special trousers.[21]

Another witness recalled that Dely had been wearing an Arrow Cross hairband![22] It is not clear what kind of hairband she thought she saw, since such hairbands did not even exist. But the intention of the survivors was clearly to prove that Piroska Dely had been a member of the Arrow Cross party. A survivor who was ushered down to the courtyard while her only son and two sons-in-law were killed in their apartment, testified in an early hearing as follows: *"I cannot recall the misery in detail. I was in a kind of unconscious state of mind."*[23] But during the next hearing she was able to give the "expected" testimony to the court. The story of the event was constructed by the survivors as a canonized narrative during the hearings. The court hearings and the discussion of the events in the house contributed to the formation of one version of the story based on the different variations of the story told by the survivors. A single version of events was constructed from the various individual testimonies, and this version was recorded in the court documents and repeated in the verdict.[24]

The most feasible scenario of the events based on the court documents is that following the report about Jews trying to protect themselves in Csengery 64 by a non-Jewish man courting the daughter of the non-Jewish housekeeper felt encouraged by the failure of Horthy's attempt to sign armistice, reported it to the nearby Arrow Cross headquarter. Piroska Dely lived nearby, at Dob utca 74, and she knew where rich Jews lived. Dely had previous experience in looting apartment buildings marked with the Star of David. In early October, she was reported to have swept up the money dropped into the courtyard by the Jewish inhabitants of a house in a neighboring street. (Her first conviction by the people's court was for this crime). Dely made use of the opportunities of this lawless period to blackmail Jewish tenants for more money. She thought the witnesses would be conveniently eliminated—either being killed on the spot or deported. As Norman Naimark has argued,[25] ethnic cleansing is always related to war; in the chaos, paramilitary units—in this case, the Arrow Cross and SS troops—become the instruments of political leaders. The role of the state and "high modernity"[26] make the targets easily identifiable.[27] A list of apartment buildings marked by yellow stars had already been compiled in order to prepare for the inhabitants' deportation. Ethnic cleansing is also associated with crimes against property, since it provides opportunities for looting.[28]

During the Dely trial there was one important political issue that needed to be resolved. It did not matter whether the witnesses recalled Arrow Cross men or SS soldiers, or both, as none of the perpetrators of the murders and the deportations, could be found after the war. The only person convicted by the people's tribunal in this case was a woman, Piroska Dely. The police was unable to arrest any of the men who actually did the shooting on October 15, 1944. Consequently, as the trial proceeded, Dely's role in the massacre received increasing emphasis. Indeed, in the end, one of the witnesses said: "What happened took place according to the will of the Arrow Cross woman. If she ordered that a person should be killed, he was taken away; if she did not want this, they did not hurt him."[29] Some witnesses like A. S. even testified at the trial that Dely had been carrying a revolver, and that she had commanded the SS troops and ordered them to shoot, and that she had done so in German.[30] We may rightly ask how a 28-year-old nurse with no military or party affiliation, who other witnesses described as a "pretty woman," was able to command a group of military men.

The "Portrait of a Beast": A Female War Criminal

During the trial and in the press coverage, Piroska Dely was portrayed as an exceptionally bloodthirsty and "unwomanly woman" who needed to be punished. The wide coverage of her case was linked with the personal quest of Andor L. and the other survivors from the house as well as the political need of the various political parties to produce quick results, thereby satisfying people's justified desire for revenge.

According to the court files, Piroska Dely (sometimes her name is spelled in the documents as Deli) was born in Jászkisér in 1913 or 1916; she had two children and an ex-husband. The court tried in vain to locate the former husband, but made no attempt to find the two children. The war was still underway and millions of people had been displaced, so the failure to locate the husband was no surprise, and subsequent files recorded him as dead. Dely worked in Budapest initially as an administrator and a factory worker and later as a nurse in the hilly Twelfth District of Budapest, where the Gestapo headquarters were situated.

Dely employed different strategies during the police interrogation. In the early interrogations, she was "stubborn" and "uncompromising." Later on, when her situation became grave, she faked heart attacks and often collapsed to make the interrogation more difficult.[31] She did not have a lawyer of her own, but one assigned to her officially, which limited her chances for a fair trial.

During the police interrogation, Dely herself also gave contradictory statements about her motivation for entering the apartment building. She said she was ordered by the SS, for whom she was working as a nurse, to act as a German translator between the SS troops and the locals. She did not seem to care that she had previously admitted that she did not speak a word of German and that the SS troops were most likely Hungarian Germans serving in the SS—who were perfectly able to speak Hungarian. She also stated during the police investigation that she met somebody on the street by accident, whose name she could not recall and who had suggested that she might get a winter coat during this action, and so she had joined in.

In the daily press, Piroska Dely was portrayed as the "Beast" of the Arrow Cross, a woman responsible for the most grave wartime massacre of civilians in Budapest. The people's tribunal exposed the image of Hungarian women, alleged members of the Arrow Cross party, who had used violence while looting. This was the first time female perpetrators were portrayed in public, and explains why, even today, the name Piroska Dely is associated with the "Women of the Arrow Cross"—even though, as I show below, she was never a member of the Arrow Cross party.

In Hungary the label "nyilas" (a member of the Hungarian Arrow Cross party) was used very freely both in the public discourse and also in the course of trials. It was very rarely the case that an Arrow Cross party card was found during a house search, so if somebody had been seen wearing an Arrow Cross armband by a witness, this was enough for the person to be identified as "a member of the Arrow Cross party" during the people's tribunals.[32] It was relatively easy to obtain an Arrow Cross armband, because neither formal membership of the party nor an admission procedure was required. Women who were regular full members of the Arrow Cross party did not serve in regular armed units. During the trials, no evidence was presented that these women had been registered members of the party. October 15, 1944 was just the beginning of the bloody Arrow Cross rule. Most of the war crimes were committed by women who were labeled in the judicial process as "Arrow Cross members" but who had not been formal members of the party. Nevertheless, they had taken advantage of the opportunity and the legitimizing umbrella of the Arrow Cross government to kill Jews and loot their property.

From the outset of the trial, Piroska Dely fiercely denied any formal affiliation to the Arrow Cross party. She testified that the Arrow Cross armband and the Arrow Cross pin were put on her jacket "quickly" and "accidentally" by an "unknown man" in front of Csengery 64. His intention had been to protect her while she entered a "Jewish house."[33] This was a very thoughtful argument; her intention was evidently to portray herself as a helpless victim with a view to receiving a milder sentence.

On February 28, 1945, Piroska Dely mentioned during the hearing that she was pregnant.[34] In her testimony, she stated the precise date of her last menstruation (December 18, 1944) and her last intercourse (December 23, 1944), thus strengthening the public's perception of her "loose morals." Her being pregnant and having two children who could not be located were reasons given for a possible pardon on April 25,

1945. This may explain why the police did not make any attempts to recover the children, because this would have weakened the argument in the eye of the public that she was a criminal. Instead of a pardon, her death sentence was merely suspended until the birth of her child.[35] The medical examination in the prison on May 8, 1945 proved that she was six months pregnant. There were some inquiries in October and again in December about whether or not she had given birth. It was only on 9 January 1946 that she was diagnosed as having a tumor rather than being pregnant.[36] Zoltán Tildy, the president of Hungary, signed the execution order on January 30, 1946.

The progression of the pregnancy was followed not only by the legal system, but also by Andor L.—who rightly did not trust in the smooth operation of the Hungarian legal system. In a letter of February 1, 1946, he informed President Tildy that Dely had been a member of the Arrow Cross party and had served in the Gestapo, ordering the murder of 18 people. In the letter, he labeled her "not a woman but a murderous beast in a human skin."[37] The execution took place on March 23, 1946.[38]

The Aftermath: The Lack of Institutionalized Commemorations

When Andor L. arrived home in February 1945 he found his apartment looted and his loved ones killed. His reaction was that this should not be forgotten. The commemoration in the case of Csengery 64 began with the identification of those who had been lost—a slow and tortuous process. A list of those who were massacred on October 15 was put together. One more name was added to the list: that of the father of Andor L., who had died of a heart attack in the courtyard after the massacre on learning that his wife had been taken away. He was the nineteenth victim on the list.

Andor L. decided to erect a plaque commemorating the murdered 18 tenants and his father. He removed the marble cover of his kitchen cupboard. He was worried that this type of marble, which was originally for kitchen use, would not be resistant to the weather conditions if placed outside. Having commissioned an engraver, he thus erected the marble plaque just inside the apartment building on the first anniversary of the massacre in 1945. The text of the plaque reads:

> To remember forever those who fell victim to Fascist persecution on October 15, 1945 (Then listing the 19). Your sacrificial death shows us how to proceed in building a free and happy Hungary. The inhabitants of the house.

The wording of the plaque is a product of communist discourse in the sense that it refers to the struggle between fascist and antifascist forces. A question it raises is how the death of people in such a manner can set an example to anyone. A belief in a "free and happy Hungary" was also mentioned in the text. In the autumn of 1945, when the plaque was erected, Hungary was under Soviet occupation, but of course it was not obvious then, as it is for us now, that this occupation was meant to be final by the Soviets.

Andor L. was a determined and skilful writer, and he had an extensive correspondence about the case with various institutions. He possessed a typewriter, and so was capable of doing so. In late October 1956, during the revolution, a relative of his saw signs of a return to the symbols and rhetoric of 1944. Andor L. decided to incinerate all the correspondence relating to the people's tribunal, and so none of the documents remain. The extensive documentation of his private initiative to punish those who committed crimes against his family disappeared during the Hungarian revolution of 1956.[39]

The events of that day underwent mediation in the family. The story of the events of the Holocaust was silenced by the surviving adults. It was a non-story in front of the children. As one of the survivors, who was four years old in 1944, said: "When my mother was 60-62, in the last five years of her life, then everything came out of her."[40] Although the witnesses did not read the records during the people's tribunal and such records were kept top secret until 1989, nevertheless the witnesses discussed the version of the events among themselves at home and with other family members—excluding their children. A consensual narrative about the event was thus formed in the privacy of families, an alternative subculture. In communist Hungary, antifascism was the official discourse, but there was only space for Holocaust victims as antifascists.[41] After 1989, the language of the "communist crimes" previously used as a minority discourse became that of the official discourse.[42] This was developed against the majority view and offered points of identification to those who demanded a revision of the history of the post-war jurisdiction process labeled as "show trials."[43] This type of interpretation challenged the previously existing, albeit limited, memory of the Holocaust. It was a predictable development, following the institutionalization of revisionist history writing. Csengery 64 is close to the newly opened "House of Terror" Museum at Andrássy 60, which offers a spectacularly revisionist history of Hungary, equating Nazism with Communism. The plaque at

Csengery 64 is just above the garbage containers at the entrance, not the most dignified location. The present residents of Csengery 64, most of whom moved into the "empty" apartments after 1945, wanted to remove the memorial plaque, using the upcoming reconstruction of the building as an excuse. The survivors, who were aged 5-16 at the time and who now live elsewhere realized in 2004 that the plaque was not on the list of municipally protected monuments. They asked, therefore, for its registration and protection.[44] On November 1, 2005, the chief architect of the district promised to put together a list of all plaques at some point in the near future, paying special attention to the one at Csengery 64. This means that the plaque was up there for fifty years without any permit or official acknowledgement.

As part of the commemoration to mark the 50th anniversary of the Holocaust, the local newspaper of the Sixth District published an article in May 2004 with a photo of the plaque. The article was full of factual mistakes. Indeed, nearly all the information about the number of people who were killed, deported, or who later returned was wrong. A correction had to be published in the following issue. Once again, the correction would not have been made without the intervention of the survivors. The main statement—which remained in the article even after the correction—recalled that those entering the house had been led by an "Arrow Cross woman." The murder and the looting in which Piroska Dely participated was a horrific event, even if she herself was not a member of the Arrow Cross party. But the newspaper article has a lesson for the theme of this paper: what will happen when all the survivors are gone? As one of the eyewitnesses told me, "I am the only one who is still alive from this story."[45] Are we losing "the" memory of the Holocaust because the framework of remembering is muting the experience?

Conclusions

The history of the post-1945 period is characterized by forgetting.[46] What is particularly Hungarian perhaps is the secrecy about the past—for which there are all sorts of reasons, such as the attempts of some Jews to keep their Jewishness from their children.[47] The same strategy—silence—has been applied by both perpetrators and victims.

We still do not know who collected and buried the dead after the events of October 15. Indeed, for a long time, the location of the graves of the massacred victims was unknown. Even today, there is still no full list available of those who were taken from Csengery 64. Some of the victims were not notified officially as dead, so they did not have death certificates until the 1970s, when such certificates became necessary for official reasons.[48] This was an attempt on the part of survivors to close the case and to conclude the paperwork that had not been undertaken after the war.

It was only in 2004 that the survivors ascertained that the victims had been buried at the "martyr" plot (no. 5c) in the Kerepesi Cemetery. In 1962, I. S., a daughter of one of the victims, officially requested a copy of the trial proceedings in order to prove that her relatives had been among the "victims." Her request was denied by the Ministry of Interior. It was only in 1972 that a copy of the transcript was sent to her to prove that her relatives were part of the "resistance" and that the SS troops (not mentioning at all the Arrow Cross troops) had been looking for weapons at Csengery 64. The responsible member of staff at the Ministry of Interior copied an extract from Dely's testimony in which she testified that the German troops had been collecting weapons in baskets from the apartment buildings they looted that night.[49] In this way, an obvious lie, fabricated by Dely to show that she had been acting under military orders, later provided legitimacy to the survivors' attempts to keep their relatives buried at the "martyr plot."[50] Paradoxically it was Dely who "made," through her testimony, heroic antifascist resisters out of the massacred Jewish civilians and secured for them a burial site of remembrance.

The process of remembering is always painful and difficult, influenced by changing power systems.[51] When cultural codes are uncertain—during political and social transitions, for instance—the process of remembering is even more problematic. Shared political frameworks disappear and the previous reference systems turn out to be meaningless. The family remains the only point of stability, while other networks are destroyed. In the case of the massacre of Csengery 64, "private memory" remained the only site for remembering. The people's tribunals were slow and imprecise, the Jewish leadership was indifferent, journalists were shallow and uncommitted, and Jewish Studies were not taught until recently.

During transition periods, personal stories serve as the only site of remembering and as a possible site for constructing and redefining a new political framework. But here I suggest differentiating between the term memory and recollection. Memory refers to an understanding of the past directed at the future, while recollection, or *zachor*, is the term that refers back in time to the demand to remember aspects which are not necessarily pleasant to remember. I argue that both memory and recollection should be present in constructing the historical canon, and that responsibility should be a part of the canon. If we define memory as referring to precise historical (and sometimes traumatic) events and experiences, we have to acknowledge that "memory" alone is unable to break out from the antiquarian approach to the historical canon, because it equates the past of events with *one* possible interpretation of telling what really happened. In such a case, individual memories are always those that are forgotten and silenced by the historical canon.

According to research on the historical consciousness of Germans, there are two tendencies in the formation of inter-generational recollection. One is that grandchildren stylize the life of their grandparents during the Third Reich as an era of resistance and heroism, and the other is that the country appears as a victim in family histories: a victim of war, rape, hunger, etc.[52] As a result of the failed people's tribunal trials, it seems that the formation of the memory of World War II follows similar paths in Hungary too.[53] After 1945, Jews in Hungary remained hurt, traumatized and silenced, while the perpetrators became convinced that they were victims of an unjust procedure and of "Stalinist Justizmord." With the collapse of communism in 1989, the competing versions of the history of the people's tribunals resurfaced. The legitimacy of the people's tribunals was once again questioned and muted.

The actions of Uncle Andi, as the survivors called Andor L., were in line with the suggestion by Hartman that the proper treatment of extremes requires an extreme representation.[54] But in the case of Csengery 64, Andor L's private commemoration—the erection of the first Holocaust plaque in Budapest—proved insufficient to prevent the construction of a divided and dichotomist memory of the massacre. Andor L. believed that after the war justice could be done by means of the available legal instruments, such as the People's Court. That this turned out to be an illusion is not his fault. It is now our responsibility to understand the consequences of a lack of consensual "sites of remembering" for the Holocaust victims. It is high time to do so because we need to think about alternative forms of commemoration—ones that last longer than the lifespan of survivors' "private" memories and that indicate what was "right" and what was "wrong" during the fateful final years of World War II in Hungary.

Appendix: Sources

Interviews

Interview with the eyewitnesses M. K., J. K., ZS. F.
1. 3rd March, 2005.
2. 22nd March, 2005.
3. 1st April, 2005.
4. 9th January 2007.

Archival Sources

Court case of Dely Piroska at ÁBSZTL (Historical Archive of State
   Security Services) V 48889, 17654/1949.
Érdi-Krausz, György, "Marble Plaque under the Gate" in: *Terézváros*
   2004. May and June.
Letter by eight survivors to the National Commemorations Committee
   in February 2004 (manuscript).
Letter by the chief architect, Laszlo Mihályfi on 1 November, 2005.
   ref. 696-2005 (manuscript).
MOL Hungarian National Archives (HNA) XIX-E-1-l-Tank-2000-
   1946.

Notes

1.   Larry May, *Crimes Against Humanity. A Normative Account* (Cambridge: Cam-
      bridge University Press, 2005), 238.
2.   Andrea Pető, Andrea "Népbíróság és vérvád az 1945 utáni Budapesten," (People's
      Tribunal and Blood Libel in post 1945 Budapest) *Múltunk*, 1 (2006): 41-72; and
      Andrea Pető,, "Blood Libel Cases in Post-Shoah Budapest. Conflicting Legal,
      Political and Private Discourses about the Holocaust" in *Holocaust Discourses,*
      ed. Luise Vasvari, Stephen Tottosy (Purdue University Press, forthcoming).
3.   May, *Crimes Against Humanity,* 22.
4.   Interview 1. A. I am grateful for the support I have received from the survivors
      whom I had to anonymize and I am referring to as A (male), B, C (females). They
      shared with me their correspondence, family photos, and documentation of the
      case.
5.   Randolph L. Braham, *Politics of Genocide: the Holocaust in Hungary* (New York:
      Columbia University Press, 1994); David Cesarini, ed. *Genocide and Rescue. The
      Holocaust in Hungary* (London, New York: Berg, 1997).
6.   Cole, Tim, *Holocaust City. The Making of a Jewish Ghetto* (London: Routledge,
      2003).
7.   Interview 1. A.

8. Interview 4. A.
9. Court case 34.
10. Vivian Grosswald Curran, "Racism's Past and Law's Future" *28 Vt. L. Rev.*683 (2004): 1
11. Pető, "Népbíróság," 2006.
12. Andrea Pető, Andrea, Patricia Chiantera-Stutte, "Cultures of Populism and the Political Right in Central Europe" in: CLCWeb: Comparative Literature and Culture: A WWWeb Journal Vol. 5.No. 4. (2003). http://clcwebjournal.lib.purdue.edu.
13. László Karsai, "The People's Court and Revolutionary Justice in Hungary, 1945-1946" in: Istvan Deák, Jan T. Gross, Tony Judt (eds.) *The Politics of Retribution in Europe. World War II and Its Aftermath*, (Princeton: Princeton University Press, 2000).
14. Andrea Pető, *Hungarian Women in Politics 1945-1951* (New York: Columbia University Press, 2003).
15. Ákos Major, *Népbíráskodás, forradalmi törvényesség*. (People's tribunals, revolutionary justice), (Budapest: Minerva, 1988), 123.
16. See the case of the Jews from Amsterdam in Leydesdorff, Selma, "A Shattered Silence: The Life Stories of Survivors of the Jewish Proletariat of Amsterdam" in *Memory and Totalitarianism*. International Yearbook of Oral History and Life Stories Vol. 1, ed. Luisa Passerini (Oxford: Oxford University Press, 1992), 145–165.
17. Interview 1. B.
18. Court case 127.
19. Court case 20.
20. Interview 1. B.
21. Ibid.
22. Court case 10.
23. Court case 81.
24. Andrea Pető, Klaartje Schrijvers, "The theatre of historical sources. Some methodological problems in analyzing post-WWII extreme-right movements in Belgium and in Hungary" in *Professions and Social Identity. New European Historical Research on Work, Gender and Society*, ed. Berteke Waaldijk (Pisa: Edizioni Plus, University of Pisa Press, 2006), 39-63.
25. Norman Naimark, *Fires of Hatred. Ethnic Cleansing in Twentieth Century Europe*, (Cambridge, Mass: Harvard University Press, 2001), 187-188.
26. James Scott, cited in Naimark *Fires of Hatred*, 8.
27. Naimark, *Fires of Hatred*, 8.
28. Ibid., 193.
29. Court Case: 11.
30. Court case 104.
31. Court case 7.
32. Karsai, " The People's Court."
33. Court case 42.
34. Court case 50.
35. Court case 92.
36. Court case 125.
37. HNS File 28.
38. HNA File 16.
39. Interview 3. B.
40. Interview 3. C.

41. Ferenc Erős, András Kovács, Katalin Lévai, "'How Did I Find Out that I Was a Jew?' Interviews" in *Soviet Jewish Affairs*, 17, 3 (1987): 55-66.
42. Gill Seidel, "Right-Wing discourse and Power: Exclusion and Resistance," in *The Nature of the Right. A Feminist Analyses of Order Patterns*, ed. Gill Seidel. (Amsterdam: John Benjamin Publishing Company, 1988).
43. Pető, *Hungarian Women;* Pető, Chiantera-Stutte "Cultures of Populism."
44. Letter by the survivors 2001 Letter by eight survivors to the National Commemorations Committee in February 2004 (manuscript).
45. Interview 1. C.
46. Andrea Pető, "Memory and the Narrative of Rape in Budapest and Vienna" in *Life after Death: Approaches to a Cultural and Social History of Europe*, ed. Richard Bessel, Dirk Schumann, (Cambridge: Cambridge University Press, 2003), 129-149.
47. Erős et al., "How Did I Find Out that I Was a Jew?"
48. Interview 1. C.
49. Court case 65.
50. Court case 217.
51. Andrea Pető, "Memory Unchanged. Redefinition of Identities in Post WWII Hungary," in *CEU History Department* Yearbook 1997-98, Budapest, (1999), 135-153.
52. Harald, Welzer, S. Moller, K. Tschuggnall, *'Opa war kein Nazi'. Nationalsozialismus und Holocaust im Familiengedächtnis* (Frankfurt: Fischer Verlag, 2002).
53. See another example of a People's Tribunal trial in Andrea Pető, "Népbíróság és vérvád az 1945 utáni Budapesten" (People's Tribunal and Blood Libel in post 1945 Budapest) in *Múltunk* 1 (2006): 41-72.
54. Geoffrey Hartman, *The Longest Shadow: The Aftermath of the Holocaust* (Bloomington: Indiana University Press, 1996), 157.

9

Recalling the Appalling: Mass Violence in Eastern Turkey in the Twentieth Century

Uğur Ümit Üngör

Introduction

The first half of the twentieth century, marked by the turn of multi-ethnic empires into nation states, saw unprecedented levels of mass violence in Europe. In the post-Ottoman areas and in modern Turkey, comprehensive policies of demographic engineering were carried out. The ethnic cleansing of Ottoman Muslims in the Balkans preceded that of the Ottoman Christians in Anatolia. Some regions, such as Bosnia, Palestine, and eastern Anatolia have suffered from prolonged crisis and mass violence at intervals throughout the twentieth century. While these policies have been researched relatively well, relatively little is known about their interconnectedness and even less about the perception of and responses to them by the population. Popular images of "spirals of violence" or "perennial hatred" do not convey even a rudimentary picture of the social and historical complexities of these events.

This chapter aims to address this gap by examining the history of violence in eastern Turkey using a longitudinal perspective. The main question in this exercise is why violence has persisted as a chronic problem in the same region in different moments and periods in history and under different regimes and generations. In order to delimit the scope, one area will be considered in detail: the Xerzan region in southeast Turkey. For multiple and complex reasons, from the late nineteenth to the late twentieth century this area witnessed levels of violence that were high even for eastern Turkey in general—this justifies a deeper focus on this region. This violence consisted of social banditry, diffuse everyday violence, massive state-sponsored violence, and organized political violence. The name Xerzan is not an official administrative name of the area, and this topographic designation is only used by locals. Due to the vagueness of topographic delineation and non-existence of precise demographic data it is difficult to map the human landscape of the region. The area of Xerzan is about as large as Corsica and covers parts of the contemporary southeastern Turkish provinces of Diyarbakır, Batman, Siirt, Bitlis, and Muş.

Approach and Sources

Three issues beset the study of mass violence, the problem of involvement and detachment being a starting point. The axis of tension between involvement and detachment as a general problem in academia has been dealt with in great precision and sophistication.[1] The study of violence is particularly problematic from this point of view. Many people find the topic intrinsically repulsive because of its grimness, and many react with strongly condemnatory emotions. Though only a certain amount of passion and involvement would determine a student's or scholar's choice for this topic, it requires a great deal of detachment to sift through multitudes of documents and memoirs detailing very intimate details of killing. In November 2004 Iris Chang, an author on Japanese war crimes in China, committed suicide, reportedly because she suffered depression emanating from her inability to cope with the horrors she was researching.[2] Robert J. Lifton confessed in the introduction to his book *The Nazi Doctors*: "I had nightmares about Auschwitz, sometimes involving my wife and children."[3] In the preface to his study *The Dark Side of Democracy*, Michael Mann, too, thanks his friends and family for keeping him "sane amid such a disturbing research project."[4] All in all, intensive research on violence is a distressful venture during which scholars need to heed theodicy, *Weltschmerz*, or callousness.

Practical difficulties are another major obstacle for the study of mass violence. The practices of mass violence demonstrate that even in highly bureaucratic and strictly formal situations, orders for killing are rarely passed down in written form. Most often, major decisions are taken orally and secretly, thus generating a paucity of key documents to work on. Even in cases where a wealth of material exists, historians seldom stumble over explicit formulations.[5] Social scientists face problems of another nature: for them it is practically impossible to carry out (group) experiments involving violence. It would be an absurdity to gauge respondents' physical and psychological reactions in an experiment during which respondents would physically injure or even actually kill other human beings.[6] Some social scientists have used substitute methods for research on matters related to violence,[7] whereas in group situations real-life simulations have been illuminating.[8]

These caveats are important and remind us to maintain reasonable vigilance when studying violence. However, they are aggrandized by a third problem: the politicization of the term "genocide" due to the identity politics of states. Robert Hayden has pointed out that "genocide has been a tool for building a number of nation-states that are now honorable members of the world community."[9] Obviously, political violence is also politically very sensitive. Governments that are not too happy with scholars searching for 'skeletons in the closet' often deny access to archival collections, libraries, or fieldwork. The opposite is also possible: governments may try to foster or manipulate research by funding politically useful research, by pushing for the establishment of academic chairs at home or abroad, or by offering scholarships.[10] Institutionalized memorialization and silencing of supposed or real historical victimization are also a function of this difficulty.

The documentation for this study originates from a variety of sources. The large body of primary documents kept at the archives of the Ottoman Empire and the Turkish Republic provide insight into state perspectives on the region. Scholarly work on the region is scant. Secondary sources that include information on Xerzan are heavily politicized, partisan and polemical, and need to be used with great care and source criticism. The few memoirs available are a useful addition to the archival materials. In their case too, the disclaimer of source criticism remains of paramount importance as they are often ridden with apologia. All reservations aside, this plurality of sources makes possible for a methodology that can provide a multi-perspective, comprehensive account of the history and the ways used to represent the past.

The study of memory proves a valuable addition to conventional historical methods as oral history is a useful and complementary method to unearth the voices hitherto unheard or silenced. However, it has its restrictions as victims of violence often repress their memories or have skewed perceptions and interpretations of the violence they endured.[11] Interviewing perpetrators of violence has been at least as difficult due to respondents' reluctance to speak out on a subject they know is morally condemning and will implicate them.[12] Moreover, building up trust requires quite some time and furthermore, in patriarchal communities, it is difficult for men to interview women. For this study, I conducted in-depth interviews with three male respondents from different occupational and ethnic backgrounds. They include a Turkish computer engineer who served in the region during the civil war between the Turkish army and the Kurdish guerrillas, a Syriac school teacher who lived in the region during his childhood and later migrated to Sweden, and a Kurdish tile merchant who lived in the region until his adolescence and later moved to Istanbul. Their common feature is that they all have strong memories pertaining to violence in the Xerzan region. The interviews were conducted in the homes of the respondents in 2002, 2004, and 2006, and recorded with their consent. Alongside these, published interviews will also be utilized.

Searching for Multiple Interpretive Contexts

In order to understand and explain mass violence, the importance of interpretive contexts cannot be overestimated. In the case of violence in Turkey, the events are wrapped up in at least three layers of context, each autonomous and complex in itself, but nevertheless nested like a Matrushka doll. The first context brings to the foreground the broad current of world history, in particular twentieth-century history. Second, there is the ebb and flow of the nascence of a Turkish nation state, roughly in the first half of that century. The third context is provided by the long-term relationship between the Kurds and the Ottoman government. Let us begin with the first layer of context, so to speak, the largest of the Matrushka dolls.

"The twentieth century," Giddens solemnly reminds us, "is a bloody and frightening one."[13] Not without reason, scholars have dubbed the twentieth century the "century of genocide"[14] Others have characterized the twentieth century as "the century of the camps."[15] Specifically, the first half of twentieth-century world history was marked by a tremendous body count resulting from wars and genocidal violence. Already in 1954, Raymond Aron recognized that the violence in this period was different from any other before. According to Aron, the new wars were "total" due to their unprecedented application of propaganda and use of bureaucracy.[16] In a lucid article Ian Kershaw paraphrases this interpretation:

[H]owever pessimistically we look back on world history in recent decades, it is plain that the ultra-violence that characterised the first half of the century had no equivalent in the second half, though the later decades could still witness the horrific episodes of violence in, for example, the Chinese Cultural Revolution, Khmer Rouge Cambodia or Rwanda. This first half of the century—or, more precisely, the years 1914 to 1950 that spanned the period from the beginning of the First World War to the end of the Second World War, embracing also its immediate aftermath, when high levels of violence against civilian populations with the resulting misery of millions continued—has indeed claim, more surely than any other period in history, to be labelled 'the era of violence'. That is to say: in these four decades of the twentieth century, violence had *epochal* character; it determined the age.[17]

Micha Brumlik identifies three fundamental aspects of this "epochal character": first, the industrial killing of non-combatants; second, the establishment of lawless enclaves embodied in concentration camps, and third, the politically motivated deportation and expulsion of indigenous peoples.[18] Aly agrees with this notion and notes about deportations: "There was nothing taboo about the forcible resettlement of population groups and entire peoples in the first half of the twentieth century. [...] Resettlement programmes were routinely justified by reference to economic and ideological arguments."[19] Hans-Lukas Kieser compares the intellectual roots of the willingness and legitimation of violence among Turkish and German intellectual and political elites in this epoch. He points out that it was especially World War I that severely brutalized the respective political cultures.[20] All in all, the period 1900-1950 merits special attention from the point of violence studies.

The second layer of context arises from the Turkish process of nation state formation, when, in the same era indicated in the above periodization, the multi-ethnic Ottoman Empire was replaced with the Turkish Republic. This revolutionary transition to a new order was managed by a generation of Turkish nationalists, and was by no means a peaceful one.[21] An incomplete list of the violent and less violent campaigns in this era would include: the 1909 Adana massacre, the violent expulsion of Balkan Muslims throughout the 1910s and 1920s, the anti-Bulgarian and anti-Greek boycotts and state terror of 1914, the 1915 deportation and genocide of Armenians and Syriacs, the 1916 crackdown on Arab-nationalist and Zionist groups, the 1921 Koçgiri massacre of Alevi Kurds, the 1920-21 Pontus massacres, the 1923 population exchange between Greece and Turkey, the 1925 massacres and deportations of Kurds, the 1934 anti-Jewish pogrom in Thrace, the 1938 massacres and deportations of Dersim, the 1942-44 persecutions and deportations of non-Muslims, and the pogrom against Greeks and Armenians in Istanbul on 5-6 September 1955.

Together, the violence and counterviolence cost millions of people of all walks of life their lives and livelihoods. Listed one by one in this "bookkeeping of death," these campaigns may seem incidental and isolated events, sudden explosions neatly encapsulated in time and space, but a closer look reveals clear ideological, motivational, and organic links and interdependencies between them. Given the status quo of isolated case studies, a broader historical-sociological contextualization seems a challenge. Were it not for the fact that almost all of these episodes of mass violence took place under Young Turk rule, the breadth and difference between each singular event would seem to preclude any interconnections. The continuity of the violence in the Turkish twentieth century is an understudied theme. This may be considered surprising, since the political and ideological continuity of the elites and its social manifestations has merited a significant amount of attention.

The longitudinal study of the history of a given society or area is a legitimate method of examining and unearthing patterns of any social phenomenon. For example, in a trailblazing analysis of modern Turkish history, Erik-Jan Zürcher convincingly emphasized the ideological and organic continuity of the Turkish-nationalist political elite in the era 1908-1950.[22] Zürcher's longitudinal study concentrates on one theme, namely that of political leadership. Although 1923 had been interpreted as a turning point in Ottoman-Turkish history, Zürcher's alternative interpretation stresses the continuity of the political elite in the period 1910-1940. Explicitly longitudinal research on the Kurds in Turkey has yet to be conducted. This is where our third layer of context sinks into place: the centuries-old relationship between the Kurds and the Ottoman state.

Since its incorporation of a large part of Kurdistan, the Ottoman Empire governed this area by proxy: Kurdish princes in charge of emirates were granted a degree of autonomy within the empire. The degree of autonomy of these emirates varied greatly and depended mostly on their geo-political significance. To a large degree, the emirates functioned as a state within a state, since they sustained their own monopoly of violence.[23] When the emirates were violently disbanded by the Ottoman state after the Tanzimat decree of 1839, it caused a disintegration of these organizational pyramids of "violence management." Large tribes residing under one chieftain broke up into a large number of smaller tribes battling each other for regional supremacy. This deconcentration and decentralization of violence led to the diffuse, anarchic use of violence, with its many vectors pointing in many different directions. This was the situation at the beginning of the twentieth century.

Xerzan in the Late Nineteenth Century

In the Ottoman system, one's religious affiliation was the most important marker of identity. Thus, precise ethnic identifications of Ottoman subjects are difficult to ascertain. It is possible to state that the Xerzan region was populated by Kurds, Armenians, Syriacs, Arabs, Yezidis, and Turks, and that it was populated by Muslims, Christians, and Yezidis—either categorization in numerically declining order. Whereas some Xerzan Kurds were adherents to one or another tribe and were semi-nomadic, others were poor peasants and paid tribute and taxes to the emirate. Most Armenians in the region were poor peasants and some migrated to urban areas to work.[24] Syriacs and Arabs lived in villages and small towns such as Hasankeyf and Beşiri. Ottoman civil administrators numbered no more than a few dozen in the small towns.

When the last Kurdish emirate was finally violently disbanded in 1847,[25] the strongest of the Kurdish tribes of Xerzan began competing among each other for power, prestige, and possessions. This involved open warfare between tribes including occasional forays into each other's villages. Murder of non-combatants was not allowed in the code of honor. One name that repeatedly appears in Ottoman state documents is the Pencînaran tribe. Its chieftain Yaşar became notorious for robbing and murdering his tribal enemies at will. After having served a prison sentence, he tracked down the police officer that had arrested him and murdered him.[26] The audacity of this act conveys his belief in his ability to resist government forces.

The Ottoman government responses to the tribal violence were by no means pacifistic. It tried to cope with the situation by reinforcing its authority in the region through sending extra gendarmes.[27] When tribesmen warred among themselves, it ordered a military operation to pacify the area.[28] The government stepped up its campaign to end banditry and tribal warfare in the region by ordering the arrest of all chieftains involved in brigandage. Negligent officials were arrested.[29]

One of the social mechanisms that rendered tribal conflicts in Xerzan enduring was the inheritance of the title of chieftain, and the accompanying responsibility to manage violence according to the tribal code of honor. In preparation for succession to the "throne," Kurdish chieftains would narrate past and present feuds to their sons and instruct them about the conduct of warfare. When Yaşar passed away, his two sons, Bişar and Cemîl, succeeded to the title of Pencînaran chieftain and literally and figuratively became brothers-in-arms. Under their rule, violence continued unabated as they wreaked havoc in the region, waging war with the Elîkan tribe.[30] This conflict grew out of the Elîkan's expanding domination in certain areas around Xerzan.[31] The government failed to capture Bişar and Cemîl due to the reluctance of gendarmes and soldiers, who feared the men and refused to pursue them into their home territory.[32] The feud between the Elîkan and Pencînaran tribes lasted for two decades and was a major source of violence in Xerzan.[33] The war was immortalized in a long lament (kilam), memorized and sung by Kurdish folk singers such as Dengbêj Şakiro, Karapetê Xaço, and Dengbêj Reşo. This way memory was transmitted and disseminated among a wider audience in Xerzan, well into the twentieth century.

According to a proverb, "when elephants fight, the grass gets trampled." Powerless peasants, whether Kurdish Muslims or Armenian Christians, suffered as a result of tribal warfare. In the late nineteenth century, several notorious chieftains held dominion over their part of Xerzan and also over the population. Their autocratic rule created conditions in which extortion and oppression of villagers was commonplace. The relationship between Kurdish tribesmen and Armenian peasants in particular was dominated by the illegal taxing of the Armenians. This tax was called "hafir" and ensured the Armenians of Kurdish protection and patronage—somewhat similar to nineteenth-century mafia practices in the Italian Mezzogiorno.[34] For example, an Ottoman government document reveals that "for a long time Bişarê Çeto has been forcibly collecting money from the Armenian and Syriac and Kurdish population of Xerzan." The government stood powerless in the face of the chieftain, who was so influential he forced a commission of villagers to petition the local government about his innocence.[35] Due to governmental inaction, Armenian guerrillas (fedais) exacted revenge by attacking the Pencînaran tribesmen, whom they considered equally oppressive. The government strove to prosecute the culprits and ordered them "delivered dead or alive."[36] The tribesmen took justice in their own hands and organized retaliatory violence, whereupon Armenian guerillas responded by developing a strategy of assassinating chieftains.[37]

Between the 1908 liberal revolution and the 1913 Young Turk coup d'état, the Ottoman government tried to solve the problem of violence between Armenians and Kurds in Xerzan by prosecuting those responsible.[38] However, neither illegal taxing nor violence decreased. The government officially prohibited the practice of illegal taxing only in November 1909.[39] In 1914, the situation reached a boiling point in the Sason area when "Armenians had to leave their villages because of oppression by the Kurds."[40] The brothers Bişar and Cemîl were still involved in extortion; because of the outbreak of World War I legal action was suspended and they evaded prosecution yet again.[41]

The break-up of the Kurdish emirates and the formation of multiple, smaller pockets of violence was one of the factors that influenced the rise of Armenian nationalism in the Ottoman Empire. "Modern" ideas about national sovereignty and independence emanating from the French Revolution, found their way into Armenian communities living in the Russian and Ottoman empires through translation and foreign missionaries.[42] Armenian nationalists argued that Armenian villagers were taxed by both the Ottoman state and Kurdish chieftains, and that violence was a legitimate method of defense. Traumatized by Greek and Bulgarian nationalist separatism, the Ottoman government was highly suspicious of these activities.[43] The conflict between Kurdish tribes and Armenian revolutionaries thus exacerbated into an Armenian-Ottoman conflict as a conflict between a minority and the state.[44]

In order to control the imperial periphery more efficiently and to stop Armenian nationalism from becoming a serious separatist threat, Abdulhamid II (1842-1918) organized a group of regiments manned by Kurdish tribesmen.[45] When the Armenian peasants of Sason, encouraged by nationalist agitators such as Hampartsoum Boyadjian and Damadian, resisted the depredations by resorting to violence in August 1894, they were set upon by regular troops and Hamidiye regiments. The ensuing battle and massacre cost the lives of thousands of Sason Armenians.[46] The breakdown of the Kurdish emirates, the rise of Armenian nationalism, the presence of foreign missionaries, and the Ottoman state response were all ingredients that contributed to the warlike atmosphere that prevailed in Xerzan at the beginning of World War I.

Xerzan in the Age of Violence, 1913-1950

During World War I, the Xerzan region was not a battlefront, even though the Russian army occupied the cities of Bitlis and Muş. Many men of all ethnic groups dodged the draft and retreated into the inaccessible mountain ranges. The war did not preclude the continuation of previous conditions of insecurity and instability. During the war, the Young Turk government intensified its persecution of Armenians. In May 1915 the government ordered the deportation of all Armenians to the Syrian desert, but by the summer of that year, the deportation had escalated into genocidal destruction. Xerzan was under the jurisdiction of Diyarbekir province, governed by the violent Dr. Mehmed Reşid (1873-1919). He organized the murder of the entire Armenian elite of Diyarbekir city on 25 May 1915 on the banks of the Tigris River, in the part of Xerzan where the Raman tribe ruled. The tribesmen assisted the killing squads in the massacre in return for booty. Due to his refusal to collaborate, the mayor of the small town of Beşiri, Sabit Al-Suwayydi was assassinated by Dr. Reşid. Then, special forces and gendarmes razed the Xerzan plateau, massacring and burning dozens of Armenian villages and shooting, hacking, and burning alive the population.[47] The Sason Armenians took up arms to defend themselves and a limited number of Armenians could escape there and find shelter.[48] This was only a "suspension of execution" as the Ottoman army, led by Mobile Gendarme Unit Commander Kâzım Özalp (1880-1968), assisted by Kurdish tribesmen, pushed the Sasonites higher up the mountains and defeated them, taking no prisoners.[49] At the end of the war, only a tiny fraction of the pre-war Armenian population remained in Xerzan.

One of the inhabitants of Xerzan was Karapetê Xaço (1908-2005) from the village of Bileyder. Karapet's entire family was murdered but he survived by hiding with his brother and two sisters. He had a beautiful voice and became "court bard" for Filîtê Quto, chieftain of the Reşkotan tribe, who rewarded him with food and shelter. After having served in the Syrian army, Karapet was "repatriated" to Armenia, where he worked for Radio Yerevan and died under dire conditions in 2005.[50]

In an interview conducted a year before he passed away, Karapet remembered that fateful day:

> I remember those days like it was yesterday. It was like the wrath of God. Death and gunpowder was raining from all over. The night before and the day it happened were even different from other days. For example, that day the sky was wrapped in a red glow. I have never seen such a fiery red sky before or after that day. It was not only human corpses that were piled on top of each other. Apart from the animals burnt to death in the stables, even the shepherd dogs tied to the garden fence were laying on the ground lifeless.[51]

On the question whether he would like to return to his village one day, the melancholic Karapet sipped his vodka and answered:

> Well my son, from Diyarbekir to Beşiri, from Reşkotan to the Batman bridge, I know the entire area village by village and spring by spring. Even now, if any man would take me by the arm and bring me there, I could name you one by one the names of all the mountains, valleys, and rivers. Ever since 1915, the year they killed my father, I have not seen the village I was born in. Of course I would like to go there and say a prayer for the souls of my mother and father![52]

Even though it would have been naive to expect that a world war would not have brought violence to Xerzan, and no matter how poetically and symbolically Karapet formulates his experiences, he was right about the apocalyptic nature of the genocide. The region witnessed a major social rupture as a result of the unprecedented violence experienced. The magnitude of the killings dramatically shifted the very ontology of the region: all of a sudden, there were no more capable peasants, millers, letter-writers, carpenters, tinners, blacksmiths, tailors, construction workers, and other craftsmen.

Whether it's about tribal warfare or the Armenian genocide, in the Kurdish laments of Xerzan violence occupies a dominant position. The following lament was often performed by Karapet, who learned it from a friend of his, a blind Armenian bard named Sakoyê Kor:

> It's *ferman* /
> It's war in Istanbul /
> They hit the Armenians in Adana /
> [...]
> Chief, I went to the hills of Bitlis /
> A crowd of Russian soldiers was there /
> The migrants left town in captivity /
> I don't know what all of this means /
> The migrants are on the edge /
> They killed all the able-bodied Armenians /
> All of these migrants are wretched in the desert.[53]

In local vernacular *ferman*, normally any Ottoman imperial edict, denotes the "edict of the Armenians" (*fermana filla*), i.e., the genocide. The "migrants" in this lament are the Armenian deportees, who were named migrants (*muhacir*) during the war. Up to the present, these laments are listened to by the locals as part of the oral tradition of Xerzan.

The establishment of the Turkish Republic in 1923 was the culmination of previous CUP policies, such as secularization and nation-building. The Kemalist abolition of the sultanate and caliphate and other reforms triggered many different responses throughout Turkey.[54] One of these involving violent resistance was the Kurdish revolt of Sheikh Said, erupting in mid-February 1925.[55] The government quelled the insurrection with violence, scorching villages and summarily executing combatants and civilians. Sheikh Said himself was arrested and hanged on 29 June 1925 with several of his henchmen.[56] The rebellion served to confirm Kemalist fears that Kurdish society was a potential separatist threat that needed to be dealt with urgently. On 8 September 1925 Mustafa Kemal personally authorized a special council to devise a comprehensive report on "reforming" eastern Anatolia. The council, known as the "Reform Council for the East" (*Şark Islahat Encümeni*), was chaired by İsmet İnönü and major positions were held by military officers such as Lieutenant General Kâzım Özalp, and Marshal Fevzi Çakmak (chief of staff).[57]

The report these men signed on 24 September 1925 foresaw a multi-track policy that would ensure the "reform"—clearly a euphemism for "containment"—of eastern Turkey. First of all, martial law would be proclaimed. Most eastern provinces, including Diyarbekir, would be reordered to form five "General Inspectorships" (*Umûmî Müfettişlik*), headed by five General Inspectors.[58] A total of seven million Turkish lira would be allocated to them to supervise the following measures: the deportation of Kurds living in Armenian villages, the settlement of Turkish immigrants in those villages, the deportation of Kurdish families deemed "dangerous," the reinforcement of military presence in the region, the complete disarmament of the population, the prohibition of the use of all languages other than Turkish, the assimilation of Kurds and Arabs through boarding schools, the prohibition of foreigners' access to the region, the construction of roads, railroads, and government buildings, and many other aspects of nation-state formation.[59]

Not surprisingly, the population of Xerzan largely rejected the attempt by the state to wrest control of the region. In 1926 clashes broke out between Sason tribes and government forces. At that time, Cemal Madanoğlu (1907-1993) was a military officer serving in Sason. His memoirs offer a unique insight into the way the military campaign was conducted. Madanoğlu remembered that before the campaign a special meeting on the Xerzan region was convened by General Inspector Abidin Özmen and General Kâzım Özalp.[60] "Utmost severity" was to be applied in order to subdue the Xerzan once and for all. According to Madanoğlu, the situation in Sason escalated when a local Kurd walked in on a lieutenant sexually harassing his wife in his own house. This was a serious breach of the patriarchal code of honor of the region. The Kurd went berserk and tried to kill the lieutenant, who fled to the roof and jumped on a pile of manure, finally escaping to his barracks.[61] This event triggered a full-scale armed clash between large and powerful tribes such as the Mala Eliyê Yûnis and the Turkish army and lasted for several months.[62] According to one Kurdish eyewitness, the Turkish army suffered an average daily loss of

40 to 50 casualties and 20 to 30 soldiers wounded.[63] Though some of the leaders were captured, taken to Diyarbekir and publicly executed,[64] in the end even Madanoğlu saw no other choice but to confess that "the pacification of Sason was unsuccessful."[65]

Frustrated by its losses, the Turkish army now resorted to more brutal measures. On 19 July 1937, the army reported to the Ministry of Interior that "the pacification required combat and clashes."[66] In practice this meant that when a village was captured, the inhabitants were killed and the village set on fire. Kurdish journalist Ahmet Kahraman travelled through Anatolia in search of Turkish soldiers who had served during the anti-Kurdish campaigns of the 1920s and 1930s.

One of his respondents, Dursun Çakıroğlu, was a retired sergeant living in Ankara. After initial reservations, Çakıroğlu began to trust Kahraman and spoke of an operation in a valley in which he participated:

> We besieged the valley in the middle of the night. Movements were detected early in the morning in the valley. One way or the other they found out about us. They started to flee under cries of "the soldiers are coming!" Our commander Deli Kemal Paşa ordered breakfast to be served. We had breakfast. Then we thoroughly surrounded the valley and advanced slowly. It was visible that there were very few men among them. They had probably fled. There were women, children, and elderly around. Some young men among them... When they finally saw us in front of them, a sudden outcry broke out. Women and children were running around, crying, groaning. Deli Kemal Paşa ordered the soldiers: "Take position!" We took position. Then he yelled: "Fire at will!" We let it loose at random. The valley turned into doomsday. Screams, moans, cries, fleeing, flights, yelling... [...] It was very bloody. Many died. Afterwards they said 600 casualties. I think there were more. There were tiny children among them. [...] For four hours we combed the place out with rifles and machine guns. Except for the 20 to 30 people we captured, nobody got out alive. In the volley fire even dogs and horses were shot. I don't know what those valley people had done wrong. They said they were Kurds. They rebelled against the government. When the sounds and twitches died down we entered the tents. Corpses everywhere... [...] Children, women and elderly had clung on to each other, dropped everywhere and died. Some friends searched the clothes of the dead and took their gold and money. [...] We set fire to the tents and left.[67]

Somber when recalling and narrating these bloody events, Çakıroğlu also noted that prisoners were taken away and executed. According to the interviewer, the old man's body language and facial expression—obviously not captured in the text—clearly revealed feelings of guilt and shame.

The violence of the 1920s is richly documented in Kurdish oral culture and remembered in detail. Seîdê Axayê Cizrawî, also a friend of Karapetê Xaço, sang the following lament about the Kemalist massacres:

> The land of the Kurds is fertile and blessed /
> It is all minerals, silver, and gold /
> What can we do, nowadays it's in the hand of others /
> Ah alas alas /
> They killed us and threw us in the rivers /
> There are no more lion-hearted valiants left among us.[68]

When local government officials found out that Cizrawî was singing this lament they ordered his arrest, so Cizrawî fled to the small Syrian border town of Qamishlo. His family members then begged the government for the decision to be revoked, to which the government agreed on one condition: Cizrawî was to sing a lament praising the government and Mustafa Kemal Atatürk. Cizrawî agreed and sang:

> Kemal, it's Kemal /
> Kemal is our father /
> He dressed us with coats /
> And placed hats on our heads.[69]

The government accepted this "apology" and allowed the man to return. Still, for decades, the laments that were sung in Xerzan by these modern minstrels remained those describing the violence.

In the eyes of the political elite, the efforts of the 1920s had been insufficient to extend Turkish state control into the eastern parts of the country, including Xerzan. On 14 June 1934, the government ratified the Settlement Law, a very elaborate legal text sanctioning the mass deportation of entire categories of peoples, from "itinerant Gypsies" to "anarchists" and "those who are not devoted to Turkish culture"; sweeping notions that most of all targeted Kurds.[70] In addition, the government prepared a report on the tribes of eastern Turkey. Noted under most of the tribes in the Xerzan region is the comment: "Participated in the Sason rebellion. Their loyalty to our motherland cannot be depended on."[71] The government believed that assimilation of the Kurdish tribesmen could be accomplished efficiently by deporting the entire tribe to western Turkey, and settling the tribesmen separately from their political leaders (chieftains, or *aghas*) and religious leaders (imams, or *shaikhs*). Thus, in the autumn of 1936 a total of 2400 men, women, and children from Xerzan were rounded up, crammed in cattle wagons, and deported.[72] Many deportees died on the way; later some returned.

A core activity in all state formation is disarmament of the population and monopolization of the means of violence in the hands of the government. Thus, in the region, security measures continued. In November 1932, the prime minister's office authorized the 7th army corps to launch a massive campaign of disarmament in the region. After several weeks, the commanding officers reported having confiscated thousands of weapons.[73] Even kitchen knives and agricultural implements were seized. After having "subdued" the tribal forces, the government proceeded to build barracks and gendarme stations.[74] It then constructed 15 police stations in the "forbidden zone" and installed 5800 phone posts.[75] Only in the summer of 1950 were the "forbidden zones" in Xerzan disbanded and locals allowed to resettle.[76]

Even though all these measures were intended to contribute to the establishment of the nation-state in Xerzan, they did not seem to succeed. Sociologist İsmail Beşikçi conducted field research on one of the tribes in the area in the 1960s. His results showed that few people spoke Turkish, and that barely half of the people in the area had even heard of the name "Atatürk."[77] Necmi Onur was a journalist who travelled through the region in the 1960s, encountered a group of women walking beside the asphalt road. When asked why they did not walk on the road, the women answered: "That road is the state's road, we refuse to walk on it."[78] Tribal identity was strong and people did not identify with the state in a positive way. In fact, tribalism was so strong that well into the 1970s, some chieftains traveled to Sweden and Germany and still managed to extort money from their former subjects who had migrated to Europe but obeyed out of tradition and fear.[79]

For the generation born immediately after this era, the memories transmitted to them about the violence was formative in the evolution of their political and cultural consciousness. Mehdi Zana (1940-), one of the most prolific Kurdish-nationalist politicians, remembered that in his childhood a man named Selimê Xerzî would recount how the government had massacred villagers in Xerzan:

> When that man told us about how in the Sason bazaar nine persons were decapitated with saws I was still a child and very much affected by the story. Also, the account of how in the village of Rabat a total of 65 people, mostly women and children were crammed into a hayloft and burnt to death caused deep changes in me. My outlook on the Kurdish nation, on my own nation was crystallizing.[80]

Even among those who chose to assimilate or wanted their offspring to do so (out of defeat, fear, and gain), traumatic memories such as these permeated the thoughts of most Kurds from Xerzan and demonstrably contributed to the development and acceptance of revolutionary ideologies of nationalist revenge. These traumatic memories provided the links between the previous violent era and the next one.

The End of Xerzan, 1984-1997

Another major watershed in the history of violence in the region was the conflict between the Turkish army and the Kurdistan Workers Party (*Partîya Karkerên Kurdistan*, PKK). The PKK grew out of a relatively small Kurdish group's frustration with what was viewed as the Turkish left's passive attitude to the Kurdish question. Its leader was Abdullah Öcalan, who conducted the party's operations until his arrest in 1999. Officially founded in November 1978, the PKK organized a clandestine movement, deploying its cadres from its political and military branches in Europe, the Middle East, and the Kurdish areas of Turkey. The party program stated that it aimed at carving out a socialist Kurdistan through a "war of liberation" against the "colonial rule of the fascist Turkish Republic."[81] On 15 August 1984, the PKK declared war on the Turkish state and its "Kurdish collaborators." Local skirmishes escalated into a large-scale conflict, lasting 13 years and causing more than 35,000 casualties.[82] Deep-seated frustration in the Turkish military led to the formation of paramilitary units that conducted brutal counter-insurgency operations and a scorched-earth campaign in 1994 and 1995. This state-sponsored terror left more than 3000 villages devastated and millions of internally displaced people in Turkey.[83] The war ended with the ceasefire of 1997 and more conclusively with the arrest of Öcalan.[84] In 2006, sporadic acts of violence recommenced in a number of regions.

Some of the heaviest battles were fought in Xerzan. Both the PKK and the Turkish state demanded support from the population. The army organized villagers to become "village guards," an auxiliary force reminiscent of the Hamidiye regiments. PKK militants would then raid those villages and commit bloodbaths.[85] But nothing compared to the massive violence committed by the Turkish counter-insurgency forces in 1994 and 1995. In Xerzan, dozens of villages were razed and hundreds of people disappeared and were murdered. One of these villages was Tanzê (official name: Heybeli), which was stormed by special forces, and given an ultimatum to become village guards. The army reportedly threatened: "Or else we'll slaughter you all." On 24 February 1994 the army shelled Tanzê, killing 9, including 3 children. One of the shells landed in front of the village mosque and ripped the imam apart. The shelling continued until most of the houses were devastated.[86]

Testimony on the extremely violent nature of the conflict is also provided by Turkish soldiers. Mehmet K. is a jovial young sound engineer whose face wears a perennial smile which discloses nothing about his harsh military experience serving as a corporal in Xerzan in 1995. When asked about his experiences in the region, he gave a cool, callous, and formal account of the proceedings:

> You know, we're driving in a convoy, fingers on the triggers, and the first truck hits a mine. The driver and the guy next to him die immediately. The first soldier that jumped out gets an artillery shell right in the face. We found nothing back from his head. He was supposed to be discharged that week.[87]

Another soldier was a guard in a barracks when a 13-year-old boy plucked a flower from the barracks' garden. The commanding officer saw this and ordered the boy arrested. The soldier remembered: "We pull him in and, as many as we are, we ram into the kid with our rifle butts and tear his mouth and face apart."[88]

The memory of Armenians was a remarkable and elusive phenomenon during the war. The Turkish army repeatedly depicted PKK forces as Armenians, insinuating that killed guerrillas turned out to be uncircumcised. The commander of an army division that attempted to raze the small town of Tatvan reportedly was yelling frantically: "You Armenian bastards, I know your mosques are really churches."[89] In the village of Tilmişar the villagers commented that in every raid, the commander would admonish them: "The terrorists in the mountains are not Muslims. They are Armenian rabble. Our religion and flag is the same. If we join forces we can root out the terrorists in two days and exterminate the Armenians."[90] The inhabitants of the village of Herêdan compared the massacre and expulsion of the Armenians in that village to their own victimization, precisely 80 years later.[91]

Kurdish laments played an important role in the transmission of previous traumatic experiences to new generations of Xerzan youth. Growing up in Xerzan in the 1970s, Erdal R. noted:

> My father used to listen to laments on an old tape recorder. But he would sit in the kitchen alone and turn down the volume really low, so we wouldn't hear it. He wouldn't allow us to listen with him. He feared that the state would hear us listening to Kurdish music. So when my father would leave the house to go to work or shopping, we would find the cassette tapes and listen to them. Me and my brothers that is. They were about the Kurdish national uprisings in the 1920s.[92]

It seems that this young man drew the historical background and legitimation for his ideological convictions in large part from these listening sessions. The envelopment of the laments in a cloud of secrecy only added to their attraction.

From the perspective of violence studies the war was an interesting development. The decisive criterion for state formation is access to a larger reservoir of violence, i.e., the replacement of former monopolies of violence with new monopolies of violence. The attempt by the PKK at undermining the Turkish state's monopoly of violence in eastern Turkey produced local, temporary successes. The PKK was at a certain time able to form a state in the bud in the Xerzan region. In 1992, the organization fully controlled certain mountainous parts of Xerzan, in which it operated as a quasi-state, practicing a form of law and taxing villagers. Turkish journalist Kadri Gürsel attested to this when he was kidnapped by the PKK in March 1995. Having had the unique chance to observe guerrillas from up close, he wrote that in personal conversations PKK-members repeatedly stated about the peak year 1992: "We were like a state back then."[93] Violence was legitimized with reference to the code of honor as well as nationalist ideology.

Currently, Xerzan is in a wretched condition. A century of violence destroyed the economic, social, cultural, and ecological foundations of the region. The entire Armenian community of Xerzan was wiped out during the genocide and simply does not exist anymore. Agriculture, horticulture, pastoralism, crafts, trade, intellectual activities function at a minimum. Much of the current population now lives in Batman, the new city in the valley south of Xerzan, or in the suburbs of Diyarbakır. Violence remains a pervasive and ongoing problem there in the form of domestic violence, tribal vendettas, organized crime, honor killings, and high female suicide rates.[94] As such, a diffuse form of violence continues, not to mention the fact that many young men and women in Xerzan remain susceptible to political violence, due to prolonged exposure to circumstances of hopelessness and nationalist propaganda.

Discussion

This chapter aimed at providing an overview of the history of violence in a small region in eastern Turkey. Although more research is needed to contextualize Xerzan within broader regional and national processes, it is still possible to conclude that the policies of the Turkish state did not succeed in integrating the Xerzan region. Some inhabitants may have jobs or own lucrative businesses in cities in western Turkey, including Istanbul. Nevertheless, violence continues to dominate the minds of the

Xerzan people, many of whom still find it legitimate to kill (or die) for causes they believe in. These beliefs are justified in terms of tradition, tribal affiliation, ideology or culture.[95] Ironically, due to the spread of nationalism, past and present victimization by rival tribes (formerly enemies) is now included in and remembered as their own.

This violence can be traced back to Ottoman-Turkish militarism. It is no coincidence that during the most violent decades of the single-party era (1923-1946) many influential politicians and parliamentarians came from a military background.[96] Ever since the *coup d'état* of January 1913, the army has remained an influential, if not dominant force in Turkish politics. Its power is so deeply-rooted in institutional structures and practices that it could intervene several times in Turkish politics without impunity.[97] It has been convincingly proven that militarism in politics does not create conditions of peaceful conflict resolution. On the contrary, it critically lowers the moral and intellectual threshold of solving political problems through outright violence.[98]

But does the answer to the question raised in the introduction lie in simple *raison d'état*, i.e., state security? Out of tradition, the population of Xerzan disregarded the state's monopoly of violence, let alone taxation and conscription. Any state would react through a campaign of pacification.[99] Therefore, more precise sociological explanations and interpretations must be sought in the red thread of violence and traumatization that runs through the Ottoman *fin de siècle*. This begins with the brutalization of political culture during the decay of the Ottoman Empire, the violent expulsion of Balkan Muslims in the late nineteenth and early twentieth century, and the response of Turkish nationalism to that experience. Heavily traumatized by this history, the Young Turk generation reacted disproportionally when confronted with what was a limited and local pocket of resistance. Ottoman traumatization fostered paranoia against nationalist separatism and strong feelings of vengeance. Furthermore, the trauma was codified into texts such as official war histories and internalized by the Turkish military milieu.[100]

"[R]ecent research suggests that trauma is contagious, transmissible from survivors to their listeners and witnesses; and, both within families and by means of wider, collective processes, to subsequent generations."[101] For the Xerzan population, this transgenerational transmission of trauma is precisely what occurred. Even though Turkish "memory managers" attempted to engineer a form of imposed amnesia on the population of Xerzan and society in general, for generations the violence was remembered in great detail in the privacy of people's homes. The laments played a crucial role in this process. The state policy of silence and denial did not contribute to heal wounds on all sides. The Armenian genocide was a seminal event for the region and is still vividly remembered with a mixture of fear, shame, and hate against the government in regional memory. The murderous campaigns of the 1920s and the deportation of their ancestors are remembered with even more bitter resentment. It was the children and grandchildren of those murdered and deported in these events that lent support to the PKK when it declared a guerrilla war against the state.

At present, these threads of traumatization are highly entangled and difficult to extricate. As Erdal R. answered sardonically the question about what it would take to engage in an open and dispassionate discussion about Xerzan's violent century: "Discussion? About violence? I wouldn't know where to begin!"[102]

Notes

1.   Norbert Elias, "Problems of Involvement and Detachment," *British Journal of Sociology*, 7, 3 (1956): 226-52; Lewis A. Coser, "Social Involvement or Scientific Detachment: The Sociologist's Dilemma," *The Antioch Review*, 28, 1 (1968): 108-13.
2.   *San Francisco Chronicle*, 20 November 2004.
3.   Robert J. Lifton, *The Nazi Doctors: Medical Killing and the Psychology of Genocide* (New York: Basic Books, 1986), 12.
4.   Michael Mann, *The Dark Side of Democracy: Explaining Ethnic Cleansing* (Cambridge: Cambridge University Press, 2005), X.
5.   Israel W. Charny, "The Study of Genocide," in *Genocide: A Critical Bibliographic Review*, ed. Israel W. Charny (London: Mansell, 1988), 1-19.
6.   John M. Darley, "Methods for the Study of Evil-Doing Actions," *Personality and Social Psychology Review*, 3, 3 (1999): 269-75.
7.   Stanley Milgram, *Obedience to authority: an experimental view* (New York: Harper & Row, 1974).
8.   The critically-acclaimed documentary movie *Das Experiment* is an example of this idiosyncratic trend.
9.   Robert M. Hayden, "Schindler's Fate: Genocide, Ethnic Cleansing, and Population Transfers," *Slavic Review*, 55, 4 (1996): 727-48, at 732.
10.   Examples include both the Turkish and the Armenian governments' manipulation of research on the Armenian genocide, Israel's sacralization and monopolization of Jewish victimhood in the Holocaust and Iran's willingness to sponsor Holocaust denial, the Ukrainian parliament's official declaration of the 1932-33 famine as genocide, and the Rwandan government's exclusion of Hutus from the category of Rwandan genocide victims.
11.   Donald E. Miller and Lorna Touryan Miller, *Survivors: An Oral History of the Armenian Genocide* (Berkeley: University of California Press, 1993).
12.   Scott Straus, *Intimate Enemy: Images And Voices of the Rwandan Genocide* (New York: Zone Books, 2006); Jean Hatzfeld, *Une saison de machettes: récits* (Paris:

Seuil, 2003); Gitta Sereny, *Into that Darkness: From Mercy Killing to Mass Murder* (New York: McGraw-Hill, 1974); Alexander L. Hinton, *Why Did They Kill?: Cambodia in the Shadow of Genocide* (Berkeley, CA: University of California Press, 2005).

13. Anthony Giddens, *The Nation-State and Violence* (Cambridge: Polity Press, 1985), 3.

14. Mark Levene, "Why is the Twentieth Century the Century of Genocide?," *Journal of World History*, 11, 2, 305-36; Eric D. Weitz, *A Century of Genocide: Utopias of Race and Nation* (Princeton: Princeton University Press, 2003); *Century of Genocide: Critical Essays and Eyewitness Accounts*, ed. Samuel Totten, William S. Parsons, and Israel W. Charny (New York: Routledge, 2004).

15. *Le siècle des camps: détention, concentration, extermination: cent ans de mal radical*, eds. Joël Kotek and Pierre Rigoulot (Paris: Lattès, 2000).

16. Raymond Aron, *The Century of Total War* (New York: Doubleday, 1954).

17. Ian Kershaw, "War and Political Violence in Twentieth-Century Europe," *Contemporary European History*, 14, 1 (2005): 107-23, at 107-8.

18. Micha Brumlik, "Das Jahrhundert der Extreme," in: *Völkermord und Kriegsverbrechen in der ersten Hälfte des 20. Jahrhunderts*, eds. Irmtrud Wojak and Susanne Meinl (Frankfurt am Main: Campus-Verlag, 2004), 19-36, at 34.

19. Götz Aly and Suzanne Heim, *Architects of Annihilation: Auschwitz and the Logic of Destruction* (London: Phoenix, 2003), 285.

20. Hans-Lukas Kieser, "Deplorable, Unavoidable, Functional, Salutary: Some Remarks on the Acceptance of Mass Violence by Turkish and German Élites in the Context of the Armenian Genocide," *Bridges*, 12, 1/2 (2005): 189-227.

21. A brief note about terminology is in order. In this chapter I will follow Zürcher's use of the term "Young Turk" to bundle together the Committee of Union and Progress (*Ittihad ve Terakki Cemiyeti*) and its descendant the Republican People's Party (*Cumhuriyet Halk Partisi*), a generation of men who ruled the Ottoman dominions in the period 1913-1950. Erik-Jan Zürcher, "The Ottoman Legacy of the Turkish Republic: An Attempt at a New Periodization," *Die Welt des Islams*, 32 (1992): 237-53.

22. Erik-Jan Zürcher, *The Unionist Factor. The Role of the Committee of Union and Progress in the Turkish National Movement (1905-1926)* (Leiden: Brill, 1984).

23. Martin van Bruinessen, *Agha, Shaikh and State: The Social and Political Structures of Kurdistan* (London: Zed Books, 1992), 179-81.

24. Vahram Shemmassian, "The Sasun Pandukhts in Nineteenth-Century Aleppo," in: *Armenian Baghesh/Bitlis and Taron/Mush* , ed. Richard G. Hovannisian (Costa Mesa, CA: Mazda, 2001), 175-89.

25. See the letters of Count von Moltke, who was authorized by the Ottoman sultan to assist the military campaign against the emir, who refused to relinquish his position: Helmuth von Moltke, *Briefe über Zustände und Begebenheiten in der Türkei aus den Jahren 1835 bis 1839* (Berlin: Mittler, 1882).

26. *Başbakanlık Osmanlı Arşivi* (Ottoman Archives, Istanbul, hereafter cited as *BOA*), DH.MKT 1498/87, 3 May 1888.

27. *BOA*, DH.MKT 1488/73, 24 January 1888, Ministry of Interior to governor of Bitlis.

28. *BOA*, DH.MKT 1555/84, 18 October 1888.

29. *BOA*, DH.MUİ 23-2/16, 29 January 1910.

30. "Şer û kilamak ji herêma Xerzan: Şerê Pencînaran û Elikan," in: Salihê Kevirbirî, *Filîtê Qûto: Serpêhatî, Dîrok, Sosyolojî* (İstanbul: Pêrî, 2001), 11-18.

31.   İsmail Beşikçi, *Doğu'da Değişim ve Yapısal Sorunlar (Göçebe Alikan Aşireti)* (Ankara: Sevinç, 1969), 78-9.
32.   *BOA*, DH.MKT 1589/66, 1 March 1889.
33.   Salihê Kevirbirî, "Deng û Awaza Xerzan," in: *Özgür Politika*, 3 January 2000.
34.   Hamit Bozarslan, "Remarques sur l'histoire des relations kurdo-arméniennes," *Journal of Kurdish Studies*, 1 (1995 [1996]): 55-76.
35.   *BOA*, DH.EUM.EMN 38/30, Vice-governor of Bitlis Mehmed Kadri to Ministry of Justice, 6 December 1913.
36.   *BOA*, İ.HUS 25/1311/Z-061, 12 May 1894.
37.   *BOA*, DH.MUİ 108/-1/34, 30 May 1910.
38.   *BOA*, DH.MUİ 120/3, 3 September 1910.
39.   *BOA*, DH.MUİ 4/-3/16, 19 November 1909.
40.   *BOA*, DH.EUM.EMN 66/15, document nos. 1 and 5, governor of Bitlis to Ministry of Justice, 12 May 1914.
41.   *BOA*, DH.EUM.EMN 89/5, 28 July 1914.
42.   Louise Nalbandian, *The Armenian Revolutionary Movement: The Development of Armenian Political Parties through the Nineteenth Century* (Berkeley, CA: University of California Press, 1963); Razmik Panossian, *The Armenians: From Kings and Priests to Merchants and Commissars* (New York: Columbia University Press, 2006).
43.   Selim Deringil, *The Well-Protected Domains: Ideology and the Legitimation of Power in the Ottoman Empire, 1876-1909* (London: Tauris, 1999), 112-34.
44.   Vahakn N. Dadrian, *Warrant for Genocide: The Key Elements of the Turko-Armenian Conflict* (New Brunswick, NJ: Transaction Publishers, 1999), 29-38.
45.   Janet Klein, "Power in the Periphery: The Hamidiye Light Cavalry and the Struggle over Ottoman Kurdistan, 1890-1914," unpublished Ph.D. dissertation, Princeton University, November 2002.
46.   Robert F. Melson, "A Theoretical Inquiry into the Armenian Massacres of 1894-1896," *Comparative Studies in Society and History*, 24, 1 (1982): 481-509.
47.   These issues have been dealt with in greater detail in my master's thesis: *'A Reign of Terror': CUP Rule in Diyarbekir Province, 1913-1923* (unpublished MA thesis, University of Amsterdam, June 2005).
48.   *United States Official Records on the Armenian Genocide, 1915-1917*, ed. Ara Sarafian (Princeton: Gomidas Institute, 2004), 364.
49.   James Bryce and Arnold Toynbee, *The Treatment of Armenians in the Ottoman Empire 1915-16: Documents Presented to Viscount Grey of Fallodon by Viscount Bryce*, ed. Ara Sarafian (Princeton: Gomidas Institute, 2005), 122-3.
50.   See the documentary by Mehmet Aktaş, *Dengekî Zemanê Bere: Karapêtê Xaço: Voice from the Past* (Belgium: Medya TV, 2000).
51.   Interview conducted in Kurdish with Karapetê Xaço by Salihê Kevirbirî in Solkhoz (Armenia) on 12 December 2001, transcribed in: Salihê Kevirbirî, *Bir Çığlığın Yüzyılı: Karapetê Xaço* (Istanbul: Sî, 2002), 53, my translation.
52.   Ibid., 37, my translation.
53.   Ibid., 34-5, my translation. See also Karapetê Xaço's two albums: *Edûlê* (Istanbul) Kom Müzik, 2001) and *Xezal* (Istanbul: Çağdaş Müzik, 2001).
54.   Gavin D. Brockett, "Collective Action and the Turkish Revolution: Towards a Framework for the Social History of the Atatürk Era, 1923-1938," in *Turkey before and after Atatürk: Internal and External Affairs*, ed. Sylvia Kedourie (London: Frank Cass, 1999), 44-66.
55.   Hamit Bozarslan, "Kurdish Nationalism in Turkey: From Tacit Contract to Rebellion (1919-1925)," in *Essays on the Origins of Kurdish Nationalism*, ed. Abbas Vali (Costa Mesa, CA: Mazda Publishers, 2003), 163-90.

56. Robert Olson, *The Emergence of Kurdish Nationalism and the Sheikh Said Rebellion, 1880-1925* (Austin, TX: University of Texas Press, 1989).
57. *Kürtler ve Ulusal-Demokratik Mücadeleleri: Gizli Belgeler - Araştırmalar - Notlar*, ed. Mehmet Bayrak (Ankara: Özge, 1993), 481.
58. For a comprehensive overview of these see: Cemil Koçak, *Umûmî Müfettişlikler (1927-1952)* (Istanbul: İletişim, 2003).
59. *Kürtler ve Ulusal-Demokratik Mücadeleleri* [n.57], 481-9, quoting the council's final report.
60. Cemal Madanoğlu, *Anılar 1911-1953* (Istanbul: Evrim, 1982), 155.
61. Ibid., 163-4.
62. Mehmûd Baksî, *Serhildana Mala Eliyê Ûnis* (Istanbul: Weşanên Welat, 2001); Reşat Hallı, *Türkiye Cumhuriyeti'nde Ayaklanmalar (1924-1938)* (Ankara: General Staff War History Department, 1972), chapter 3.
63. Osman Sebrî, *Şerrên Sasûnê (1925-1937)* (Istanbul: Pêrî, 2005), 58.
64. Ibid., 45. One of the chieftains executed was Cemîlê Çeto. His brother, Bişarê Çeto, later lamented that the government had used the Kurds in the Armenian Genocide, only to take care of the Kurds later. To comment on this presumed stupidity he reportedly rhymed: "Bişarê Çeto / ji kerê keto" (Bişarê Çeto / descendant of a donkey).
65. Madanoğlu, *Anılar* [n.60], 261.
66. *Başbakanlık Cumhuriyet Arşivi* (Republican Archives, Ankara, hereafter cited as *BCA*), 30.18.1.2/77.66.10, 19 July 1937.
67. Interview conducted in Turkish with Dursun Çakıroğlu by Ahmet Kahraman in Ankara in 1990, transcribed in: Ahmet Kahraman, *Kürt İsyanları* (Istanbul: Evrensel, 2003), 215-6.
68. Kevirbirî, *Karapetê Xaço* [n.51], 59, my translation.
69. Ibid., 60, my translation.
70. The law was published in the official gazette: *Resmi Gazete*, no. 2733, 21 June 1934.
71. See the demographic data and comments on the Alikan, Beleki and the Xerzan tribal confederation in: *Aşiretler Raporu* (Istanbul: Kaynak, 1998), 262-3, 264, 265-6.
72. Selahattin Çelik, *Ağrı Dağını Taşımak: Çağdaş Kürt Halk Direnişi; Siyasi, Askeri, Ekonomik ve Toplumsal Sonuçları* (Frankfurt: Zambon, 2000), 24.
73. *BCA*, 30.10.0.0/54.359.14, 29 November 1932; 30.18.1.2/37.41.11, 13 May 1933.
74. *BCA*, 30.18.1.2/84.66.10, 14 July 1938.
75. *BCA*, 30.18.1.2/92.98.14, 11 October 1940.
76. *BCA*, 30.18.1.2/123.53.20, 1 July 1950.
77. Beşikçi, *Doğu'da değişim* [n.31], 200.
78. Necmi Onur, *Şark cephesinde yeni bir şey yok... (Röportajlar)* (Istanbul: Belge, 1972), 169.
79. Interview conducted in Turkish with Feyyaz K. in Stockholm on 23 May 2004.
80. Interview conducted in Turkish with Mehdi Zana by Şeyhmus Diken, published in: Şeyhmus Diken, *Amidalılar: Sürgündeki Diyarbekirliler* (Istanbul: İletişim, 2007), 135-58, at 136.
81. Konrad Hirschler, "Diskursive Räume in der PKK: Eine Studie zur kurdischen Geschichtsschreibung,": *Kurdische Studien*, 2, 1 (2002): 63-79. This discourse changed after Öcalan's arrest.
82. Ali Kemal Özcan, *Turkey's Kurds: a theoretical analysis of the PKK and Abdullah Öcalan* (London: Routledge, 2006).

83.   Vedat Çetin, *Yakılan / Boşaltılan Köyler ve Göç* (Ankara: Öteki, 1999); *"Zorunlu Göç" ile Yüzleşmek: Türkiye'de Yerinden Edilme Sonrası Vatandaşlığın İnşası* (Istanbul: TESEV, 2006).
84.   See the memoirs of Öcalan's lawyer: Britta Böhler, *De zwerftocht van een leider: achter de schermen van de zaak-Öcalan* (Amsterdam: De Arbeiderspers, 2000).
85.   See the collection of very disturbing pictures in a volume published by the Turkish general staff: *Anadolu'da Akan Kan* (Istanbul: n.p., 1992).
86.   Turkish Human Rights Foundation, *Annual report* (Istanbul: İHD, 1994), 62.
87.   Interview conducted in Turkish with Mehmet K. in Ankara on 21 July 2006.
88.   Nadire Mater, *Mehmedin Kitabı: Güneydoğuda Savaşmış Askerler Anlatıyor* (Istanbul: Metis, 1999), 152.
89.   "Turkije walst Koerdische dorpen in ijzingwekkend tempo plat," in: *Trouw*, 12 January 1994.
90.   Zülküf Kışanak, *Yitik köyler: bin yılların mirası nasıl yakıldı?* (Istanbul: Belge, 2004), 129.
91.   Ibid., 85-7.
92.   Interview conducted in Kurdish with Erdal R., Istanbul, 18 August 2002.
93.   Kadri Gürsel, *Dağdakiler: Bagok'tan Gabar'a 26 Gün* (Istanbul: Metis, 1996), 63.
94.   The suicides of young women are most probably 'stimulated' by male family members and are little more than honor killings. United Nations Commission on Human Rights, *Press Release*, 31 May 2006. See also: Müjgan Halis, *Batman'da Kadınlar Ölüyor* (Istanbul: Metis, 2001).
95.   Martin van Bruinessen, "La natura e gli usi della violenza nel conflitto kurdi," in: *Uomini in armi*, eds. Marco Buttino, Maria Cristina Ercolessi and Alessandro Triulzi (Napoli: l'Ancora, 2000), 99-113.
96.   Naim Turfan, *Rise of the Young Turks: politics, the military and Ottoman collapse* (London: Tauris, 2000), 429-44; Handan Nezir Akmeçe, *The birth of modern Turkey: the Ottoman military and the march to World War I* (London: I.B. Tauris, 2005), chapter 7.
97.   George S. Harris, "The Role of the Military in Turkish Politics," *The Middle East Journal*, 19, 1 (1965): 54-66 (part 1); Ibid., in: *The Middle East Journal*, 19, 2 (spring 1965): 169-76 (part 2).
98.   Samuel E. Finer, *The man on horseback: the role of the military in politics* (London: Pall Mall Press, 1962).
99.   Johan Goudsblom, "De monopolisering van georganiseerd geweld," *Sociologische Gids*, 48, 4 (2001): 343-59.
100.   *Bir Zümre, Bir Parti: Türkiye'de Ordu*, eds. Ahmet İnsel and Ali Bayramoğlu (Istanbul: Birikim, 2004).
101.   Selma Leydesdorff et al., "Introduction: Trauma and life stories," in *Trauma and life stories: international perspectives*, ed. Kim L. Rogers, Selma Leydesdorff and Graham Dawson (London: Routledge, 1999), 17.
102.   Interview conducted in Kurdish with Erdal R. in Istanbul, 18 August 2002.

10

Multiple Framings:
Survivor and Non-Survivor Interviewers in
Holocaust Video Testimony

Michele Langfield and Pam Maclean[1]

Motivated by a desire to preserve a "living" record of Holocaust experiences, organizations throughout the world have initiated programs
to collect video testimonies of Holocaust survivors. Underpinning these
programs is the belief that Holocaust video testimonies provide "direct"
access to the memories of survivors, giving the impression that viewers too can relive these horrific events. Like any film footage, however,
video testimonies are the products of a complex process of construction
that, while dependent on the witness to events, is also structured by the
camera operator, the editor and, as this chapter indicates, an interviewer,
whose task is to solicit the survivor's story, usually as part of a larger
oral history project. Analysis of the construction process is central to
understanding what is being told and why.

In comparison with audio-only Holocaust testimony, video testimony
possesses several additional elements.[2] Interviewees are "in the spotlight"
so to speak, on camera, their emotions, reactions and "performance" visu-
ally recorded by a camera operator who further constructs and constrains
the entire process. The increased exposure and heightened sensitivity
of the interviewee, together with the traumatic nature of events being
related, makes the relationship between interviewer and interviewee all
the more important. Familiarity by the interviewee with the genre of
television interview also influences how an interviewee will respond. The
viewer too, has sophisticated expectations of the video medium. Unlike
some audio-only testimonies, which place priority on the transcript as
the primary document, video should be used in the original.

By examining a selection of video testimonies held at the Jewish Holocaust Museum and Research Centre (JHMRC) located in Melbourne, Australia, this chapter focuses specifically on the role played by the interviewer in framing the witness's story. Community volunteers, some but not all of whom are survivors, conduct the interviews. We ask whether survivor interviewers are more effective than non-survivor interviewers in dealing with traumatized respondents. Do they establish a particularly empathetic relationship towards fellow survivors? Or does the non-survivor occupy an "objective" position that enables a more distanced approach to be taken?

The Problem of Mediation

Oren Stier disagrees with the assumptions reached by Lawrence Langer and Geoffrey Hartman, that video testimonies allow the viewer direct access to Holocaust experience, arguing instead that videos perform "mediatory and representative functions."[3] Stier shows how multiple contexts affect the recording of Holocaust video testimonies, framing what the witness remembers and tells. Witness agendas may complement the specific objectives of collecting institutions, whose set interview protocols provide a narrative script. Conversely, respondents may actively undermine these agendas. In addition, viewers bring their own expectations to their reception of Holocaust accounts. Thus, Stier questions the fundamental notion of the "autonomous" witness and views their testimonies as ensnared within a complex web of mediation. Both the witness and the interviewer make choices that help shape the final structure and content.[4]

While these choices may be conscious or unconscious, memory and narration, as Mary Chamberlain and Selma Leydesdorff observe, are the inescapable products of social and cultural mediation: They are fashioned by "socially and culturally specific ... 'frameworks'" that are a prerequisite for remembering. Without such structures, recollection would be impossible. "Memories are, therefore, always mediated ...they are not only mediated but also censored, publicly and privately, officially and unofficially."[5] The oral history interviewer, thus, plays a pivotal role as gatekeeper of memory and it is curious that, in contrast to the notion of the Holocaust witness, which has been highly theorized, the function performed by the interviewer in soliciting Holocaust testimony, has been relatively neglected.[6]

The general oral history literature has long acknowledged that interviewers are never neutral players.[7] Through their questioning, their role in the collection, creation, control and direction of the data is critical and can facilitate or impede the outcome. The doyen of oral history research, Ronald Grele, comments that soliciting memory is a fragile process that requires a "skillful interviewer" and a "good storyteller" to "in tandem, recreate the sense of the past."[8] Chamberlain and Leydesdorff observe that: "In the beginning it [oral testimony] is, as Bakhtin (1981) pointed out, dialogic and never finished. That is, the interviewer or historian is engaged with the informant or the subject in negotiating and creating a text."[9] Critical to the dialogical text-creating process—what Mary Marshall Clark terms the "representation" of events—is the capacity of the interviewer to "listen" to what is said. Thus, "the story of the life is represented by the narrator, shaped by the hearing of the interviewer, and is an artifact of both imaginations."[10] Clark's observation is particularly helpful in the analysis of the interviewer in the JHMRC video testimony collection. In a number of instances, misunderstandings (leading sometimes to open friction) arise between interviewer and interviewee when the interviewer's recapitulation of remarks made by the interviewee does not (in the mind of the interviewee) accurately reflect what was said. Only when a shared understanding is reached can the interviews proceed.[11]

The social and cultural capital brought by the interviewer to the interview is frequently ignored. According to Dale Treleven, such neglect is the norm, even from such sophisticated oral history theoreticians and practitioners as Grele and Michael Frisch who, while acknowledging the role of the interviewer, fail "to reveal much knowledge about context and its connection to content based on their field work experiences."[12] A notable exception is Alessandro Portelli who emphasizes the significance of the social and personal relationship between the two speaking subjects in an interview.[13] Treleven's comments preface a discussion of his almost sixty-hour long series of interviews with close friend, American social reformer, Frank Wilkinson. Reflecting on the interview, Treleven concludes that, "The most critical contextual element in an oral history interview is the relationship between interviewer and interviewee. Mutual respect, rapport, and trust are essential if substantive, meaningful information is to emerge.… When the principals are close friends, the relationship fosters special opportunities but also presents unique challenges."[14]

Sidney Bolkosky and Henry Greenspan acknowledge that the role played by the interviewer in Holocaust oral testimony has been sadly neglected. To gain insight into the interview process, they questioned previously interviewed Holocaust survivors about their experience of being interviewed. Bolkosky and Greenspan conclude that from the perspective of the interviewee, not only can "good" interviews be differentiated from "bad" ones, but also the quality of the interview fundamentally influences what is told.[15] While our study focuses on the interviews themselves and specifically on video testimony, we reach similar conclusions: the interviewing context profoundly affects the content of the interview, how the interviewee relates his or her story, and how the viewer interprets the account given. More radically than Bolkosky and Greenspan, our discussion calls into question the heuristic value of categorizing interviews as "good" or "bad," as such. Instead, we are interested in the dynamics of the interview process and what this process reveals beyond the literal "content" of the interview.

The JHMRC Video Testimony Collection

In "conventional" large-scale oral history projects, an academic designs the project to meet a specific research objective in order to create data to "present to the researcher."[16] By contrast, the JHMRC collection is a community project that arose out of the need of survivors to speak after decades of silence. Recording of survivor testimonies began in 1987, initially on audiocassette and from 1992 on videotape.[17] By 2007, some 1400 testimonies had been recorded. Phillip Maisel, himself a survivor and interviewer, has been the lynchpin of the project. When not interviewing, Maisel is present during the majority of interviews, behind the camera, monitoring the situation, occasionally asking questions and, where necessary, assisting with translations and giving counsel. He constitutes a third participant with considerable influence over the finished product and, like the interviewer, is by no means a neutral figure. Indeed, Maisel's multiple involvements epitomize the at times blurred role played by survivor interviewers.

Although it was hoped that the video testimony collection would be useful to researchers, the project has not been designed to satisfy a specific research agenda. Instead, it performs multiple purposes. On one level, its function is commemorative. It honors those murdered in the Holocaust, recalls prewar Jewish life and bequeaths a tangible legacy to survivors' families and the Jewish community as a whole. Survivors can also find the process of recounting long-repressed stories therapeutic, when barely believable events are confirmed as having really happened. The interview legitimates their experiences, while tending to survivors' pain. Finally, the video testimonies perform a broader evidentiary function, documenting the "facts" of the Holocaust in order to counter denial and anti-Semitism.[18] Because the JHMRC interviewing process serves far more than a clinical, social science-oriented purpose, expectations of academic research, such as the systematic noting of specific responses to interviewing, for example, "long pauses," may appear trivial.[19] In this way its purpose differs from that of the purely academic or single-purpose project.

In the case of JHMRC testimonies, the interviewer (an unpaid, non-academic volunteer who may be a survivor) deals with the profound problem of how to solicit long-repressed, traumatic memories. Reactions such as silence, hesitation or aggression may be the norm and seem barely worth noting.[20] Instead, the interviewer may scarcely be able to keep track of convoluted narratives recounting unbelievable stories, entangled in a labyrinthine web of chronological and geographical detail.[21] While trying to follow the flow of events, the interviewer must provide balm to tortured spirits.

While many interviewers at the JHMRC are survivors who are uniquely placed to create a shared narrative with their interviewees, understandably, some may lack a comprehensive knowledge of the Holocaust, and, despite undertaking research, find it difficult to grasp experiences that do not conform to their own. They may also be less detached and feel that their status as survivors entitles them to query what the interviewee remembers and may actively dispute the interviewee's account. The interviewers may move between the frame of facilitation and the frame of witnessing. How then does the survivor interviewer influence the shape of the video testimony? How does the interviewee respond to another person's story impinging on their own, and does this compromise the integrity of the interviewee's experience? Alternatively, where conflict exists between interviewer and interviewee, does the viewer learn more about the discursive fluidity of experience by watching its validity being negotiated than is apparent in the ideal oral history interview?

Other interviewers, while not survivors themselves, have close links to the JHMRC. They may be closely related to Holocaust survivors or may know the respondent personally and, as Treleven observes, such relationships may have a profound effect. Finally, when interviewers and interviewees are drawn from a relatively limited social group, the possibility of cross-pollination of accounts cannot be overlooked.[22]

The impression should not be given that interviewing has taken place without careful planning or training. All interviewers receive training and those considered unsuitable are removed from the interviewing roster. Interview preparation is based on extensive advice from institutions such as Yad Vashem. Interviewers follow a predetermined protocol for questioning survivors.[23] Respondents are first asked about their family background and their childhood memories. Further questions relate to their lives before the Holocaust and the effects of increasing anti-Semitism. They then move on to experiences during the Holocaust, post- (or where relevant pre-) war migration and the effect of the Holocaust on survivors' subsequent lives. Interviewees are asked to comment on the factors which they believe contributed to their survival and finally to leave a message for future generations.[24] The structure of the interview clearly circumscribes the autonomy of the witness and interviewer and is deliberately designed to control the direction taken by the narrative. Within these constraints, interviewers often encourage the interviewee to speak freely, however, interviewers frequently return to issues they believe have not been adequately covered.

Engaging in the process of "representation" referred to earlier, interviewers also seek to clarify statements and make sense of first-person accounts by placing them within a chronology and ordering them into a comprehensible narrative structure. Here the interviewer not only attempts to confirm that they have "heard" correctly, they consciously place themselves in the position of the viewer to whom the meaning of the events recounted may need to be explained. Although such interpolations sometimes interrupt the flow of memory and shift the emphasis away from what the witness wants, above all, to put on record, ultimately interviews need to generate meanings that are recognizable to potential viewers. Barry Godfrey and Jane Richardson argue that to be made relevant and meaningful for others oral accounts need to be simplified, structured into a coherent narrative, and stripped of references that relate only to the individual interviewee.[25] The interviewer plays a pivotal role in this process of placing the personal, "timeless" story within a broader, historically "fixed" context.[26] Given the complexity of the "twisted road" taken by Holocaust events, choosing a single metanarrative is problematic.[27]

The JHMRC interviewing protocol presupposes a specific Holocaust metanarrative and this frames the choice of questions. The sequence of events referred to begins with Hitler's seizure of power in Germany, proceeds to the escalating persecution of German Jews, the invasion of Poland and sometimes the Soviet Union. Ghettoization, deportation to camps, death marches, liberation and post-Holocaust life are major chronological markers. While this metanarrative is particularly applicable to the experience of Jews in western Poland, interviewers who are unfamiliar with alternative Holocaust stories may fail to understand what they are being told and are unable to adjust their questioning. In the worst cases, the interviewer is left asking meaningless questions that literally render the survivor speechless. Rosa's interview, discussed below, exemplifies this. Many of her problems in responding reflect the interviewer's lack of knowledge of the rapid progression of the Holocaust in Hungary, where the concentration, ghettoization and deportation process was concertinaed into a few weeks from March 1944. The interviewer's constant querying of Rosa's recall, whether in relation to the looseness of ghetto organization or her relatively lenient treatment in Auschwitz-Birkenau, not only reflects his ignorance of the broader historical literature, but maybe also a failure of imagination. The latter may prevent him from "hearing" what Rosa is trying to say.[28] He "misframes" Rosa's story.

The following in-depth analysis of selected JHMRC video testimonies examines how, in practice, the interviewer elicits, frames and structures Holocaust memory through a comparison of survivor and non-survivor interviewers.[29]

Survivor Interviewers: "Sharing" a Story?

Not only did a survivor interviewer conduct Samuel's and Saba's video testimonies, but also, in both cases, the interviewers shared the experience of extended periods of ghettoization. Indeed, Samuel's interviewer also came from Vilna. Does this mean that the results were especially revealing?

There is a noticeable rapport between Samuel and his interviewer.[30] Their personal exchanges suggest that they are good friends and Samuel's interview is far more relaxed and conversational than many other JHMRC testimonies. To some extent, the interviewer was also a witness to the events being related by Samuel and more explicitly than some interviewers contributes to the construction of a shared narrative.[31] Thus, the interviewer has almost as much to say as the interviewee, asking leading questions, completing sentences, coaxing, prompting, translating, giving and explaining answers, elaborating, and at times refuting what is being recounted. The United States Holocaust Memorial Museum in Washington's published guidelines to conducting interviews with Holocaust survivors explicitly counsel against arguing with respondents and warn against the insertion of personal preoccupations into the interview.

These guidelines, however, assume that the interviewer is an outsider:

> We try to understand from the inside as if we were there—much like the musician playing a piece of music. But we are always outsiders, even while we share an intimacy with the interviewee. It is important to balance our ability to listen empathetically with our ability to listen carefully and critically.[32]

In the case of the interview with Samuel, the blurring of the distinction between insider and outsider results in the creation of a far richer and detailed testimony, despite the violation of the "rules."

While the interviewer makes his position as an insider absolutely clear, he does not neglect his duty to connect private reminiscence with public history. In setting the scene of pre-ghetto life in Lithuania, he pointedly states: "I know because I was there but people who are listening to the tape in years to come might not know it, so the more details you can give about the period the better." In another instance, he asks, "What were you getting [for food]? *I* know, but what were you getting?" When questioned about the executions at Ponary,[33] Samuel replies, "Nothing." Rather than proceeding, the interviewer gives his own explanation for Samuel's ignorance: "You didn't want to believe." He suggests to Samuel that "it wasn't knowledge but a feeling; you had an inkling." It is unclear if the interviewer is construing Samuel's motives, or speaking about himself. Later in the interview when discussing the concentration camp, Stutthof, where Samuel was deported in late 1944, the interviewer (who was also there) comments, "You said something about crematoria." Samuel replies, "Crematoria, there wasn't there." The interviewer responds gently, "There were. You didn't see them. It was not like in Auschwitz—extermination—but bodies of the people were buried in crematoria. It was separate." Then, almost by way of apology, he adds, "But this is not important" and moves on.[34]

The skill of the interviewer in differentiating between his position as witness and as historian is reflected in the quality of Samuel's testimony that seldom rises above the level of personal anecdote and the interviewer's constant attempts both to place the anecdotal within a broader historical framework, and to seize upon fragments of previously unknown information. He becomes very excited by Samuel's revelation that he had seen his personal friend, Hirsch Glik, a leading Vilna resistance figure and poet. Samuel responds with surprise (almost irritation) that his comment about Glik solicited such an interested reaction from the interviewer—an exchange that illustrates the tension that can exist between personal memories and the "structures of social memory."[35]

In the case of Saba's interview, both interviewer and interviewee are key figures at the JHMRC.[36] Saba appears reticent and defensive throughout the interview. As a museum curator, Saba seems skeptical of the validity of oral history, constantly interpolating physical documents into the interview in order to "prove" that her recollections are accurate. The interviewer is also keen to gather information, but what she wants to find out is often beyond Saba's recall.[37] Indeed, there is a palpable sense of competitiveness and tension between the two whose origins may lie in their different experiences of ghettoization. Unlike many of the Lodz ghetto's inhabitants, Saba, protected by her aunts who secured for her a relatively comfortable position, gives the impression that she avoided the privations suffered by others. The unspoken text here is that her family must have held some sort of privileged position in the ghetto that the interviewer subconsciously resents. Although these issues are not addressed directly in the interview, they may account for both Saba's reluctance to discuss her period in the Lodz ghetto and the interviewer's dissatisfaction with her answers.

Like the interviewer, Saba was transported to Auschwitz-Birkenau and her experiences there become a further source of tension. Saba, whose incarceration in Auschwitz-Birkenau occurred very late in its operation, claims to have had no knowledge of the exterminations. She was neither subjected to a selection, nor did she work. Instead, she was held in Auschwitz-Birkenau for a fortnight before being sent to Stutthof concentration camp.[38] Her interviewer (like other interviewers) returns to a key question over and over again, pursuing what seems to become an *idée fixe*.[39] She constantly asks Saba about her lack of knowledge of the gassing of Jews in Auschwitz-Birkenau. She struggles to accept that Saba could have been in Auschwitz-Birkenau without being aware of the extermination of Jews. Saba's response illustrates the difficulty experienced by interviewers when the story being told does not follow their internalized script and, in the case of survivor interviewers, does not conform to their own experiences. Only when Saba moves to later events that deviate from the interviewer's experiences does the focus totally shift to Saba's unique story, which reached a horrific climax on the last day of the war, when the SS abandoned shiploads of prisoners in a barge in the Baltic Sea, shooting them as they tried to swim ashore.

The interview appears particularly confronting for Saba and suggests that the notion that the insider occupies a peculiarly empathetic position is more complicated than might be expected. Rather than accepting and giving priority to the informant, this interviewer finds it difficult to disentangle her personal interests from those of the interviewee.[40] She gives a running summary and evaluation of the interview, the only interviewer in this testimony sample to do this.[41] The interviewer's understandable concern with Auschwitz-Birkenau is again evident in her interview with fellow survivor, Ludwig.[42] Desperate for information, she is anxious to discover how and why things were different from when she went through the camp. Imposing her own agenda, she begins to ask Ludwig questions that directly relate to herself, for example, "How come when I came to Auschwitz our transport was not processed and we got a tattoo without any papers?" whereupon Ludwig, who tattooed prisoners in Auschwitz-Birkenau, clarifies the situation. Parts of the testimony become a comparison of their experiences, each feeding off the other and seeking each other's reactions, more for the interviewer's benefit than for the interviewee's, with the result that the interview is skewed away from Ludwig's particular experience as the focal point. Unlike the interview with Saba, however, Ludwig's interview is conducted in a relaxed, almost conversational manner.

Similarly, Samuel's interviewer demonstrates an easy rapport during his interview with Zina, as she recounts her experience of the Holocaust in Latvia.[43] Although not from Vilna, Zina, like the interviewer, was imprisoned in Stutthof. The questioning is ordered, gentle, even protective.[44] It is interspersed with comments such as "this is a very important part," that internally prioritize the information. The narrative is relatively free flowing until Zina begins to talk about Stutthof. At that point, the interviewer becomes increasingly involved, calling for more detail about the routine in the camp with either leading questions or closed questions that require only yes or no answers, for instance: "Did you get soup or bread or coffee?" and "At Appell they called you always by numbers?" Here the survivor interviewer influences *how* the events are retold, rather than leaving the survivor narrator to recount the story as she has remembered it. The interviewer stresses the urgency of preserving accurate details of Stutthof for the historical record. When the questioning moves to liberation and postwar settlement experiences, it again becomes open and detached. Throughout the interview, the interviewer intervenes when he believes that vital information must be captured. Similarly, while filming Stephanie's interview (discussed below), he interrupts to make sure that details of Mengele's criminal "research" on twins are accurately documented.

While survivor-to-survivor interviews set up a particular dynamic of trust and enable previously repressed information to be revealed, discussion of common experiences may result in a contestation of what occurred. What happens when survivor interviewers question survivors whose Holocaust experience differs from their own?

When interviewing Alex who lived through the German occupation of the Netherlands the interviewer maintains the normal structure of the interview, but also allows Alex to indulge in long sections of monologue that include many anecdotes. Alex reveals much about his pre- and postwar life in the Netherlands, as well as events while in hiding during the occupation. He is encouraged to fill in perceived gaps in public knowledge, with statements like: "We don't know anything about Jewish life in Amsterdam." Questions are prefaced with statements on which Alex is expected to expand, for example: "There were two types of Jews, people who lived always in Amsterdam and those who were recently coming from the East." Alex is asked how the occupation affected this situation. Nonetheless, Alex maintains almost complete control throughout the interview, which is summed up in the concluding frame. When invited to give a message to his children, he responds, "No message for my children. I wanted to say to my great grandchildren...." Where the interviewer has no direct experience of the events described, he seems less interventionist than in the interviews with Samuel and Zina and has far less influence in shaping Alex's narrative. His position as survivor-interviewer is not as evident.

Cesia's testimony revolves around her life in the Krakow ghetto, her subsequent escape to the countryside and involvement with a resistance group in the forest.[45] There is the suggestion of an existing friendship with this same interviewer. The questioning once again is very sensitive, the interviewee responsive. At one point, however, Cesia begins to talk about her marriage and her strained relationship with her husband's family. She stops herself: "But you don't want to hear it yet." The interview proceeds but again Cesia comes back to her personal life: "[He] married me without telling his parents about it. They were religious and I wasn't ... you don't want me to talk about it," whereupon the interviewer suggests a break.[46] Cesia, however, insists on continuing. "No, I just wanted to finish this part because then we can talk about something else." In a few rushed sentences she says what she wants to say and then, "Now we can make a break ... there's not much more from then on to tell." (This is despite the fact that the testimony has by then only covered the years up to early 1943.) Intriguingly, she is asked immediately after the break, "How did you meet him and how did your life change when you met him?" Maybe some renegotiation over content has occurred and, although the relationship between interviewer and interviewee is less comfortable than before, the testimony continues productively for another two hours.

Stephanie's testimony recounts her experiences in Theresienstadt, Auschwitz-Birkenau, the death marches and, finally, the Malchow concentration camp.[47] Her Holocaust is far removed from that of her interviewer who fled persecution in Germany prior to the outbreak of war and there is no sense of an exchange of experiences. The interviewer lacked knowledge about the "family camp" established specifically to house Jews deported from Theresienstadt, and, understandably, the interviewee had little specific knowledge of the background to its establishment. The subsequent dialogue of the deaf reinforces how important the role of the interviewer is in mediating between private reminiscence and public history.[48]

Although the interviewer begins by saying that the main focus of the interview will be on the "war years," it is clear that this term is shorthand for the Holocaust. The interviewer prefaces the interview by saying: "I know this is very difficult for you," and is cautious and hesitant in her questioning, in contrast to Stephanie who appears calm and refers to herself as "optimistic" with a Pollyanna philosophy on life (although her usually confident demeanor dissolves during the most upsetting parts of her testimony, when her voice drops to a barely audible whisper). While the interviewer's questioning can be pre-emptive as she talks over the respondent, at the end of a topic she asks whether Stephanie has anything further to add. Like many other interviewers, she focuses particularly on the relevance of Jewishness in various situations; questions whose significance seems to escape the highly assimilated Stephanie. Because Stephanie, a twin, was a victim of Mengele's medical experiments, the interviewer barely touches on the gassing of Jews and keeps returning to Stephanie's knowledge of Mengele's practices. Possibly this reflects a tendency in oral testimony to talk about the "sensational."[49] Little in the interviewer's personal Holocaust experience could have prepared her for Stephanie's account and Stephanie herself answers questions by referring to her subsequent visits to museums that have helped her to place Mengele's program in a broader historical context.

Where the Holocaust experiences of interviewer and interviewees are significantly at variance, the authority of the insider perspective may be diminished, especially if the survivor lacks specific knowledge of what is being described.

Non-Survivor Interviewers: A Search for Understanding

Non-survivor interviewers find themselves in a difficult position. Lacking the authority and/or empathy of survivor interviewers, they also may not have the depth of knowledge and research skills of academically trained interviewers.[50] Interviews with witnesses whose stories fall outside the metahistorical framework inherent in the interviewing protocol can present particular difficulties.

Take Joseph's interview for example.[51] Joseph, from Czechoslovakia, has relatively poor English skills and is fairly unforthcoming. His relationship with the female interviewer is stilted and uneasy. The resultant interview is formal, precise and very slow moving, with long, deliberate pauses between questions. The main problem, however, which is not acknowledged (and maybe not recognized) by the interviewer, is that while the setting of much of Joseph's story is Auschwitz-Birkenau, because Joseph was incarcerated as a political prisoner, rather than as a Jew, his account does not constitute the "standard" Holocaust narrative. Joseph, who was arrested with four fellow school students, continuously denies any anti-Nazi political activity. As a political, rather than Jewish, prisoner he enjoyed a privileged position working in "Canada" (the warehouse holding arriving prisoners' goods) and acting as a factotum to SS officers. Although he witnessed the mass murder of Jews, his fate was not theirs.

Hans is interviewed by a male non-survivor,[52] whose interviewing style varies considerably between, and within, testimonies.[53] This interviewer consistently reveals the problems associated with trying to interview without sufficient historical knowledge and preparation.

In the early part of his interview with Hans, a *Kindertransport* child refugee who arrived in England in May 1939, the interviewer is methodical and non-committal, moving directly from one question to the next. Hans confides his despair at his inability to get his mother out of Germany before war broke out. A long discussion follows on the nature of Hans' lifelong guilt, with the interviewer analyzing the situation and trying to counsel him. The tone of the interview changes when Hans suggests that the London Blitz occurred in 1941. The interviewer challenges the accuracy of Hans' recollection and lectures him about the chronology of the war. This confuses Hans, who begins to check the personal documents he had brought with him to try to confirm what he remembers. The narrative is disrupted and the relationship between the two participants becomes noticeably cool as the interviewer, having forgotten the original reason that Hans took out his papers, starts examining and summarizing some of the documents, regardless of their relevance to the date of the London Blitz. The camera, now focuses on the interviewer, reinforcing that he has usurped center stage. The examination of photographs and documents, usually left to the end of the testimony, may have been a conscious strategy by the interviewer to verify the evidence of the witness.[54] To Hans, however, the interviewer's dragooning of the documents indicates indifference to his personal story and effectively silences him.

For some time, Hans remains preoccupied, tight-lipped and evidently puzzled, flipping through other documents, still looking for the detail that would verify his version of events. He appears resigned and bored, to the extent of checking the time on his watch. These mood changes and emotional responses would not have been so obvious in an audio-only testimony. Finally the interview resumes but the normal sequence of questions has been lost. Later the interviewer comments, somewhat insensitively, that because his father died during *Kristallnacht*, Hans was lucky that, being partly orphaned, he was eligible for the *Kindertransport* program. Hans does not share this view. At the end of the interview he returns to his documents, repeating much of what was covered earlier by the interviewer, so as to give his own view of how to interpret them.

Ironically, the interviewer's own understanding of events is inadequate. His suggestion that Hans should have arranged his mother's emigration is ludicrous, given, as Hans tried to explain, the restrictive conditions governing emigration.

In the case of Luba,[55] this interviewer responds quite differently. This may be because the interviewee is female or because, like the interviewer, she is a lawyer. Another contributing factor could be the nature of Luba's story, which is primarily situated in the Soviet Union where she escaped following the German invasion of Poland. Because her direct experience of Nazi persecution was limited and her suffering occurred at the hands of the Soviet regime, the question protocol left the interviewer with little space. Luba seems happy to fill in the blanks.

Luba was not subjected to an interrogation or ignored, as happened to Hans. She is very forthright, highly intelligent, articulate, confident, composed and not easily intimidated. As she talks about finding her brother after the war, she responds quickly with: "Just a minute. I want to say a few words," when interrupted by another question. She controls the interview at all times. Her testimony is extremely well informed and insightful, presenting what Portelli might call "self-reflexive thick dialogue."[56] Rosa's interview covers the late persecution of Jews in Hungary and her deportation to Auschwitz-Birkenau.[57] Although events in Hungary deviated in significant respects from the Poland-centered metanarrative, sufficient parallels exist to enable this same interviewer to imagine that he has expertise. He is particularly assertive with Rosa, but this is understandable because he is compensating for a reticent interviewee with somewhat limited English and he does most of the talking. He asks long, closed or leading questions soliciting the monosyllabic answers, "yes" or "no." The interview is labored and sometimes insensitive and this is compounded by Rosa's limited recall or understanding of events at the time. According to the interviewer, she and her family should have known what was happening. He asks why she lacked curiosity: "Well, you would have heard—this is the middle of 1944—that the Germans were killing the Jews by that stage" to which Rosa responds, "There was not much news coming through." He upsets her with his persistence, reminding her that she was not a child, but an adult of 24 or 25 by the time she was deported to the Hungarian ghetto of Sopron and then Auschwitz-Birkenau.

In response to Rosa's account of her uncle and aunt's suicide in Budapest, the interviewer questions her credibility: "That's a strange step, to commit suicide, even if you lose your family." He tells her that, in comparison with other interviewees, she is very lucky, since she "only" stayed at Auschwitz-Birkenau for three to four weeks, was never starving and, although her father perished, her mother and sister survived, as did many family members. Rosa disagrees, responding that more members of her large family died than survived. The lack of awareness by Hungarian Jews of the Holocaust is well documented and the interviewer's judgmental tone cannot be justified. Indeed, Saba's story corroborates Rosa's account of her inactivity at Auschwitz-Birkenau.

Rosa's interview can be compared with Zygmunt's, which was also conducted by the above interviewer.[58] Zygmunt survived by escaping from the Warsaw ghetto and concealing his Jewish identity. Although subjected to dreadful conditions in forced labor camps, his persecution as a non-Jewish Pole was preferable to that of other Jews. In a quite formal interview, the interviewer is assertive and persistent. In relation to certain issues, particularly how little Zygmunt appeared to know about what was happening to Jews in Poland, he provides a further example of an interviewer clinging to an *idée fixe*. Given Zygmunt's renunciation of his Jewish identity this seems a somewhat disingenuous concern that finally sparks the answer, "No, I was probably stupid at this time." When he later mentions that he was constantly thinking of his family in the ghetto and wanted to save his sister, he is asked, "So you think she [your sister] was more important than saving your parents?" When Zygmunt replies, "Please don't give me such a question," the interviewer responds, "You have to ask these strange questions." A connection is only established when Zygmunt recalls Mauthausen, which the interviewer has also visited.

Finally, Leo's interview with a female, non-survivor interviewer (whose interviewing has not previously been discussed) is quite different from any other interview.[59] Although Leo's description of the Holocaust in Poland is prompted by the usual questions about his early life and family, the interview is quickly transformed into a monologue that describes various brutal episodes experienced in a series of concentration camps. Leo has his own agenda and resents being interrupted, so the interviewer, perhaps in deference to the trauma Leo has suffered, abandons the normal set of structured questions. Leo is impervious to questioning. Having previously written down his story, he views his task as giving the "highlights." He assumes that the viewer can always consult the written text for further details so when the interviewer tries to clarify the chronology of events, he disregards her saying, "I cannot tell you everything in detail—it would be too long." Their relationship is tense and he frequently pre-empts her reaction to what he is relating. The result is a disjointed and non-sequential testimony, which is difficult to follow and has almost no input from the interviewer at all.

Volunteer, non-survivor interviewers must compensate for lack of personal experience and authority with a thorough knowledge of the background to the events being described in the video testimonies. They are especially at risk of misunderstanding what is being recounted if it does not fit neatly into the framework of the question protocol or the accepted metanarrative. Rapport can quickly dissolve, followed by conflict over what occurred, or, even worse, silence. Only the strongest of survivors assert their story, regardless of the interviewer.

Conclusion

Video testimonies are subject to certain types of framing and varying degrees of intervention and control and this is evident in the case of the video testimonies held in the JHMRC. The interviewer knowingly or unknowingly, mediates, intervenes and provokes and can indeed significantly compromise the integrity of the interviewee's testimony. The empathetic survivor interviewer may have an advantage over the non-survivor interviewer but this may introduce other problems. The non-survivor interviewer may be more objective, but lack the necessary breadth of knowledge to engage in a meaningful dialogue with the respondent.

In order to fully appreciate Holocaust video testimony, an understanding of the dynamic relationship between interviewer and interviewee is vital because the first person to speak in an interview is the interviewer, who begins the conversation, "defines the roles, and establishes the basis of narrative authority."[60] It is this authority that distinguishes the oral testimony from an autobiography, as it is the interviewer who (generally) takes the initiative rather than the interviewee.[61] This chapter has shown that the analyst of Holocaust video testimony must also seize the initiative by paying careful attention to the role played by the interviewer in shaping the presentation of Holocaust testimony.

Notes

1. This chapter was originally presented at the Australian National University Humanities Research Centre Conference, Testimony and Witness from the Local to the Transnational, 14-16 February 2006. Research was funded by an Australian Research Council Linkage Grant.
2. See Michele Langfield, "Capturing the Intangible: Holocaust Survivor Testimonies Held in the Jewish Holocaust Museum and Research Centre, Melbourne," *Oral History Association of Australia journal* 28 (2006).
3. Oren Baruch Stier, *Committed to Memory. Cultural Mediations of the Holocaust* (Amherst and Boston: University of Massachusetts Press, 2003), 70.
4. Ibid., ch. 3. For a discussion of how the narrator's perspective may be placed in the foreground see Rita Charon, "Narrative Medicine: Attention, Representation, Affiliation," *Narrative* 13, 3 (2005).
5. Mary Chamberlain and Selma Leydesdorff, "Transnational Families: Memories and Narratives," *Global Networks* 4, 3 (2004): 229.
6. For example, Nanette C. Auerhahn and Dori Laub, "Holocaust Testimony," *Holocaust and Genocide Studies* 5, 4 (1990); Michael Bernard-Donals and Richard Glejzer, *Between Witness and Testimony. The Holocaust and the Limits of Representation* (Albany: State University of New York Press, 2001); Geoffrey H. Hartman, *Scars of the Spirit. The Struggle against Inauthenticity* (London: Palgrave Macmillan, 2002); Dori Laub, "An Event without a Witness: Truth, Testimony and Survival," in *Testimony. Crises in Witnessing in Literature, Psychoanalysis, and*

History, ed. Shoshana Felman and Dori Laub (New York and London: Routledge, 1992).

7.   See Andrea Fontana and James H. Frey, "The Interview. From Structured Questions to Negotiated Text," in *Handbook of Qualitative Research*, ed. Norman K. Denzin and Yvonna S. Lincoln (Thousand Oaks, London, and New Delhi: Sage, 2000), 646. The authors note that "increasingly, qualitative researchers are realizing that interviews are not neutral tools of data gathering but active interactions between two (or more) people leading to negotiated, contextually based results."

8.   Ronald J. Grele, "On Using Oral History Collections: An Introduction," *The Journal of American History* 74, 2 (1987): 572.

9.   Chamberlain and Leydesdorff, "Transnational Families," 232.

10.   Mary Marshall Clark, "Resisting Attrition in Stories of Trauma," *Narrative* 13, 3 (2005): 296.

11.   For the importance of a "collaborative" approach, see Henry Greenspan and Sidney Bolkosky, "When is an Interview an Interview? Notes from Listening to Holocaust Survivors," *Poetics Today* 27, 2 (2006): 435-6.

12.   Dale E. Treleven, "Interviewing a Close Friend, First Amendment Activist Frank Wilkinson," *The Journal of American History*, 2 (1998): 611.

13.   Alessandro Portelli, "Oral History as Genre," in *Narrative and Genre*, ed. Mary Chamberlain and Paul Thompson, (London and New York: Routledge, 1998), 30.

14.   Treleven, "Interviewing a Close Friend," 611.

15.   Greenspan and Bolkosky, "When Is an Interview an Interview?"

16.   Grele, "On Using Oral History Collections," 570.

17.   Judith E. Berman, *Holocaust Remembrance in Australian Jewish Communities, 1945-2000* (Nedlands, WA: University of Western Australia Press, 2001): 105-12.

18.   Phillip Maisel, "First Hand: The Holocaust Testimonies Project," in *Reflections. 20 Years Jewish Holocaust Museum and Research Centre*, ed. Stan Marks (Elstern-wick: Jewish Holocaust Museum and Research Centre, 2004), 73-4. Also Deborah Schiffrin, "Linguistics and History: Oral History as Discourse," in *Georgetown University Round Table on Languages and Linguistics 2001. Linguistics, Language, and the Real World: Discourse and Beyond*, ed. D. Tannen and J. E. Alatis. (Washington, DC: Georgetown University Press, 2003).

19.   See Vansina, "The Documentary Interview," 11-12.

20.   Also, Laub, "An Event."

21.   See David Wolgroch, "Holocaust Testimonies: The Interviewer's Perspective," *Cahier international : études sur le témoignage audiovisuel des victimes des crimes et génocides nazis/International journal : studies on the audio-visual testimony of victims of the Nazi crimes and genocides* 5 (September 2000).

22.   Vansina, "The Documentary Interview."

23.   Before their interviews respondents fill in a questionnaire summarizing the main details of their lives and outline where they experienced the Holocaust. Interviewers frequently refer to this before asking questions. Greenspan and Bolkosky, "When is an Interview an Interview?" review the literature that suggests that interviewers frequently deviate from "formal" interview scripts, 433-5.

24.   See Stier, *Committed to Memory*, 75-6. Stier describes similarly structured question protocols used in other Holocaust testimony collections.

25.   See Barry S Godfrey and Jane C Richardson, "Loss, Collective Memory and Transcripted Oral Histories," *Social Research Methodology* 7, 2 (2004): 144. Also Dan Goodley, Rebecca Lawthom, Peter Clough & Michele Moore, *Researching*

Life Stories: Method, theory, and analyses in a biographical age (London, New York: RoutledgeFalmer: 2004).

26. Clark, "Resisting Attrition," 298. See also Godfrey and Richardson, "Loss, Collective Memory," 149.

27. Karl A. Schleunes, *The Twisted Road to Auschwitz: Nazi Policy toward German Jews, 1933-1939* (Urbana, IL: University of Illinois Press, 1990).

28. See Charon "Narrative Medicine": 263-4.

29. We would like to acknowledge our two research assistants, Donna-Lee Frieze and Janette Sato, for help in the selection of relevant JHMRC video testimonies. Their observations have proved invaluable and have been incorporated into our discussion.

30. Video testimony No. 433, 9 November 1993.

31. For example, Henry Greenspan, *On Listening to Holocaust Survivors. Recounting Life History* (Westport, CT and London: Praeger, 1998), chapters 1, 2, 6 and 7.

32. Joan Ringelheim, Arwen Donahue, and Amy Rubin, *Oral History Interview Guidelines* (Washington: United States Holocaust Memorial Museum, 1999), vii-viii. See also Vansina, "The Documentary Interview," 10.

33. Approximately 70,000 Jews from Vilna and the surrounding area perished in Ponary between 1941 and 1943. See Rachel Margolis and Jim Tobias, eds., *Die geheimen Notizen des K. Sakowicz. Dokumente zur Judenvernichtung in Ponary 1941-1943* (Frankfurt am Main: Fischer Taschenbuch Verlag, 2005), 11.

34. Here the interviewer plays a restorative role by helping the interviewee understand the context of his pain, as envisaged by Clark, "Resisting Attrition," 298.

35. See Godfrey and Richardson, "Loss, Collective Memory," 144.

36. Video testimony No. 261, 1 January 1993.

37. Greenspan and Bolkosky, "When is an Interview an Interview?" express surprise that survivor interviewees place so much emphasis on accurately establishing the chronology of events, 237.

38. For the changes in routine in Auschwitz-Birkenau during its final period of operation see Andrzej Strzlecki, "Evacuation, Liquidation and Liberation of the Camp," in *Auschwitz. Nazi Death Camp*, ed. Franciszek Piper and Teresa Swiebocka (Oswiecim: The Auschwitz-Birkenau State Museum of Oswiecim, 2004), 270-1.

39. She does this also in her interview with Ludwig, asking several times for him to explain when and why he changed his name. That interviewees find interviewer preoccupations annoying is strongly evident in Greenspan and Bolkosky's study, "When is an Interview an Interview?" 443-6.

40. See Alessandro Portelli, *The Death of Luigi Trastulli, and Other Stories: Form and Meaning in Oral History* (Albany, NY: State University of New York Press, 1991): 54.

41. See for example, Video testimony No. 779, 3 July 1996.

42. Video testimony No. 761, 8 May 1996.

43. Video testimony No. 1077, 25 April 2001, 2 May, 3 May 2001 (three parts).

44. According to Greenspan and Bolkosky, interviewees considered that a "gentle," co-operative, approach produced the "best" interviews, "When is an Interview an Interview?" 440-3.

45. Video testimony No. 703, 7 November 1995.

46. It is common practice in the interviews for breaks to be taken when respondents are distressed, or simply because interviewing has occurred over an extended period.

47. Video testimony No. 478, 10 March 1994.

48. Greenspan and Bolkosky find that the ideal interviewer contextualizes individual memory within broader historical context, "When is an Interview an Interview?" 442.

49. Vansina, "The Documentary Interview," 10.

50. Ringelheim, Donahue, and Rubin, *Oral History Interview Guidelines*, ch. III, 'Conducting research'; Treleven, "Interviewing a Close Friend," 616.

51. Video testimony No. 691, 12 October 1995.

52. Video testimony No. 836, 17 November 1996.

53. Although not a survivor, this interviewer has a close relationship with an uncle who is a survivor, personal communication to Pam Maclean from Phillip Maisel, 31 January 2006.

54. See Vansina, "The Documentary Interview," 12.

55. Video testimony No. 383, 11 July 1993.

56. Portelli, "Oral History," 31.

57. Video testimony No. 754, 21 April 1996.

58. Video testimony No. 297, 14 March 1993.

59. Video testimony No. 738, 10 March 1996.

60. Portelli, "Oral History," 28. See also Grele, "On Using Oral History Collections," 570.

61. Portelli, "Oral History," 28. Paradoxically Leo's usurpation of the interviewer's authority disempowers his ability to tell his own story.

List of Contributors

Nanci Adler is associate professor at the Center for Holocaust and Genocide Studies, an organization of the Royal Netherlands Academy of Arts and Sciences and the University of Amsterdam, and one of the editors of *Memory and Narrative*.

Jacob R. Boersema is a doctoral candidate at the Amsterdam Institute for Metropolitan and International Development Studies at the University of Amsterdam. His Ph.D. thesis, "Afrikaners after Apartheid," investigates discourses of identity and belonging among white Afrikaans speaking people in post-Apartheid South Africa. He has master's degrees in human geography from Utrecht University and in history from the University of Amsterdam. This chapter is based on his master's thesis on the Rwandan Genocide.

Mary Chamberlain is professor of modern social history at Oxford Brookes University and former co-editor of Transaction Publishers' *Memory and Narrative Series*.

Jan K. Coetzee is professor of sociology at Rhodes University, Grahamstown, South Africa. He specializes in qualitative methodology and in the narrative study of lives. His publications include *Fallen Walls* (2004) and *Development: Theory, Policy, and Practice* (2001).

Jim House is senior lecturer in French Studies at the University of Leeds (UK). His research interests include the history and memory of Algerian migration to France and of colonial and post-colonial violence in France and Algeria. With Neil MacMaster, he is the author of *Paris 1961: Algerians, State Terror, and Memory* (2006). He is currently preparing a study of the history and memory of shantytowns in Algiers, Casablanca, Paris, and Marseille (1930-1975).

Michele Langfield is associate professor in the School of History, Heritage and Society, Faculty of Arts and Education, Deakin University, Melbourne, Australia. Her research interests include migration, ethnicity, identity, and cultural heritage. She is the author of *More People Imperative: Immigration to Australia, 1901-39* (1999), *Espresso Bar to EMC: A Thirty-year History of the Ecumenical Migration Centre* (1996), and co-author with Peta Roberts of *Welsh Patagonians: The Australian Connection* (2005). She has edited a collection of essays entitled *A Question of Ethics, Personal Perspectives* (1999).

Selma Leydesdorff is professor of oral history and culture at the University of Amsterdam. She is one of the editors of *Memory and Narrative*. She has published extensively on the history of Jews in Amsterdam (*We Lived with Dignity*, 1994), Holocaust memories, and trauma. Her present research has brought her into several public arenas, including print journalism, where she has written on the role of the Dutch army in Srebrenica. Though her arguments have found an audience in Holland, her work on Bosnia is far better received outside the country. Her recent work, based on interviews with the women of Srebrenica, is expected to be published in New York and Sarajevo.

Pam Maclean is senior lecturer in the School of History, Heritage and Society, Faculty of Arts and Education, Deakin University, Geelong, Australia. Her major research interest is modern Jewish history, with an emphasis on the Holocaust, German-Jewish relations during the First World War and Australian-Jewish history. Since 2003, together with Assoc. Prof. Michele Langfield, she has been part of an Australian Research Council funded project analyzing Jewish Holocaust video testimonies. Her publications include: "'You Leaving Me Alone?' The Persistence of Ethics during the Holocaust." *Cahier International,* 12 (2006): 23-36.

Norman M. Naimark is the Robert and Florence McDonnell Professor of East European Studies at Stanford University, where he is also senior fellow of the Hoover Institution and the Freeman-Spogli Institute for International Studies. He is the author and editor of a number of books, among them *The Russians in Germany, A History of the Soviet Zone of Occupation* (1995) and *Fires of Hatred: Ethnic Cleansing in 20th Century Europe* (2001).

Leyla Neyzi, an anthropologist and oral historian, is associate professor in the Faculty of Arts and Social Sciences at Sabancı University, Istanbul.

Hessel Nieuwelink graduated in 2006 in Holocaust and Genocide Studies and International Relations from the University of Amsterdam. He currently teaches social studies at the Amsterdam Faculty of Education. His chapter is based on his Master's thesis, entitled "Contribution of an International Tribunal: Conversations with Rwandans" (in Dutch).

Ulla-Maija Peltonen is director of the Literary Archives of the Finnish Literature Society and a lecturer (docent) at the Institute for Cultural Research at the University of Helsinki. She is author of *Naisia turvasäilössä* [Female political prisoners in Finland 1930-1944] (1989), *Punakapinan muistot* [Memories of the 1918 Civil War] (1996), *Muistin paikat* [Sites of Memory: On Remembering and Forgetting the Finnish Civil War] (2003) and is co-author of *To Work, to Life, or to Death: Studies in Working-Class Lore* (1996). She is co-editor of *Muistitetotutkimus* [Oral History Research: Methodological issues] (2006).

Andrea Pető is associate professor at the Department of Gender Studies at the Central European University where she teaches courses on the social and cultural history of Europe. Her books include: *Women in Hungarian Politics 1945-1951* (2003), *Geschlecht, Politik und Stalinismus in Ungarn. Eine Biographie von Júlia Rajk. Studien zur Geschichte Ungarns, Bd. 12* (2007). Presently she is working on gendered memory of World War II and political extremisms.

Christoph Thonfeld is post-doctoral fellow at Trier University. He is also co-editor of *Werkstatt Geschichte* since 2002. His research interests currently include the history and memory of forced labor in Nazi Germany, the history of migration, and the history of denunciation in 20th-century Germany.

Uğur Ümit Üngör is lecturer in International History at the University of Sheffield (UK) and staff member of the Center for the Study of Genocide and Mass Violence. His main area of interest is the historical sociology of mass violence and nationalism in the modern world. He has published on genocide in general, and on the Rwandan and Armenian genocides in particular. At present he is revising his Ph.D. thesis, titled "Young Turk Social Engineering: Genocide, Nationalism, and Memory in Eastern Turkey, 1913-1950."

Geoffrey T. Wood is professor in human resource management at the School of Management, University of Sheffield, UK. He specializes in trade unionism and industrial relations. His latest book is *Industrial Relations in Africa* (2007).

Index

accounts of survivors, ix
accusation, 25, 39n16, 74, 112, 113
activism, 101, 102, 115, 139, 144-146
activists, xv, xvi, 100-115, 139, 144-146
African National Congress (ANC), 101, 104, 111, 114, 115
African Union, 12
afterlife, xiii
aftermath of genocide, 129
Albright, Madeline, 6
Algeria, 137, 139-143, 145-147, 149, 150
Algerian War of Independence, 138-141, 145, 147, 148, 150
amnesty, 88, 138
Anatolia, 175, 186, 187
anonymous, 85, 121
antifascist, 168, 170
apartheid, xv, 99-101, 104, 106, 115
Arab Worker's Movement, 144
Armenia, 184
Armenian genocide, x, xvii, 9, 15, 17, 185, 194, 197n64
army
  Bosnia-Herzegovina, 3
  Bosnian Muslim, 3, 21
  Bosnian Serb, 3, 4, 6, 34
  Dutch, 3, 4, 21, 23, 25
  French, 141
  Ottoman, 184
  Russian, 183
  Rwandan, 123
  Serbian, 3, 4, 9, 13
  South African, 103
  Syrian, 184
  Turkish, 178, 186, 187, 190, 191, 193
arrests, 109
Arrow Cross (party), 158-164, 166, 167, 169, 170
articulation of experience, 139
Arusha Peace Accord, 48
atrocity, ix, xiii, xvi, xviii, xix, 21, 23, 25, 95, 126, 132, 133

audience, x-xii, 104, 144, 182
Auschwitz, 17, 70, 176, 205-208, 210, 211, 213
authorities, 44, 50, 51, 53, 57, 90, 101, 104, 105, 107, 111, 113, 127, 135n15, 141

Balkans, 6, 15, 17, 175
Biko, Steve, 103, 112
Black Local Authorities, 101-103, 106
bodily memory, 142, 152n25
Bosnia (Herzegovina), 3, 6, 8, 9, 11, 12, 16-18, 19n13, 83, 94, 95, 175, 220
Botha, P.W., 100, 114
boycotts, 46, 100, 102-104, 107, 111, 179
Budapest, xvii, 158, 159, 161, 165, 166, 171, 213
Bush, George W., 10, 11
bystanders, 24, 119-121, 129, 157

camp system, 88
Cape Province, 100
censure, xii
Chang, Iris, xxn14, 176
chaos/chaotic, xi, 25, 33, 36, 55, 164
Chetniks, 25
churches, 53, 108, 191
civil war, 41, 42, 44, 61, 66, 68, 75, 85, 87, 94, 95, 122, 140, 178
coexistence, 25, 30, 66
Cold War, 6, 138, 161
collaborators, 24, 84, 87, 190
collective memory, xiii, xv, xvi, 15, 69, 140, 157, 158
colonial, xvi, xvii, 139, 141, 144, 145, 150, 190
commemoration, 22, 28, 143, 148, 167, 169, 171
committees, 106, 107, 109, 111
Communist party, xvii, 62, 88, 111, 144, 160
communist, xvii, 4, 87, 159, 168

community, xiv, xvi, 13, 14, 41-43, 45, 47, 48, 51, 54-57, 68, 100-102, 105, 106, 111, 113, 120, 125, 130, 137, 141, 177, 192, 200, 202
compensation, xvi, 126
concentration camps, 65, 67, 68, 70, 71, 74, 75, 85, 94, 95, 179, 206, 207, 210, 214
consensus, ix, 10, 23, 41, 88, 132
courts, ix, xvi, 7, 12, 15, 157, 160
crime, xvi, xix, 10, 12, 13, 15, 17, 19n20, 30n26, 63, 74, 91, 124, 125, 129, 132, 133, 136n51, 147, 157, 158, 160-162, 164, 166, 168, 176, 192
criminal character, ix
Croatia, 18, 83
culture, xii, xviii, xix, 7, 16, 21-23, 37, 70, 78n41, 103, 122, 135n15-16, 179, 187, 188, 193

Dachau, 85, 88
Darfur, xiv, 8, 11, 12, 19n21
Dayton Accords/Agreements, 8, 17, 19n13
democracy, xii, 41, 44, 99, 108, 114, 141, 145, 146
denial, 43, 68, 194, 203
denunciation, 85-87
deportation, 5,‐7, 8, 11, 62, 90, 92, 95, 97, 158, 162, 164, 179, 183, 186, 188, 194, 204, 205, 213
deprivation, 110
detention, 6, 101-103, 108-115, 142
diaspora, 16, 139
distortion of memory, xvii
Dutchbat (Dutch army), 3, 4, 11, 19n19

economic processes, 99
emigration, 141, 143, 212
emotions, ix, xii, xiii, xv, 24, 30, 36, 65, 67, 72, 176, 199
empathy, xi, 211
empowerment, 123
emptiness, 23, 32, 33
enemy, 23, 34, 35, 37, 49, 88, 90, 96, 131
epistemological testimony, 66
ethnic cleansing, xiv, 6-11, 16-18, 164, 175
ethnicity, 41
European Union (EU), 8, 9, 12, 17, 18
executions, 6, 13, 57, 88, 140, 161, 167, 184, 206

experiential memory, 66
eyewitness accounts, x, 24, 26, 39n26, 73

fear, xv-xvii, 5, 44, 48, 52, 53, 56, 65, 67, 86, 89, 95, 108, 110, 112, 115, 120-122, 127, 142, 185, 189, 194
Finnish Civil War, 61, 66
Finnish-Russian border, xv, 62
FLN (Algerian National Liberation Front), 137, 138, 140, 141, 144-146, 149
forced Labor, xv, 83-87, 89-97, 98n26, 158, 162, 213
Fortunoff Video Archive, xviii
fragmentation, xii, xvi, 23, 25, 36, 72, 115, 206
France, xvi, xvii, 138-150
French government, xvi, 146
French Revolution, 183
frozen memories, 23

gacaca, xvi, 120, 121, 124-126, 129, 132, 133, 134n4
gender, 159, 161
generation, xvii, 71, 98n31, 105, 107, 111, 140, 144, 145, 150, 171, 175, 179, 189, 191, 193, 204
Genocide Convention of 1948, 8, 11-13, 19n20
Genocide, ix-xi, xiii, xiv, xvi, xvii, xix, 6-18, 19n20, n21, n23, 20n28, 22-25, 37, 38n5, 39n16, 41-43, 52-57, 66, 75, 119, 120-131, 133, 134, 135n16, 177-179, 185, 192, 194,
Germany, 8, 83-87, 89, 90, 92-97, 157, 159, 189, 204, 210, 211
Gestapo, 165, 167
ghetto, 34, 158, 204-207, 209, 213, 214
glasnost, xii
Gorbachev, Mikhail, xii
grassroots, xv, 99, 107, 115, 147
gulag, 75, 76n3, 85

harkis, 140
hatred, 5, 22, 30, 33, 34, 37, 52, 87, 122, 135n16, 137, 175
historical consciousness, xix, 145, 171
historical experience, 68
historical source, xii
Hitler, Adolf, 204
Holbrooke, Richard, 19n13

Holocaust, xvii-xix, 8, 9, 15, 24, 75, 143, 157-160, 168, 169, 171, 194n10, 199, 200-206, 209-211, 213-215
honor killings, 192, 198n94
human rights, 9-12, 69, 109
Hungary, xvii, 157-162, 166-168, 171, 172, 205, 213
Hussein, Saddam, 10
Hutus, 44, 49, 50, 52, 55, 56, 122, 125, 129, 131, 194n10

immigrant, 145, 168
incarceration, 110, 115, 207
individual memory, xiii, 42, 68, 218n48
informers, 112, 113, 115
Ingria, 61
insider-outsider position, xviii
institutionalization of revisionist history, 168
insurrection, 99, 102, 103, 114, 185
Interahamwe, 45-49, 51-57
international community, xiv, 8-11, 16, 22, 23, 36, 52
International Court of Justice, 17
International Criminal Court, 12
International Criminal Tribunal for Rwanda (ICTR), 121, 123, 128
International Criminal Tribunal for the Former Yugoslavia (ICTY), 12, 13, 15
International Forced Labourers Documentation Project, xv, 83
international intervention, xiv, 8, 12
interrogation, 27, 64, 84, 92, 105, 109-112, 162, 165, 212
interviews, xiii-xvi, 24, 25, 27, 42, 61, 70, 83, 89, 93, 94, 119, 121, 139, 148, 159, 172, 178, 200-202, 204, 205, 209, 211, 216n7, 217n46
involvement, xv, 45, 57, 92, 100, 102, 105, 112, 114, 176, 202, 209
Iraq, xiv, 10

Jewish Holocaust Museum and Research Center, xviii
Jews, xvii, 15-17, 71, 75, 158, 159, 164, 166, 169, 171, 204, 205, 207, 209-211, 213
juridical, 7, 12, 22, 65, 66, 76, 147
justice, xvi, 15, 86, 119-121, 126-129, 134, 146, 158, 160, 161, 171, 182

Karadzic, Radovan, 13
Kemal, Mustafa, 186, 188
KGB, 69, 84, 92.
Khmer Rouge, 179
killing, xiv, xvii, 3, 7-14, 19n21, 21, 24, 29, 30, 37, 41, 51, 52, 54, 55, 87, 119, 122, 123, 131, 138, 140, 147, 176, 179, 184, 185, 192, 198n94, 213
Kindertransport, 211, 212
Kinyarwanda, 121
Kosovo, 9, 28
Krakow ghetto, 209
Kristallnacht, 212
Krstic, Radislav, 13, 14
Kubuhoza, 45, 46
Kurdish nationalism, xviii
Kurdish question, 190
Kurds, xvii, 178-183, 186-189, 197n64

Lemkin, Raphael, 7, 12
Levi, Primo, 24, 74, 75
life story(ies), xi, xii, xvi, 25, 36, 83, 102, 106, 108, 109
London Blitz, 211, 212
longitudinal, 175, 180
long-term effects, 84

Malchow concentration camp, 210
mass atrocity, ix, xiii, xix, 126, 132, 133
mass graves, 6,
mass killing, xiv, xvii, 8-12, 19n21, 21, 24, 122, 123
mass movement, xv, 99
mass repression, vii, x, xi, xix, 83
mass violence, vii, ix, xiii, xvii, xix, 24, 175, 176, 178, 180
massacre, xiv, xvii, 5, 10, 13, 15, 16, 19n19, 21, 22, 26, 34, 56, 138, 143, 146-148, 159, 161, 162, 164, 167, 169, 170, 171, 179, 183, 184, 187, 189, 191
media, 41, 44, 93, 138, 145, 146, 150
mediation, 10, 168, 200
medical experiments, 210
memoirs, ix, xii, 176, 177, 186
memorialization, xiv, 177
memory, vii, ix-xvii, 15, 23, 24, 30, 32, 33, 36, 37, 42, 43, 67-69, 72, 76, 88, 94, 103, 115, 138-140, 142-146, 148, 149, 152n25, 157-161, 163, 168-171, 177, 182, 191, 193, 194, 200, 201, 204-206, 218n48

Mengele, Josef, 208, 210
metanarrative, 204, 205, 213, 214
methodology, xi, 37, 42, 177
micro history, xi, xiv
micro level, xiv
migrant, 102, 137, 138, 140, 141, 144-146, 148, 150, 151n20, 185, 186
militarization, 101
military, xviii, 5, 8, 9-12, 14, 22, 41, 44, 48, 49, 52, 53, 55, 63, 73, 84, 85, 89, 103, 123, 138, 165, 170, 181, 186, 190, 191, 193
Milosevic, Slobodan, 9, 13, 15
minorities, xvii, 96, 101
Mladic, Ratko, 4, 5, 9, 11, 13
moral judgment, 74
Mouvement Démocratique Rwandais (MDR), 44-51, 54, 56, 57
Mouvement Révolutionaire National pour le Développement (MRND), 44-50, 53, 56, 57
Muslim, 3-6, 8, 11, 13, 14, 16, 21, 22, 28-30, 36, 175, 179, 181, 182, 191, 193

narrative, x, xi, xiii, xv-xviii, 16, 21, 25, 30, 36, 42, 43, 65-69, 71-75, 84, 85, 114, 115, 119, 145, 146, 149, 160, 164, 168, 200, 203-205, 208, 209, 211, 212, 215
nation-state, xvii, 177, 186, 189
NATO, 3, 4, 8, 9, 12, 17
Nazi Germany, 83, 85, 97, 157, 159
Nazism, 168
neighbors, xiv, 25, 27, 29, 30, 31, 36, 37, 47, 52, 61, 131
NKVD, 92
Nuremberg Trials, 12

objectivity, 72
Obrenovic, Dragan, 13, 14
Öcalan, Abdullah, 190
oppression, 105, 106, 113, 182
oral culture, xviii, 187
oral history, 199-203, 207
oral sources, x, 42, 72
organized crime, 192
Ottoman Empire, 177, 179, 180, 183, 193

pain, xi, xii, xvi, 21, 22, 25, 32, 34, 73, 140, 142, 202, 217n34
Papon, Maurice, 137, 147, 149
paramilitary, 3, 5, 164, 190

peace(ful), 5, 8, 15, 19n13, 25, 30, 48, 102, 109, 115, 122, 123, 131, 133, 137, 159, 179, 193
perestroika, 62, 69
perpetrator(s), ix, x, xiv, xvi, 10, 12, 15, 24, 42, 43, 58n9, 119-121, 125-134, 135n15, 157, 158, 161, 162, 164, 166, 169, 171, 177
PKK (Kurdistan Workers Party), 190-192, 194
pogrom, 179
police, 3-5, 10, 50, 86, 91, 102-105, 107-110, 112-115, 137-142, 145, 147, 149, 150, 159, 161-165, 167, 181, 189
political culture, 122, 135n15, 179, 193
post-colonial, xvii, 150
Potočari, 4, 5, 11, 15, 21, 26, 28-32, 34, 35
prison camps, 62-64, 69, 71, 72, 74, 75
prosecution, 13, 126, 127, 129, 132, 183
psychological consequences, xvi, 84, 94, 113, 126, 131, 177
psychotherapy, xi
public discourse, 166
punishment, 63, 84, 98n26, 109, 126-129, 132-134
purges 62, 69

racial persecution, 92, 94
racial segregation, 105,
racism, 44, 52, 141, 145, 146
rape, 5, 10, 11, 27, 31, 93, 119-121, 171
reception (of memory), 150, 200
recognition, xiii, 10, 17, 98n31, 139, 146, 147
reconciliation, xiii, xvii, 68, 119-121, 129-134, 136n63, 157
recovery, 124, 126, 146
Red Army, 90, 92, 95, 154, 159, 160, 161
Red Cross, 35
refugee, 3-6, 8, 11, 12, 22, 27, 30-33, 50-54, 211
religion, 29, 191
repression, vii, xi, xvi, xix, 43, 83-86, 89, 96, 99, 105, 107, 108, 137-139, 140, 143, 145, 147-150, 151n2
reprisal, 86, 93, 105, 137
resistance, 3, 4, 56, 99-102, 104-110, 145, 170, 171, 185, 193, 206, 209
retaliation, 87, 120, 129, 130
revisionist history, 168

Robben Island, 110-112
Runda, 41-45, 47-57
Rwanda, X, Xiv, 7, 9, 11, 41-44, 48, 52, 53, 119-123, 126-129, 132-134, 135n15, 179
Rwandan Patriotic Front (RPF), 43, 44, 46-50, 52, 56, 122, 123, 127, 129, 134n11
    rebel army of, 44

safe areas, 3, 11, 18n1, 21, 22
Sarajevo, 8, 15, 16, 22, 23, 26, 27
scars, 112, 113, 115
security forces, 100, 137, 140
separation, 21, 30, 32
sexual abuse/violence, xvii, 120, 141
Shalamov, Varlam, xv, 75
shame, xii, xvii, 70, 92, 120, 187, 194
show trials, 168
Siberia, 62-64
silence, xvii, xix, 25, 67, 69, 71, 75, 92-94, 120, 138, 139, 142-144, 146, 147, 150, 169, 194, 202, 203, 214
silent knowledge, 67, 74
site of worship, 17
sites of memory, xiii
slave labor, xv, 88, 98n26
Slovenia, xv, 83-85, 88
Solzhenitsyn, Aleksander, xv, 75
Sopron ghetto, 213
South Africa, 99-101, 110, 111, 114-116
South African Police, 103
Soviet Union, 61, 62, 83, 86, 89, 90, 96, 159, 204, 211
Soweto uprising, 99
Srebrenica massacre, 18n1, 19n19, 21, 26
Srebrenica, xiv, xv, 3-17, 18n1, 19n13, 20n28, 21, 22, 24, 26-31, 34-36
SS troops, 159, 163-165, 170, 204, 211
Stalin, Josef,
    death of, 86, 91
    labor camps of, 61, 75
    nationalist policies of, 62
    purges by, 68, 69
Stalinism, xii, 161, 171
State of Emergency, 107-109, 114
strategy, 48, 88-90, 92, 100, 115, 139, 148, 157, 169, 182, 212
subjective information, ix
subjectivity, ix, x
survival, 13, 23, 25, 32, 37, 71, 204
survivors, ix, x, xii-xiv, xvi,-xix, 15, 22, 23, 25, 26, 33, 36, 37, 43, 75, 92, 95, 119-122, 124-126, 128-134, 157, 159, 160, 162-165, 168-172, 193, 199-205, 209, 214
Survivors of the Shoah Visual Foundation, xviii

terror, 10, 65, 67, 115, 137, 142, 143, 179, 190
testimony, ix, xi, xviii, 65, 66, 71, 75, 113, 119, 121, 127, 139, 140, 143, 144, 146, 147, 149, 162, 163, 166, 170, 191, 199-203, 206, 208-210, 212-215
Theresienstadt ghetto, 210
Third Reich, 83, 87, 90, 97, 171
torture, 5, 6, 29, 94, 109-112, 115, 119 137
totalitarian, 74
trade unions, 101, 103, 106, 108
traitors, 49, 70, 87
transitional justice, xvi, 134, 158, 160
transmission of memory, 143
trauma, xi-xiii, xv, xix, 25, 26, 31, 36, 43, 67, 68, 136n63, 143, 159, 193, 214
traumatized memory, xi, xiv
trial, 13, 15, 85, 88, 101, 108, 111, 126-129, 134, 147, 149, 158, 161, 162, 164-166, 168, 170, 171
truth commissions, xiii, xvi, 133, 134
Turkey, xvii, 175, 176, 178-180, 185, 186, 188, 190, 192
Tutsis, 42, 44, 48-57, 58n9, 122, 123, 125, 129

U.N. Convention on the Prevention and Punishment of the Crime of Genocide (1948), 7, 8, 11-13, 19n20
U.N. Security Council, 6, 19n20
    Resolution 819, 18n1
    Resolution 1564, 18n12
UDBA police force, 86
underground (resistance), 101, 107
United Democratic Front (UDF), 103, 106, 109
United Nations (U.N.), 3, 4, 7, 9, 10, 14, 21, 22, 27, 34, 35, 52
United States Holocaust Memorial Museum, 205
UNPROFOR (U.N. Protection Force), 3, 6

Vichy France, 147

victimization, 177, 191, 193
video testimony, xviii, 199, 201-203, 215
vigilantes, 102, 104
victims, ix, x-xiii, xv-xvii, xxn14, 7, 9,
    14-16, 24, 26, 37, 43, 69, 75, 83, 85,
    88, 126, 131, 146, 158, 161, 168-171,
    177, 194n10
violence, vii, ix, xiii-xix, 7, 9, 10, 24, 30,
    41, 42, 48, 53, 57, 65, 67, 68, 102, 104,
    120, 131, 137, 138, 140-146, 149, 150,
    151n20, 166, 175-183, 185, 187-190,
    192-194

war, xvi-xviii, 6, 12, 13, 16, 17, 20n28,
    21-23, 26, 28, 29, 31, 34, 36, 41, 42, 44,
    49, 55, 62, 64, 67, 68, 71, 75, 87, 91,
    92, 94-96, 121, 122, 129, 137-142, 144,
    145, 147, 148, 150, 157, 160, 161, 164,
    165, 170, 171, 178, 182-185, 190-192,
    194, 207
    World War I, 147, 179, 183
    World War II, xiv, xv, xvii, 7, 8, 12,
        21, 34, 62, 66, 67, 75, 84, 85, 93-
        96, 159, 161, 171, 179
war crimes, 12, 13, 15, 39n26, 158, 160,
    161, 165
war criminal, xvii, 5, 13, 159, 161, 165
Warsaw ghetto, 213
wartime experience, 140-143, 146, 147,
    149
Wiesel, Elie, 71, 75

Xerzan, xvii, 175-178, 181-186, 188-194

Youth, 42, 45, 46, 50, 102, 104-106, 111,
    113, 191
Yugoslavia, xv, 7, 12, 13, 16, 39n26, 83-
    86, 94, 96